the Genealogy
HANDBOOK

the Genealogy HANDBOOK

The complete guide to tracing your family tree

ELLEN GALFORD

Editorial Consultant: *Ancestry.com*

Reader's Digest

The Reader's Digest Association, Inc.
Pleasantville, New York • Montreal

First printing in paperback March 2005

A Reader's Digest Book
Conceived, edited, and designed by
Marshall Editions
The Old Brewery
6 Blundell Street
London N7 9BH

Copyright © 2001 Marshall Editions

Project Editor	Judith Samuelson
Art Editor	Patrick Carpenter
Picture Editor	Zilda Tandy
Designer	Helen James
Proofreader	Maggie McKormick
Indexer	Dorothy Frame
Production Controllers	Claire Armstrong, Nikki Ingram
Editorial Assistant	Ben Horslen
Editorial Coordinators	Ros Highstead, Gillian Thompson
Art Director	Dave Goodman
Editorial Director	Ellen Dupont

Reader's Digest Project Staff

Editorial Director	Fred DuBose
Senior Designer	Judith Carmel
Contributing Editor	Leslie Gilbert Elman

Reader's Digest Illustrated Reference Books

Editor-in-Chief	Christopher Cavanaugh
Art Director	Joan Mazzeo
Director, Trade Publishing	Christopher T. Reggio
Editorial Director, Trade	Susan Randol
Senior Design Director, Trade	Elizabeth L. Tunnicliffe

All rights reserved. Unauthorized reproduction, in any manner, is prohibited.

Library of Congress Cataloging in Publication Data
Galford, Ellen.
    The genealogy handbook : the complete guide to tracing your family tree /
Ellen Galford.
        p. cm.
    Includes index.
    ISBN 0-7621-0645-X (paperback)   ISBN 0-7621-0308-6 (hardcover)
        1. Genealogy. 2. United States—Genealogy—Handbooks, manuals, etc. I. Title.

CS47 .G35 2001
929'.1—dc21   00-062693

9 8 7 6 5 4 (hardcover)
9 8 7 6 5 4 3 2 1 (paperback)

Reader's Digest and the Pegasus logo are registered trademarks of
The Reader's Digest Association, Inc.
Originated in Singapore by Chroma Graphics
Printed and bound in Singapore by Star Standard Agencies (Pte) Ltd

Jacket Credits t = top; c = center; b = bottom; l = left; r = right
Front cover photographs: tl Philip Letsu, tcl & tcr Hilary Mandleberg, tr Horace
Bristol/Corbis, bl Bob Rowan; Progressive Image/Corbis, bcl The Stock Market,
bcr Michael Fall, br Elise See Tai

Back cover photographs: tl Hulton-Deutsch Collection/Corbis, tcl Philip Letsu, tcr Mario
Santos, bl Meena Bangay, bcl Michael Prince/Corbis, bcr Mario Santos, br John Barlow

Contents

CHAPTER ONE

GETTING STARTED

You are about to embark on a fascinating journey.
Genealogy—the exploration of family history—is one of the
world's fastest growing pastimes. But this is far more than a
hobby: It will help you discover more about who you are.

There was a time when only a handful of people knew about their ancestors. For the majority of families, the past was a closed book. They might recall the names of great-grandparents or hand down a few traditions, but the lives of previous generations remained a mystery. For those who were interested in family history, there was little access to official data.

Today, all that has changed. There is more data available—and more ways to find it—than at any time since records began. The fruits of new technology—ranging from the Internet to digital photography—speed up research and make it easy to share data from all corners of the world. And perhaps most important is the change in our perceptions: The lives and experiences of ordinary people—in every era and every society—are seen to play as vital a role in human history as the deeds of heroes, presidents, or kings.

Enthusiasm for genealogy has generated a wealth of new ideas and methods for accessing not only official documents but other fascinating facts and images from our past. Although the procedures for recording and obtaining information vary from one country to another, the tools and techniques remain the same no matter where you live or where your ancestral roots lie.

This book will show you how to begin the search, how to navigate around the obstacles, and how to enjoy, share, and preserve your discoveries. It will guide you through the complex maze of official and unofficial sources, introduce you to like-minded people with research notes to share, and provide tips for making the most of today's resources—from family history societies to rare archives to Internet sites covering all corners of the world.

Genealogy is an exciting fusion of living history, written records, and family lore. During your research you will experience the wonder of finding old photographs, personal diaries and albums, and forgotten heirlooms from the past. It is your responsibility to tell your children and grandchildren about their family heritage and let them share in the joy of your historical finds.

What Are You Looking For?

We are all descended from a vast collection of ancestors: Even if you count back to your great-grandparents, you will find eight different family lines to follow. When you consider that each of these individuals had another eight great-grandparents, you may feel as if you are standing at a crossroads at the center of a bewildering number of streets. How do you decide which way to go?

- Male lines of descent are traditionally easier to research than females

- There are records relating to the underclass of society—the poor, sick, criminal, and the elderly—in many countries

When you start researching, do not try to pursue all directions at once. Be patient! With more experience, you will find it easier to research more than one line at a time without becoming overwhelmed or discouraged. Most seasoned genealogists say that the best advice for beginners is to start simply and stick to one line.

Stay Close to Home

You will have the best chance of success if you select the branch of the family that you know most about already, or for which you have good sources of information—such as elderly relatives. By starting with a line for which you already have some information, you will feel a greater sense of achievement early in your research. The process of confirming facts you believe to be true is good practice for using official sources and obtaining vital records.

Before you start researching, decide whether you want to trace the female or maternal line—your mother's mother's

---

RESEARCH NOTES

FAMILY RESEARCHER *Barbara Green*

FOCUS OF INQUIRY *Hidden Histories of the Poor*

When Barbara Green found records for her nineteenth-century ancestors, she saw that they lived in the poorest neighborhood of the Scottish city of Glasgow. Barbara also found that the family moved regularly from one slum tenement to another, and had come over from northern Ireland in the 1850s to escape the potato famine.

"I realized," says Barbara, "that vital records are only the beginning. I wanted to put flesh on the bones." Barbara found ways that the poor interacted with officialdom—and how these encounters were recorded. In Glasgow, Barbara found records showing her ancestors' receipt of social welfare: One female, abandoned by her husband, was forced to seek shelter, along with her two children, in the notorious poorhouse.

Inspired by her discoveries, Barbara followed trails for different family lines—this time in southern

Since the nineteenth century, tenement blocks have been home to the poorest residents of Glasgow.

England. Here she found the story of another woman forced into the poorhouse: While staying in this cheerless place, the woman gave birth to an illegitimate daughter. While on vacation in Australia, Barbara took her research to the Sydney public library. There, she found records of a man born in the same small English village as her other ancestors and who bore the same surname. This ancestor had been sent to Australia sentenced to seven years' penal servitude for the crime of stealing chickens.

SEARCH TIP Records relating to society's underclass may show your ancestry to be more colorful than you imagined.

RESEARCH NOTES

FAMILY RESEARCHER *Garvin Brown*
FOCUS OF INQUIRY *Proud Kentucky Roots*

Garvin Brown's roots go back to colonial times. In 1742, James Brown from Glasgow, Scotland, crossed the Atlantic to work in the Virginia tobacco trade. James's sons sought their fortunes in the wilderness of Kentucky, walking the trail first established by frontiersman Daniel Boone. One brother, James, built what was said to be the first house in the territory, but died young in battle with the Cherokee.

Garvin became fascinated by his family's history as a boy, listening to stories at the Thanksgiving table. He heard many tales, such as the story of a teenage ancestor who defended his mother and sisters against Yankee soldiers while his father was away fighting for the Confederates.

In the nineteenth century, one of Garvin's great-great grandfathers—George Garvin Brown—proposed a new way to sell bourbon, safely sealing the liquor in glass bottles, rather than drawing from unsealed barrels. Brown's innovation planted the seed that made the family what it is today: They built a distillery in Louisville and founded the firm that now owns the famous Jack Daniels brand. "The rest," says Garvin "is history."

Inspired by his legacy, Garvin researched historical Kentucky texts, interviewed relatives, and hunted around family graveyards for more vital details. He carried his explorations farther back in time, discovering a Scottish ancestor beheaded for his religious beliefs at Glasgow Cross during the turbulent days of the Reformation.

SEARCH TIP Talk with, and listen to, as many older relatives as you can find. Do not be shy about approaching them: Seize every opportunity to find out what they know about bygone generations. Also, seek out records relating to your female ancestors, especially their maiden names. These details will provide vital leads to hundreds of new family lines of descent, that may easily be "lost," says Garvin, "in the macho mists of time."

The town of Louisville, Kentucky, where George Garvin Brown (right) built his first distillery and established a family business which still thrives today.

mother, and so forth—or the male or paternal line, working backwards from son to father. This choice may depend on your own gender, on the relatives to whom you feel closest emotionally, or on the branch that fascinates you most.

Some newcomers to genealogy find it easiest to start with the male line of descent, on the grounds that they are likely to be working with a single surname. But if, like many people, your childhood brought you into closer contact with your mother's side of the family, you may feel that the maternal line provides a more hospitable territory for initial exploration, even though the records may be harder to source.

Keep Track of New Leads
During your investigations, you will find information on branches of the family that you are not in the process of researching. Make a note of these details, including exactly where you found them, so you can return to them later. There is nothing more frustrating, farther down the research road, than realizing you have lost essential information because it did not fit into your research needs at the time, and you did not record how to find it again. It is more efficient to research one branch of the family at any one time, rather than juggling many unconnected leads.

Your Place in History

When we trace our history, we come to understand the past in a very personal way. History comes alive when we learn about our ancestors: The places they came from, the dates they moved—voluntarily or otherwise—their culture, occupation, and even the illnesses or injuries from which they died. These details tell us about their lives, and also something about ourselves.

● The more you know about the era in which your ancestors lived, the more empathy you will have with their lives and experiences

Historians tell the tale of a royal wedding in medieval Scotland, when a court bard regaled King Alexander III and his bride by reciting the names and great deeds of the groom's earliest ancestors: The first name mentioned in the story was that of an Egyptian princess named *Scota* who left her father, the Pharoah, to elope with a Greek prince. This legend illustrates that ever since human beings first sought to rule over others, nobles have used their family connections and blood lines of descent to assert rights to land and power.

Today, we appreciate that history does not belong only to the mighty and the powerful of society: Each person has played his or her own unique part in the story, and all our ancestors have been shaped by the times and environment in which they lived. All of our ancestors are equally valid and, as ethical genealogists, we should not judge our forebears by their social or economic status.

The political map of the world is ever-changing, and country borders have altered dramatically over the last few centuries. When researching, it is important to appreciate the effect of war and political upheaval on past generations.

The Impact of World Events

The inconsistency between an ancestor's nationality stated at birth (Austrian) and at death (Italian) may be explained by the fact that, in the interim, part of this territory was ruled by both nations.

If you know the approximate years when your ancestors lived and died, and have some idea of where they came from, you can gain insights by reading a history book focusing on that particular time and place.

You may find, for instance, that a forebear's departure from rural Ireland to the industrial city of Liverpool, northern England, coincided with the devastating failure of the Irish potato crop during the nineteenth century. Or, the extended gap between the year that a

History can also shed light on joyous events

Chinese great-grandfather arrived in the state of California and the later entry date of his wife and children may speak volumes about the harsh social and economic constraints placed on foreign Asian workforces during the nineteenth and twentieth centuries.

Family history can also shed light on joyous events: A Mississippi couple's move northwest to Missouri in the late 1860s may indicate that they were no longer slaves of the South and were free to migrate north. An Englishwoman's spate of newborn babies in

Your ancestors may have lived through events that we can only read about in history books. The eyes of these children reveal a multitude of emotions: At the time of this photo, their father was serving in the German Army during World War I.

the late 1940s, may signal the return home of her soldier-husband after the end of World War II in 1945.

Treat the issues of war, hardship, and social or political oppression with tact and sensitivity. These events do not only affect those who experienced them firsthand, but also the descendants of those involved, some of whom you may need to contact during the course of your research. Read about the subject or event in question, since this will equip you with the knowledge to tackle this part of your history and help you discuss the issue with relatives or other contacts.

RESEARCH NOTES

FAMILY RESEARCHER *Guy Lee (with William Wong)*
FOCUS OF INQUIRY *Using History to Find Leads*

When Guy P. Lee was two years old, his father was killed in an automobile accident in San Francisco. In the 76 years since then, Lee never knew what his father looked like. No family member had ever taken a picture of Guy's father.

A few months ago, Lee's niece told him about the United States National Archives and Records Administration office in San Bruno, just south of San Francisco, where thousands of original files are kept of Chinese immigrants during the late nineteenth century and first half of the twentieth century, all victims of the 1882 Chinese Exclusion Act. Meticulous records were kept of Chinese immigrants to determine if they should be excluded from entry to the U.S.

Guy and his 74-year-old wife, Rose, drove to San Bruno, hoping to find a photo of Guy's father. With the help of an archives technician, they found the file of his father, and for the first time in his life, Guy P. Lee saw what his father looked like, in two small photographs shown on the immigration documents. "I was so surprised, so happy," he

The first time Guy saw his father was on the immigration document recording his arrival in the United States.

said. When he gazed upon his father's image on an original photograph, tears welled up in his eyes. "It was absolutely something. I've been looking all these years for a picture of my father," Lee said.

SEARCH TIP The historical context in which your ancestors lived can suggest new leads regarding the location of vital records. The U.S. National Archives and Records Administration office in San Bruno is a useful treasure trove for Chinese-Americans and other immigrants who arrived at West Coast ports. Archive centers in areas with concentrations of a particular ethnic group may hold similar records.

Your Place in History

Ethical and Medical Issues

You will soon discover that genealogy is more than the collection of names and dates. You are opening a window into people's lives. Whether you are gathering information from close relatives or researching documentary evidence of bygone generations, be prepared for surprises.

● **Consult modern medical reference books for details of hereditary diseases that are common among particular ethnic groups**

You may discover ancestors with whom you have an astonishing amount in common—or find evidence of medical conditions handed down through generations. You might encounter those who committed crimes or lived by a moral code different from your own. But no matter what you discover, always employ the most important research tool—an open mind.

Handle With Care

No human being is perfect and not every person shares the same system of values: What one person treats as a humiliating secret, another may see as a cause for pride and celebration.

If you are dealing with past generations, these discoveries may not cause any difficulty. But it is also possible that you will uncover information that living relatives find embarrassing or shocking. Be as tactful as possible and make every effort to respect the privacy of those who could still be distressed by this knowledge. Here are some of the sensitive issues you may encounter:

Financial and Legal Matters

Bankruptcy
Business failure
Eviction or dispossession
Unpaid debts
An ancestor deliberately cut out of a will
Trouble with the law
An ancestor found guilty of a crime
An ancestor sent to jail
An ancestor in a financial, political, or other public scandal
Military desertion

Love and Marriage

Divorce
Children conceived or born out of wedlock
Same-sex partnerships
Arranged marriages (where love matches are the norm)

An ancestor's diary may reveal private emotions and unknown secrets that may alter your understanding of your family history. If the information is of a sensitive nature, consider carefully with whom you share it.

Marriages based on love (where arranged marriages are the norm)
Desertion of a spouse
Bigamy
Cohabitation out of wedlock
Marriage when one or both parties are under-age according to convention
Marriage with someone considered socially unacceptable, crossing religious or cultural divide.

Genes and Genealogy

Just as our ancestors bequeath us such traits as eye color or hair texture, they also leave legacies that may affect our health, either by passing on hereditary conditions or—more positively—an ability to resist disease. For this reason, one of the most fascinating and useful aspects of genealogy is to ascertain information about the health of previous generations. In many cases, the specific medical conditions that affected our

Medical Terminology

TUBERCULOSIS, CONSUMPTION	Bacterial diseases affecting, among other parts, the lungs or the lymph nodes. Also called Phthisis, Scrofula, and The King's Evil.
TYPHOID FEVER, ENTRIC FEVER	Infectious disease, spread by bacteria in food or drink, causing fever and intestinal inflammation.
TYPHUS	Unrelated to typhoid, but the terms are frequently confused. Typhus is caused by microorganisms generally carried on lice or fleas, and manifest in the form of delirium, prostration, and fever.
CHOLERA	Infectious disease spread by fecal contamination of water supply. Also known as Winter Fever or Summer Complaint.

ancestors were caused by environmental, social, or economic factors rather than by inborn propensity to disease. The short lifespans recorded on tombstones speak volumes about the dangers faced by women in childbirth, the high rates of infant mortality, and the vulnerability of anyone living in overcrowded conditions in times where sanitation was primitive and modern principles of hygiene unknown. However, a visit to an ancestral burial plot or a look at the vital records of previous generations can also deliver encouraging news: You may find that you are blessed with ancestors who stayed hale and hearty throughout their life and survived well into old age.

A valentine card or love letter may reveal your ancestor's innermost emotions. Treasure these items and the sentiments they contain.

Your ancestor's military service may have been a period of national glory and success, but it may also have been a time of personal humiliation, injury, desertion, or emotional trauma.

13

Basic Research Skills

Information is the lifeblood of genealogy. Once you get started, names, dates, research sources, and stories will start coming at you from all directions. Make sure you do not drown in a sea of paper or lose vital facts jotted down on an envelope—set up, and stick to, a system for recording and organizing your notes and archive material.

Official documents may seem indecipherable at first, but after reading them carefully a few times, you will be able to find the relevant data and transcribe or abstract the text.

Never skip this step, since you may need to return to this source again in the future. For reference, keep a separate "Contacts File," giving the names, numbers, mailing addresses, and E-mail addresses for all the individuals and institutions that have given—or are likely to provide—useful information. Keep a chronological research log or running diary of places visited or people consulted, commenting on how you found the source, and tips for the future, such as directions to a hard-to-find location.

No matter how exciting the prospect of discovering your family history, always temper your enthusiasm with common sense. Even though a lot of information is available without charge, avoid investing in expensive software, or subscription fees or search fees for items that you may not need.

The Library: A Key to Many Doors

One of the most useful starting points for your genealogical journey is your local public library. Even if you are not an experienced library user, you will soon find that librarians are generally helpful by nature. They will explain how to use the computerized catalog to request items and how to find items on the shelves.

On-line Catalogs and Inter-library Loans

On-line catalogs usually arrange their collections in three ways—by the author's surname, by title, and by subject—with the entries for each category listed in alphabetical order. Libraries often have agreements with other libraries to borrow items from each other's collections. Public libraries usually have access to libraries in

● Read the publicity leaflets of record offices before you visit them; these will help you plan your visit efficiently, saving you hours of effort

Note-taking and Manual Skills

Even if you plan to work on computer, there will be situations in which you have to take notes by hand. A basic stationery kit should include pens, soft pencils, a soft eraser, a pencil sharpener, and ruler. Pencils are essential for working in archive centers.

Use a ring binder that takes a regular size of paper, and always use the same size of paper. This will make it easy to divide notes into sections, and move material between files. Keep plenty of paper on hand, and take a good supply when traveling.

Label all notes with names, dates, and locations. At the top of each page of notes, write the surname of the family it covers, along with the date and place the information was collected. Do not put information about more than one family on a single page. When taking notes from a document, identify the title, date, author, location, catalog reference number, and library classification number, as appropriate.

Research Budget Considerations

COMMUNICATIONS	Mailing costs for letters you write and for documents ordered by mail; long-distance telephone calls.
STATIONERY	Notebooks, writing equipment, files, and storage facilities.
TRAVEL	Fuel, fares, parking fees, meals, and accommodation.
RESEARCH	Fees for accessing and duplicating documents and microfilms.
RECORDING EQUIPMENT	Photographic, video, and audio equipment; tapes and film processing.
ORGANIZATIONS AND READING MATTER	Fees for genealogical magazine subscriptions and reference books. Membership fees of genealogical societies: Be sure these bodies offer genuine help before you sign up.
COMPUTER EQUIPMENT	Hardware, software, and peripherals. Upgrades and external storage facilities, such as CDs.

● Many record offices and archives have descriptions of their records, public access policies, hours of operation, and full addresses available on their websites

the same county or state, and academic libraries can often access material from other academic libraries in the same country. So even if you cannot find the publication close to home, you may be able to order it from elsewhere. Ask the librarians for more details on inter-library loans.

Trawling for Treasures
Even small libraries are likely to have a genealogy section, containing a selection of guides. Many will also have a local history section. The librarian will show you where these are kept, or you can check the subject index in the library catalog to see the extent of the collection. The library may also subscribe to genealogy magazines.

As you explore your ancestry further, you may have questions about the places from which your ancestors came or the events that affected their lives. For this type of information, look in the library reference section for encyclopedias, history books, old maps, and atlases.

Commercial and residential telephone books are an essential reference for family researchers, as are published listings of public organizations throughout the country. Copies of these directories are available from major libraries, and the data can also be found on the Internet.

Larger libraries often contain archive material relating to the history of the surrounding area, such as newspapers, letters, and journals. If your ancestors lived for a long time in the place where you are now—or if you are visiting a library in another town—you could find them mentioned in these sources. Be sure to ask the librarian for any assistance you need.

With hours of library research ahead of you, try to make yourself as comfortable as possible in this environment and learn the working practices of the institution.

CHAPTER TWO

INTERVIEWING

The best place to start your research into family history is close to home. Your own relatives—parents, grandparents, aunts, uncles, and cousins—are likely to be your most valuable resource. Older family members in particular form a living link with the past and must be carefully encouraged to shed light on the family's history.

Your elderly relatives are probably the most qualified individuals to explain the connections between branches of your extended family.

Even those with failing memories will have some recollections of their own childhoods, good and bad episodes in the family's history, memories of work and home in a vanished era. They may also be able to pass on anecdotes about distant ancestors, as told to them by their own grandparents.

Trusty Allies

Family gatherings are rich sources of information. When far-flung kinfolk join together—whether to celebrate a wedding

or to comfort each other at a funeral—the conversation often turns to the old days, with favorite tales retold and memories shared.

But these informal encounters are only a starting point. Once you have decided to explore your roots in a more systematic manner, the best place to begin is by interviewing those relatives who are willing to share what they know. There may be some who are reluctant—with or without clear reasons—to speak of the past, and their refusal should be respected. But most relatives will be delighted to help. No matter how wide the age gap, or how different your lifestyles, your family is something you have in common. Where key elders are deceased, seek out close friends, who may know almost as much as living family members.

Enriching Experience

This chapter will help you make family interviews as fruitful as possible. An interview can be an enriching experience for both parties and provide vital data for your family research.

Following the life of Ada Porter, these images make an ideal talking point for an interview. Top left: Ada standing with her mother and four siblings. Top right: Ada photographed as a young woman. Bottom left: Ada's daughter Peggy holding her son, Graham, outside the family home. Bottom right: Peggy standing with her grown-up son, Graham, at a family wedding.

Recording Equipment

The most effective way to preserve the information you gain from an interview is by audiotaping the session and taking notes at the same time. Used together, notes and audiotape will provide a fail-safe system, making sure that no valuable fact or memory is lost. You may only get one chance to interview a key relative or friend, so it is vital to make the most of any meeting.

● Try out your writing and taping equipment before the interview to make sure everything works

● Always allow yourself plenty of ruled writing paper

● Avoid personal stereo tape players, since these are not designed for recording voices; dictating machines are more suitable

Your choice of notebook is vital to successful interviewing. Experienced interviewers prefer to use a traditional reporter's or stenographer's spiral-bound notebook that flips open from the bottom, since it is portable and comfortable to hold. Others prefer one that opens from the side, with holes punched to allow insertion into a ring-binder. In either case, ruled pages are essential for keeping your notes legible.

Always allow plenty of paper for each interview. Begin each session on a new page, with a note of the interviewee, the date, and the location. If there are other people present who may be taking part in the conversation, be sure you make a note of their names, too. Otherwise, it may be hard to identify all the speakers when you listen to a tape at a later date.

One Side or Two?

When taking notes, it is up to you whether or not you write on both sides of a sheet: Using only one side makes sure every item is visible, and that no details are forgotten; writing on both sides saves paper and keeps your collection of bulky notebooks to a minimum. In either case, make sure you have plenty of pages available to avoid running out of paper halfway through the session.

Tape Recording

The most suitable recording equipment is a fully portable cassette recorder with a noise-reduction system.

Dictating machines are ideal for recording interviews. However, their small-tape format means they are difficult to copy onto traditional audiotape.

A traditional shorthand notebook is still the most popular kind, since the pages can be quickly turned and the ruled paper keeps your notes neat and legible.

If you hope to do a lot of interviews, opt for the best quality you can afford. Avoid personal stereo tape players, since these are rarely capable of producing good sound quality. Stereos with a socket that allow connection to an external microphone system may give better results.

If you have bought a new tape player especially for your research, study the instruction manual carefully, and do at least one dry run to make sure you know how it works before you use it for an interview. This will help prevent problems on the day.

Microphones

The most effective microphone is a clip-on type that attaches to the speaker's lapel or tie, placed about 9 inches (23 cm) from the speaker's mouth. If your tape player records in stereo, employ two small, clip-on microphones—one for your interviewee, the other for yourself. If you are using a free-standing microphone, or one built into the recorder, think carefully about where you place it. Avoid hard work surfaces, which may pick up echoes and vibrations that will interfere with the audibility of your tape. Position the microphone on a flat but padded surface, such as a smooth cushion or the arm of an upholstered chair.

To make sure the cassette does not stop unexpectedly, place it where you can see, at a glance, that the tape is still running smoothly, and remember to check from time to time.

Location

The place where you record the interview is as important as the equipment itself. Avoid rooms with windows opening onto busy roads, children's play areas, or back yards where electrical mowers or power tools are in use. Kitchens, too, are generally unsuitable. The tape player will inevitably pick up echoes bouncing off the hard surfaces, as well as the hum of refrigerators. Throughout the house, even sounds that most people hardly notice, such as a ticking clock or a creaking rocking chair, can create unacceptable distractions on a tape. Once you have considered these technicalities, be sure your subject is at ease with the location: Let them decide which chair they find most comfortable, and work around this when positioning your equipment and yourself. Neither the interviewee nor the interviewer should have to raise their voices to be heard.

Always accommodate the equipment to the person

Sound Checks

Before beginning an interview, it is important to do a sound check. Switch on the tape player, make sure the tape is running forward, and ask your interviewee some simple question, such as, "What is the weather like?" or "What did you have for breakfast?" Immediately play it back, to be sure that you are satisfied with the position of the microphone and the recording level. You may wish to ask them to change position slightly in order to improve the recording level of their voice.

Always accommodate the equipment to the person, rather than the other way around. The more relaxed the interviewee feels, the better your results will be. It may take a few minutes for your interviewee to become accustomed to speaking on tape, but as long as you explain its purpose and resist fussing over the equipment, they will soon forget their inhibitions.

● Small clip-on microphones are specifically designed to pick up the voice of the person to whom they are attached

● Always conduct a sound check before starting an interview to ensure the microphone is positioned correctly and the recording level is satisfactory

Professional Hint

Do not rely totally on taping interviews, since recorded voices can become inaudible, batteries fail, tapes tear, machines break down. Similarly, if you take notes entirely by hand, you may find that it is almost impossible to concentrate simultaneously on asking questions and accurately writing down the answers once the conversation begins to flow.

Use a good quality pen that you find easy to handle and does not smudge. To be on the safe side, take along a couple of spare pens as well. Make sure your notes are legible.

Always take spare batteries to every interview and check frequently during the session to be sure that the tape is running smoothly. You may prefer to use rechargable batteries as a long-term option.

Videotaped interviews are not generally recommended for those new to interviewing. It is impossible to concentrate on the subject at hand if you are also operating a camcorder. And even if you have a helper to perform this function, you may find that his or her presence will distract and inhibit an interviewee.

Planning an Interview

Whether you are recording the reminiscences of a well-loved grandparent or gathering data about an unfamiliar branch of the family from a distant cousin whose name you didn't even know until last week, advance planning will help make the most of any encounter. Since an interview is, essentially, a conversation aimed at increasing your knowledge about your roots, the best way to achieve this is to make sure the encounter is a pleasant experience.

● Before an interview, write a list of the things that you would like to learn from the interviewee

● When arranging an interview, be considerate and realistic about the demands you make on your subject's time

One of the secrets of interviewing is the questioner's ability to put himself in the place of the person he is talking to. To get an idea of what it feels like, ask someone else to interview you about your own life and family history. Go through the questions you plan to ask others in the course of your research.

Next, build on this experience by interviewing a close family member, such as a parent or a sibling. Treat it as a dry run that will increase your confidence when you finally set out on the interview trail.

Before you set up an interview, take stock of what you already know and what you would like to find out. Write a questionnaire, listing your questions about names, places of origin, dates and details of births, marriages, and deaths. Some genealogists like to send this questionnaire to interviewees in advance, while others feel

Do not hesitate to ask your interviewee if they can shed any light on inherited family heirlooms or mystery people in group photographs. Remember to take these items along to the interview.

> Go through the questions you plan to ask others

this is too formal and prefer to bring a list of questions to ask on the spot. Vague requests to "tell me about your grandparents" are unlikely to prove productive. Even if your purpose is the search for specific names, dates, and places, allow time for unscripted conversation: The most valuable things you learn may come from unexpected directions.

Be Diplomatic

Whichever approach you choose, treat your prospective interviewees with tact and sensitivity. Make it clear how much you value their assistance, and reassure them that you will respect whatever boundaries they set. It is easy for an innocent question to revive long-buried tensions, even if those involved in the conflict have been dead for decades. However, many people will speak freely if they know you will be discreet.

Elderly people may find prolonged conversations tiring and draining. Set limits in advance—one hour at most—depending on the individuals in question.

Let the Interviewee Retain Control
The interviewee should always feel at ease and in control of the situation. Often, the most comfortable place for an interview is in the subject's own home, or in the house of a close relative. Although it is easiest to conduct an interview one-to-one, there are times when the presence of a relative or friend may help break the ice and move things forward, especially if you do not know the person you are interviewing. However, if a second person is present, be sure they do not, even with the best of intentions, "hijack" the interview. If they have something useful to add, arrange a separate session with them alone.

Professional Hint

If you are hoping to interview a person who lives in a nursing home, residential care facility, or is in the hospital, always discuss your intentions in advance with the staff. Private spaces in these facilities are not always available, but it should be possible to arrange the use of a room where you can both relax and not be interrupted. A clear and coherent interview is much more likely with the benefit of peace and quiet.

The Importance of Photographs
Another useful conversational trigger is a selection of photographs. If you have pictures of people that you have not been able to identify, be sure to bring them along. You may find that your relative can help solve the mystery and remember new information with vivid detail.

Also, ask a helpful third party to photograph you and your interviewee together, and be sure to send your relative a copy as a memento of the occasion.

- Even very elderly relatives will be stimulated and charmed by family photographs, so take along a selection of snapshots, including those about which you hope to gain more information

- Arrange for someone to photograph you and the interviewee together as a record of the event

The physical surroundings shown in photographs can conjure up background information about the social and economic lifestyles of past generations.

Interview Guidelines

You may only get one chance to interview a particular relative, so it is vital you make the most of the meeting. With careful planning and consideration, you will be able to maximize the amount of information gained—from key facts to peripheral details—in order to further the course of your family research.

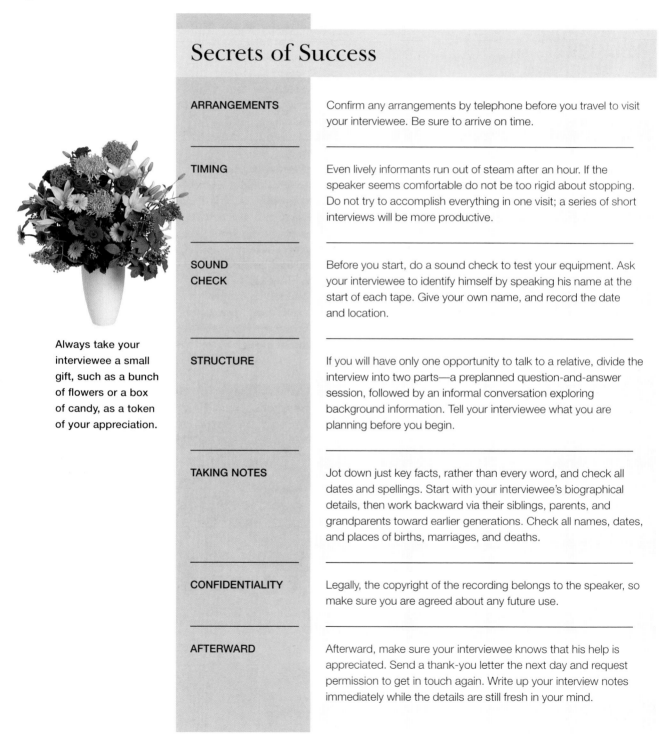

Always take your interviewee a small gift, such as a bunch of flowers or a box of candy, as a token of your appreciation.

Secrets of Success

ARRANGEMENTS

Confirm any arrangements by telephone before you travel to visit your interviewee. Be sure to arrive on time.

TIMING

Even lively informants run out of steam after an hour. If the speaker seems comfortable do not be too rigid about stopping. Do not try to accomplish everything in one visit; a series of short interviews will be more productive.

SOUND CHECK

Before you start, do a sound check to test your equipment. Ask your interviewee to identify himself by speaking his name at the start of each tape. Give your own name, and record the date and location.

STRUCTURE

If you will have only one opportunity to talk to a relative, divide the interview into two parts—a preplanned question-and-answer session, followed by an informal conversation exploring background information. Tell your interviewee what you are planning before you begin.

TAKING NOTES

Jot down just key facts, rather than every word, and check all dates and spellings. Start with your interviewee's biographical details, then work backward via their siblings, parents, and grandparents toward earlier generations. Check all names, dates, and places of births, marriages, and deaths.

CONFIDENTIALITY

Legally, the copyright of the recording belongs to the speaker, so make sure you are agreed about any future use.

AFTERWARD

Afterward, make sure your interviewee knows that his help is appreciated. Send a thank-you letter the next day and request permission to get in touch again. Write up your interview notes immediately while the details are still fresh in your mind.

Possible Pitfalls

FOCUS

Avoid vague, open-ended queries, such as "What was life like during the 1940s?" Keep to the point.

FLEXIBILITY

Do not be too rigid. If your interviewee veers from answering your questions, take advantage of this opportunity to gain background information. However, if you find the discussion drifting into completely irrelevant areas, ease the speaker back to the subject at hand.

ETIQUETTE

Do not offer your own opinions unless you think it may help the speaker to remember more. If the speaker mentions a name you do not know, contradicts what has been said already, or gives information you believe is incorrect, do not interrupt. Make a note of these anomalies and come back to them later. Give your informant plenty of time to think before answering. Do not be deterred by spells of silence, and do not distract the speaker by switching off the tape during pauses. It is better to waste tape than to derail a train of thought.

Let the interviewee speak his mind, even if his views are opposite to your own. Always keep your facial expression and voice calm and neutral during the interview.

TIMING

Do not tire out the interviewee. If the speaker's voice starts dropping off at the end of sentences, suggest a short break with refreshments. Alternatively, suggest resuming the conversation at a later date.

TACT

Do not pressurize the interviewee. If your informant is upset by recollections, switch off the tape and take a short break. When, and if, he is prepared to continue, do not return to the subject that caused the distress. You may gain more information from another person who is less involved. If there are difficult subjects, introduce them late in the interview, once more straightforward questions have been answered, and you both feel at ease. If you plunge into problematical areas too early, you may find that the session comes to a premature end. It is better to give up the quest for certain information than to risk alienating a useful source.

Do not forget to take plenty of refreshment breaks so you and your interviewee do not become tired.

Formulating Your Questionnaire

- Use the interview as an opportunity to check existing information

- Use mementoes and photographs to help your interviewee recall family details

- Ask your relative to spell out any unusual surnames or proper names

- Make sure only one person speaks at a time, so you do not end up with a garbled recording

Every family is different and, apart from the inevitabilities of birth and death, few lives stick to a standard script. But there are certain kinds of information that form the building blocks of all genealogical research.

Used as a guide, the list of questions on these pages will help you make the most of your interviews. Feel free to add more questions which relate more directly to your family experience and background. Use every interview as an opportunity to check existing data. Few memories are entirely reliable, and errors have a way of sneaking into the family history—an incorrect birth date, confusion over different people with the same first names, inconsistencies caused by multiple marriages or the presence of stepchildren, bureaucratic mistakes in official records.

Your first set of questions should supply concrete facts. See the chart below for details of the required information.

Childhood toys are particularly emotive and can help your interviewee "turn back the clock."

Facts and Figures

NAMES AND RESIDENCE	What is your full name and nickname? When and where were you born? What are your parents' and siblings' names and nicknames? Where and when were they born? List all the addresses where your family lived.
SCHOOLING, PROFESSION, AND STATUS	Where and when did you go to school and college? Did you do occupational training or military service? If so, when and where? List your qualifications or military offices. Are you single or have you had spouses? What were their names, birthplaces, and occupations? If you married, when and where did the ceremony take place? If your spouse is deceased, when did he or she die? If you have been divorced, indicate when and where.
OFFSPRING, SIBLINGS, AND PARENTS	Name your children. Details, as above, of their birth dates and birthplaces, education, occupations, spouses, and children, plus marital or death details. Details, as above, about your siblings and parents.
MIGRATION	Did your parents come from another country? If so, where and when? What was their port of entry?
ANCESTORS	Do you know any biographical details, as above, for your grandparents, aunts, uncles, great-aunts, and great-uncles? Can you provide any information, however brief, for generations before them?

After asking your questions, you might also ask permission to look at any family papers or memorabilia. In addition to official material such as birth or marriage certificates and diplomas, he or she may also have family photographs, newspaper clippings, letters, wedding invitations, postcards, or vacation souvenirs that not only generate recollections, but form a rich historical archive in their own right. This information forms the basis of your family archive and may be collated at a later day, with the permission of the owner. See Chapter Four for more details on preserving archive material.

War mementoes stir strong feelings and are always treasured possessions.

After asking your basic questions, move on to discuss broader topics of the family background and lifestyle.

Home Life

What sort of house did you live in when growing up? Was it owned or rented? What rooms did it have? What sort of outdoor space? What was the furniture like? Were there pictures on the walls or any other forms of decoration? Describe the street and neighborhood where you lived.

Religion, Culture, and Leisure

Were you brought up to practice any particular religion? Where did you worship? What religious observances and customs were part of your family life?

If your parents or grandparents came from other countries, what languages were spoken at home? What stories did they tell you about life in the places they came from?

What were family meals like? How was the shopping done? Who cooked? What special dishes were served for celebrations, religious holidays, or other special occasions? Who visited for these occasions?

What were your favorite toys, games, and pastimes? What did you and your siblings do for entertainment? Where did your family take vacations, and what sort of activities did you do there?

How did your family react to major news events? How were they affected by war, natural disasters, economic depression, or national politics?

Social Status and Discipline

Was the family poor, rich, or somewhere in between? Was there a sense of social status? What sort of transportation did the family use? Did they have a car? Were your parents strict or easy-going about bedtimes, manners, chores, and teenage dating?

Were you, your parents, and/or your siblings involved in community activities, such as clubs, lodges, or volunteer work?

Your Ancestors

Did your parents, grandparents, or other family members tell you about earlier generations? Did they pass on tales of descent from famous people, dramatic experiences in their lives, or exotic descriptions of life in another country?

- Do not forget to check the details of stepchildren, since offspring from second marriages often use different surnames

- Background questions will not only give you a vivid sense of the lives led by your ancestors, but may also suggest directions for further exploration

A family album or scrapbook is an invaluable trigger to recovering lost memories, factual data, and family stories.

Alternative Interview Formats

Sometimes it is not possible to interview relatives face-to-face. And, in an increasingly mobile society, families are widely scattered. The person likeliest to have the information you need may live on the opposite side of the world, or be someone you have never met. But it is still possible to establish friendly and fruitful connections.

These two photographs, taken 25 years apart, show the same four siblings. They make an ideal memory aid for an interview by mail, since they encourage memories from different stages in the children's family lives.

- When making contact with a relative via letter, first explain who you are

- Reassure any prospective informants that you will treat any information with discretion

A telephone call out of the blue could start you off on the wrong foot with your interviewees. If possible, make the initial contact by letter or E-mail.

When writing, first explain who you are, how you are related to your subject, and how you obtained his or her name and address. If appropriate, pass on greetings from the relative who has put you in touch. As a friendly gesture, enclose a couple of photographs, such as a picture of yourself or of someone the subject already knows.

State Your Aim

Explain your interest in the family history, but do not include a barrage of questions at this stage. Ask if they would be prepared to answer your questions either by letter, E-mail, or by telephone. If they agree, go ahead and submit your questions.

Be Diplomatic

If interviewees express reservations about sharing information, reassure them about your discretion. Indicate that you will not press them on any subjects and explain how helpful you would find it to obtain even a few basic facts—a name, birth year, or a place of origin may be all that you need. If they refuse outright to help you, do not pressure them. You may find other leads elsewhere that are equally useful. Keep informants posted on the progress of your research.

Crossing the Language Barrier

If your relative does not speak your language, ask if there is another family member or friend who does, and who can translate the letter you are sending, as well as any reply. If you cannot find anyone with these skills, it may be possible to find a native speaker living nearby, or someone fluent in the language you need. A foreign language teacher in a local school, a university student, or a foreign exchange student may be willing to assist, either for the pleasure of using their skills or in exchange for a reasonable fee. Telephone directories list professional translators or translation agencies. If you live in, or near, a large city, contact the diplomatic mission or the cultural attaché of the relevant country.

Keep informants posted on the progress of your research

Drafting Your Questions

It is better to start by sending a single sheet of basic questions, and then, if your informant is willing, follow up with questions on less essential matters. From the list of questions suggested on pages 24 and 25, select those you think only this particular relative can answer. Do not waste time on details you can easily find elsewhere. Write out each individual question separately. Number each question individually and group under the sub-headings relating to the relative in question—your subject, their parents, siblings, and offspring. Even though this preparatory task may seem time-consuming, it is well worthwhile, since it will make the questionnaire quick and easy for your subject to use, make sure each category is answered, and enable you to assess the facts you need at a glance.

If you are writing your questionnaire by hand, be sure to make a few photocopies of the document before mailing it to your interviewee, just in case you need to send it again to someone else.

- When you are interviewing a relative through the mail, it is best to write out each question individually

- Spend time preparing a questionnaire template that you can reuse as necessary

RESEARCH NOTES

FAMILY RESEARCHER *Hilary Mandleberg*
FOCUS OF INQUIRY *Family Split by Cold War*

Londoner Hilary Mandleberg knew that her maternal grandfather, Joseph Loshakov, emigrated from Russia to England in 1913, along with his sister, Zisl, and brother, Meier. But when World War I broke out, Meier returned to Russia to fight for his homeland. Afterward, he remained there, marrying his sweetheart, Rosa, and raising a family. Until World War II, the English and Russian branches of the family kept up a sporadic correspondence, but once the Cold War split Europe, contact ended.

In 1968, Hilary was studying Russian at Cambridge University, England, and rapidly became fluent. At a family gathering, her mother's brother, Asher, produced the last-ever piece of correspondence from the Soviet Union, a postcard dating from 1945 and bearing an address in Baku in the southeastern part of the Soviet Union. Out of a sense of curiosity, Hilary wrote a note to the address, sending "Greetings from your family in England." She received a response, in a shaky, spidery hand, from Rosa, the widow of her great-uncle Meier. Rosa passed Hilary's address to

Loshakov family c. 1950. *Clockwise from back left: Meier Loshakov, Zoya Loshakova, Helena Loshakova, Abraham Loshakov, Leonid Loshakov, Rosa Loshakova.*

her son, Leonid, a Russian language teacher. In 1977, despite the travel restrictions imposed on Soviet citizens, Leonid and his wife, Rimma, were allowed to visit London for a reunion with three generations of cousins.

The Baku family members have now immigrated to the United States. Additional Russian relatives have contacted Hilary, who is continuing her family research.

SEARCH TIP Follow up all known addresses and contact names, since they may provide unexpected leads from previously untapped sources.

CHAPTER THREE

COLLECTING INFORMATION

Written documents and visual records are the lifeblood of genealogy, with religious, social, and professional records forming the bulk of family archives. Unofficial records, such as photographs and mementoes, are also key archive material.

Written documents contain the vital information reflecting life's major events, from birth to marriage to burial. They provide data on ownership of property, qualifications, memberships, rewards and punishments, migration, military or government service, census data, taxation, welfare benefits, voter registration, plus other aspects of public and private life. Details of your relatives—even those belonging to earlier generations or coming from societies where few records were kept—may not have slipped through the net.

Documentary evidence is not restricted to pieces of paper signed and sealed by government or religious representatives. Personal letters and photographs, family Bibles, even the epitaphs carved on tombstones are valid documents, too.

Source material appears in a variety of forms, from handwritten property deeds and census returns to family photographs and Bibles. A basic comprehension of these materials will help you build a detailed picture of the past.

Search and You Will Find

Once you know where and how to look, you are almost certain to find concrete information about your family. There are hundreds of places to try, ranging from well-organized public records offices to piles of paper in the attic of an elderly relative. Faced with so many possibilities, you may feel, at first, as if you are searching for a needle in a haystack. However, you will soon become familiar with a range of official and unofficial sources and learn how to search effectively.

Primary and Secondary Sources

Documentary evidence generally falls into one of two main categories: primary and secondary sources. Primary sources are those where information is derived directly from people involved in an event; secondary sources are those produced at a later time, or based on data supplied by other people. Assess each document on its own merits, considering why it was created and whether the information it contains came from a reliable source.

Starting the Search for Data

You have decided which family line you want to investigate. You have interviewed relatives to verify what you already know, and to gather information about names, dates, places, and other pertinent details. You know what part of the country, or where overseas, your parents, and possibly your grandparents, came from. Where do you go next?

● Read the publicity leaflets of record offices before you visit them; they will help you plan your visit efficiently, saving you hours of effort

● Many record offices and archives have descriptions of their records, public access policies, hours of operation, and full addresses available on their websites

● Be sure to ask staff to help you access and understand your family records

The challenge for a novice genealogist is knowing where to start. Although there may seem to be an overwhelming number of options, your initial steps should be clear and well defined. By identifying the gaps in your knowledge, you can devise a clear plan of action and work toward accessing concrete information and new leads.

Official documents may seem indecipherable at first, but after reading them carefully a few times, you will be able to use them to further your research.

Devising a Research Plan

ASSESSMENT

Working back as far as you can go, prepare a separate sheet of paper or file card for each family member. Head each one with the individual's full name. Then list the vital details you have already. Work line by line, in chronological order, filling in birth-related information—date, place, and parents' names. Move on to the names, dates, and places of any marriages, and ending with dates and places of death and burial. Work only on one side of the paper, adding supplementary cards or pages later if necessary.

IDENTIFY GAPS

Use your initial records to sketch out a rough family tree. Write your name and those of your siblings on a line at the top of the page, with birth, marriage, or death dates under or alongside each name. On the line below, do the same for your parents, then set out another line for your grandparents. Blank spaces will probably begin to appear around here. Work down the page for earlier generations.

ACTION

Make a "shopping list" of the data you need, beginning with your own generation, then working your way backward.

Starting With the Basics

DOCUMENT ALL SOURCES

Access the certificates for your relatives' births, marriages, and deaths. These documents are known as *vital records* or *civil registrations*. Originals are held in record offices at local, regional, or national level, but many people have copies at home. So before you order extra copies, check your family papers and ask your relatives to do the same. List the places where key events occurred in order of proximity from where you live. Start your research close to home.

TAKE AN ON-LINE SHORT CUT

Many library and archive catalogs, and genealogical databases, are available via the Internet. These can be searched on home computers and at libraries. They are organized chronologically and by name, and indicate where vital documents are located.

WORK BACK IN TIME

Investigate one person's vital records at a time, working back in time generation by generation. If a record office has data on more than one relative, save time by listing every person whose records might be found, so you can view as many documents as possible during a single visit.

- Begin your search using vital records, making sure you have asked all your family members what documents they have already

- Use your initial records to draft a rough family tree

- Save time by listing every family member whose records might be found in one archive center

Advance Preparation

MAKING CONTACT

Telephone public record offices or archives in advance. Make sure you know where they are, what hours they are open, and what fees they charge. What are their rules for visitors? Do they ban pens, insisting that notes be taken in pencil only? Do they allow laptop computers?

TIME FRAME

Are there particular days or certain times that are overly busy? If possible, arrange your first visit for a quiet period, when staff have more time to help you find your way around.

RESTRICTIONS

Ask how many documents you can order at one time. Can you order documents before your visit? How long will you have to wait for your request? Will you see the original documents or copies? Will you have to wait to use a microform screen?

Birth Records

A birth certificate or a baptismal record will give you information about an individual's birth and immediate ancestors. Details vary depending on where and when it was compiled. For instance, your maternal grandmother's birth certificate may reveal the name of your great-grandparents, their place of birth, parents' occupation, and the family place of residence.

Christening photographs are a common visual record of births, while engraved silver christening spoons or other heirloom gifts are kept in families and passed down from generation to generation.

● When consulting indexes of birth registrations, you may need to extend your search to cover a period of three to sixth months after the birth date

● Most countries allow a certain number of days or weeks to elapse before registration of birth is required

The date of birth is the crucial starting point for finding birth certificates. However, documents are usually filed according to the date the birth was registered, not the date of birth. Check with your record office as to their particular filing system: Some record offices group records by yearly or quarterly period with the alphabetical surnames listed within each volume. If you do not know the exact date of birth but are sure of the district, you will have to search through records for a range of years until you uncover the details of the person you are seeking.

Where Were They Born?

Births are registered by the place of birth, rather than the parents' address. Even before the introduction of hospital births, women did not necessarily bear children at home. And, since the advent of modern transportation, registration may be some distance from the family home.

What's in a Name?

Birth registrations are listed by surnames, followed by given names. But, especially in older documents, spelling of the family name may differ from the version you know. If you cannot find the one you are looking for, check likely alternative versions—the name *Smyth*, for instance, may have been inscribed as the more common *Smith*, or a *Cohen* as a *Cohn*. When dealing with names beginning with the prefix *Mc* or *Mac*, search for both spellings.

Redefining Given Names

Treat given names with caution. The one given by parents at birth and inscribed on the birth record may not be the name by which this person was known.

First names are frequently swapped with middle names, or abandoned altogether for alternatives that the owner prefers. So if you think that the family name, the chronology, and the location make sense, do not automatically reject a birth with an unfamiliar name. That listing for a mysterious *Lena*, for instance, might turn out to be the person everyone always called *Hélène*. Nor did every family manage to settle on a name at the time of registering the birth: You may find records that note

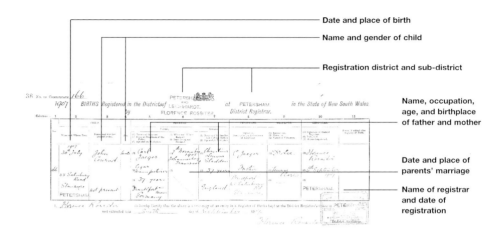

Date and place of birth

Name and gender of child

Registration district and sub-district

Name, occupation, age, and birthplace of father and mother

Date and place of parents' marriage

Name of registrar and date of registration

Birth records vary from country to country, but all contain basic information regarding the sex and name of the baby, and parental details available at the time of registration. This Australian certificate reveals that the parents were relatively old when the child was born and were not, themselves, born in Australia.

only the sex of the child. In some cases, births are registered twice. This can occur when the parents were unmarried at the time of the birth, but formalized their union later. You may find birth records under the mother's maiden surname and again under the paternal surname.

Baptismal Records

Before the establishment of state registers, the only official note of a birth in some countries was a certificate of baptism, kept in the parish church. Even after public registration began, these records continued

to be maintained. Obviously this resource is only relevant for those living in times and places practicing infant baptism. If this is the case, you may be able to pursue your searches farther back in time than any state archives allow. In England and Wales, for instance, parishes were first ordered to keep baptismal records in 1538, although few extant registers date from as early as this. In Scotland, the Presbyterian church began its baptismal records in 1553. In the U.S., the earliest records go back to the 1620s. These are sometimes still held by the churches or stored in libraries.

REGISTER OF THE CIVIL STATE FOR BIRTHS

1888 No. 461 Avram Rotinberg

From the year one thousand eight hundred and eighty-eight, month November day five, hour one in the afternoon. Certificate of birth is Avram Rotimberg, of sex masculine, born the four the current, hour nine in the evening in house No. thirty-eight, from this town, colour of red, son legitimate of Mr. Cunea Rotimberg of thirty-six years, librarian, and Sabina Rotinberg of thirty-one years, religion Mosaic, living in Roman. Following the declaration made by the father, in the presence of Mr. Simon Cramer, of fifty-one years, business-man, living in Roman and Moise Berman, of fifty years, business-man, living in Roman, who have signed this document, according to which it is binding together with us and with the declarant making a statement according to the law of our signatory Ton Georgiu Pioneam, Member Community ? of the City Roman. I declare that I have seen the child at the house of his parents.

M Berman

S Roneprey ?

K Ruthenberg
Member Comis. Inter,

T.G. Pioneam

Romanian birth certificates were traditionally issued in a short form, shown left, and also a long form, transcribed on the right. The question marks indicate illegible handwriting.

Adoption Issues

Visual records of children raised in orphanages and other charitable organizations are usually limited to formal group photographs. These were usually produced for the benefactors of such institutions, rather than for the children or their families.

● Documentation relating to fostering and adoption is usually restricted or sealed entirely to protect the rights of the child and the birth and adoptive parents or guardians

Access to adoption records differs greatly between countries. Britain, for example, grants adopted children the legal right to seek information about their birth families, while many states in the United States keep this data sealed. Even if you were not adopted yourself, your research may involve ancestors who were either adoptees or gave up offspring for adoption. In these cases, it may be difficult to follow the trail, and you may have to work around official records.

Adoptions on the Record

Legal adoption, by order of the court, is a relatively modern institution. In England and Wales, for instance, it was established in 1927, while in Scotland and Northern Ireland it began in 1930. By contrast, Canada passed its first adoption law as early as 1873 in New Brunswick.

Records of adoptions by court order are held in the same government registries as other vital family records. Access restrictions surrounding adoption certificates are designed to protect the privacy of the birth parents and adoptive parents, as well as the

child. Although details differ from one country to another, adoption certificates are likely to record the child's birth date, the date of the Adoption Order, the name of the court where it was made, the child's adoptive name (which often includes a new first name), and the adoptive parents' names, address, and occupations.

Tracing Birth Parents

In many countries, once an adopted person has reached the legal age, usually 18, he is allowed to learn his original birth name, and to obtain his birth certificate. For some people, this document provides all the information they need; those who wish to make contact with birth families are offered support from an adoption counselor and given access to the register that matches up their own name with the names of birth family members. These may be parents or other relatives of the birth family, including those linked by marriage.

If you are trying to research adoptions that took place before the process of legal adoption was introduced, you may have to

look in several different directions. Some adoptions were arranged by public officials dealing with orphans, paupers, or those otherwise on the margins of society; others were handled by charities or churches. If you know the area where the adoption took place, you may be able to find records of the charities that were involved. The search becomes easier if you know the child's birth name and date, since this will lead you to a birth certificate. Probate and guardianship records can also provide useful clues.

Churches have traditionally played a key role in arranging adoptions. Depending on the year and the location, a church will hold a range of documents—from public baptism records to private letters between the supervising priest and the parents. You may be asked to wear cotton gloves when viewing these old records to prevent the paper from deteriorating.

● Until modern times, children born out of wedlock were often regarded as an uncomfortable embarrassment, and their existence may be denied in family records

● The closest ties made by children raised in orphanages were often with their fellow residents; these friends, or even their own relatives, may be the most reliable sources about an adopted ancestor

RESEARCH NOTES

FAMILY RESEARCHER *Hilary Bird*
FOCUS OF INQUIRY *Adoption Search*

In 1976, a new English law made it possible for adopted adults to access their adoption files. With the support of her adoptive parents, Hilary Bird began to seek her birth mother. The process proved to be more difficult than she had ever anticipated.

Bureaucratic errors and plain bad luck caused Hilary's quest to drag on for 10 years. Hilary's mother had already died by the time Hilary found her. In spite of this tragedy, Hilary was determined to research her origins. She knew from her adoptive parents that her mother was from eastern Europe, and assumed, from her surname, that she was Polish. But when Hilary finally received her adoption file, she found that her mother was from Estonia.

In 1998, Hilary was visiting friends in Moscow. There, her friend Ravi introduced Hilary to the Internet as a means of learning about her ancestors. Hilary swiftly found her way to a website, run by the university in the Estonian city of Tartu, with a section entitled *How to Trace Your Estonian Relatives*. Hilary keyed in her mother's surname and birth date and obtained six contact addresses. She wrote to them all and eventually received an answer from her second cousin, Merike. Merike welcomed Hilary to a huge new extended family that had lived in the same rural area since 1756. "Your mother and my aunt used to take the cows to pasture together," said Merike. In 1999, Hilary visited Estonia for an emotional family reunion. She was welcomed by delighted aunts and cousins, a great feast, and copious amounts of Russian champagne. It was a turning point for all of them. Hilary now also uses her original first name, Annaliese.

SEARCH TIP About her research, Hilary says "I found parts of me that I didn't even know existed. I feel much more a whole person, and much happier. It's good to know what your roots are. But it has also made me appreciate my adoptive parents even more."

From left to right: Merike, Hilary's second cousin; Hilary; Aunt Maret, Hilary's mother's sister; Ilona, wife of Hilary's first cousin, Kalle; Kalle, Hilary's first cousin.

Marriage and Divorce Records

Depending on their origin, marriage documents take you several steps back into the past. If, for example, you have your grandmother's birth certificate, it will give you her parents' names. With these names, you can usually find that couple's marriage record, and often learn your great-grandmother's maiden name and the names of two great-great-grandparents.

● Traditionally, a married woman has taken the surname of her husband, but not all her personal documentation may reflect this change in identity

● Only the marriage certificate can be taken as absolute proof that a marriage has taken place

Before the establishment of civil state registers, marriages were controlled by religious organizations. Prospective spouses had to work through preliminary steps, each one marked by its own paperwork, before they could tie the knot. For this reason, you will come across a variety of different documents.

Marriage-related Documents

MARRIAGE BOND

An agreement, sealed by a financial exchange, confirming that a marriage was planned between two parties.

MARRIAGE BANNS

Banns are public declarations affirming a couple's intention to marry. These are also known as proclamations (Scotland) and contracts (Quakers).

MARRIAGE LICENSE

An official document, issued by religious authorities and later by the state, giving permission for a wedding to take place, indicating that the couple has satisfied whatever legal requirements the community imposes.

MARRIAGE CERTIFICATE

The document recording that the marriage ceremony has been carried out. Depending on date and place, this may be held either in the civic register or in religious archives. This is the only document that can be taken as absolute proof of a marriage.

Some couples will have more than one marriage document reflecting separate religious and civil ceremonies. These two documents refer to the same marriage—one is a civil Australian marriage certificate and the other is the Jewish record, or *Ketubah*.

Apart from the certificate, marriages generate other forms of documentary evidence. If your ancestor was married in a church or other house of worship, records may include not only the registration of the marriage itself but those for the posting of banns and other preliminaries. In Jewish communities, a marriage is marked by the production of a contract, confirming the

Marriage records involving servicemen or servicewomen are often kept separately from regular civic records—always check with your records center before starting your search.

obligations of both parties. This document must be kept safely, since it confirms the Jewish identity of the bride's children and will be needed by them in order to arrange their own marriages. These documents are often highly decorated.

Even if no religious records can be found, a newspaper announcement—though only a secondary source—may also provide details, such as the names of the parents and the newlyweds' occupations. The announcement may be accompanied by an account of the wedding itself, which may provide names of key guests and members of the wedding party, and insights into the family's social standing and the bride's taste in gowns and flowers.

Divorce and Annulment Papers

Divorces alert you to potential confusions in family records, such as the existence of more than one wife and different parentages of half-siblings or stepchildren who share the same surname. They also may contain information on the ages of the divorcing parties, personal wealth, and even the grounds for bringing the marriage to an end. Procedures for ending a marriage have changed dramatically in recent times. The regulation of divorce has passed from ruling religious authorities to the state and reflects a significant shift in social attitudes.

Until the middle of the nineteenth century, and in some countries later, civil divorce was very rarely granted. Divorce might be granted only by the highest religious bodies or, as was the case in England until 1858, by the arranging of an individual private Act of Parliament. Even after divorces became easier to obtain, they were overseen by different governmental departments. For this reason, the location of divorce documents—whether in court records or in civic registers—varies according to the time and place where the marriage was dissolved.

MRS. RALPH P. DUPONT

Newspaper social columns are an excellent source of marital information, but must be regarded as secondary sources.

Death Records

Documents related to death offer a range of research opportunities. They include registrations and burial records, newspaper obituaries, condolence letters, memorial plaques and charitable donations, religious items, and documentation from insurance or pensions.

- The written information surrounding a person's death should never be taken as gospel truth

- Unsuspecting next of kin may pass on incorrect information, even names and dates

- Look for obituaries and death notices in back issues of national, local, and ethnic community newspapers, particularly in the town where the death took place

Death documents—like birth and marriage records—may lead you to names of relatives from previous generations and provide information about their occupations, birthplaces, and residences at the time of their deaths. Official registrations provide the person's age at death and also the cause of death, which may give you insights into your ancestors' health and average life spans.

In the United States, death certificates may also include the names and birthplaces of the deceased's parents. When researching your immigrant ancestors, these details may link you to a country of origin.

Questions of Reliability

Even official death records may contain errors. Frequently, the details entered on the death certificate come from a bereaved

Deceased relatives are rarely forgotten by their next of kin, especially when they are included in family portraits taken after death.

relative who is too traumatized to think clearly, or a doctor or undertaker who has only limited knowledge of the individual. Family members do not always have the correct information, either because the details have been forgotten or the facts they have turn out to be wrong. Younger relatives may misspell the names of grandparents they never met, or the deceased may have used a different name from the one on his or her birth certificate.

People sometimes even rewrite their own life stories, making discreet adjustments to birth dates or marriages, or concealing facts about their origins. They carry these

Even official death records may contain errors

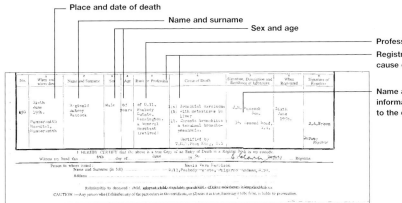

Place and date of death — Name and surname — Sex and age — Profession — Registration district and cause of death — Name and address of informant, and relationship to the deceased

Although death certificates vary between countries, most contain basic facts about the deceased. These are usually provided by a surviving spouse or child.

secrets to their graves. Meanwhile, their unsuspecting survivors pass on the false information they have been given, unwittingly setting traps for future genealogical researchers.

What the Papers Say

Anyone who has ever had his or her name in the newspapers knows that they are notoriously prone to error. The person submitting a funeral announcement to the press may get a birth year wrong, or accidentally omit a name from a list of surviving relatives. And even if the original facts are right, typographical errors frequently creep in, distorting dates and spellings almost beyond recognition. Some well-known people have even discovered their obituaries published while they are still alive. Bearing this in mind, an obituary is still a useful tool for accessing information about a person's life.

Other Trails to Follow

Death records can be difficult to find, since people do not always die close to home. If a person dies in a hospital, for instance, the death will be registered according to the location of the hospital, rather than the residence. To find the death records, you might have to check towns or counties in the area surrounding your relative's home.

If you know that a relative was killed in a war, died abroad, or was buried at sea, you may be able to consult indexes in public archives, although these are not necessarily comprehensive. In Great Britain, for instance, comprehensive records exist for the deaths of military personnel, merchant seamen, diplomatic employees, colonial governments, and other categories of British nationals who died abroad.

Rituals of Faith

Religious memorial customs generate specific documents which include the date and place of death, and details of relatives. Roman Catholics often leave bequests to fund masses on the anniversary of a death, and these are recorded in Mass Intention Books.

Jewish mourners light memorial candles on the anniversary of a close relative's death, according to the Hebrew calendar. At the time of the funeral, leaflets may be given to mourners, listing the future dates when this annual ritual should be performed. Synagogues may also send yearly letters reminding mourners of the date of the anniversary.

In Victorian England, money was sometimes allocated in a will for the purchase of special black jewelry to be worn by the chief mourners.

Child mortality rates remained extremely high well into the twentieth century. Handwritten in the late nineteenth century, this family record of child birth and death dates reveals many who died at birth or from childhood diseases.

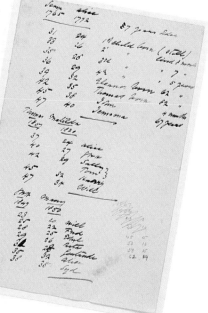

Cemetery Records

- The supervisors of cemeteries and crematoriums keep records of the people or ashes buried on site, although over the years older records may have been lost or destroyed

- Do not assume that gravestones show the correct information about the deceased, since surviving relatives and stone masons can make errors

- Do not visit graveyards alone

- Undertakers' records are useful for establishing or confirming funeral dates and details

Before the registration of vital records, grave inscriptions often provided the only record of names, dates, and other family connections. Although texts on tombs hark back to ancient times, gravestones only became common in the eighteenth century, and their cost often put them beyond the reach of all but the élite. Wooden crosses with painted names had to suffice for those of modest means. However, even for more recent generations, the inscriptions, decorations, and locations of graves can provide insights about the deceased or the relatives who arranged the burial.

Here Lies …

A visit to a family grave may be your easiest way of discovering the birth and death dates of the deceased, plus the names of spouses

Jewish gravestones may be inscribed with either Hebrew text or the vernacular language of the deceased.

Visiting a Churchyard

EQUIPMENT	Take a notebook and pen to record information notes, and also a camera to photograph gravestones.
OPENING HOURS	If you wish to visit a cemetery that is still in use, telephone the cemetery office in advance to check opening hours and establish the whereabouts of the grave you are looking for.
DOCUMENTATION	Cemetery records, held in the office, should not only provide names and dates, but also the locations and plot numbers of individual and family burials. Check the access to these records before your visit.
LOCATION	Always discuss security with the cemetery management in advance. Take someone with you on your visit, and visit at a busy time when other people are around.
ETIQUETTE	Check the conventions of the organization in charge of the cemetery. Some establishments require a modest dress code.

and children, and even birthplaces. You may also learn about the personality, beliefs, and tastes of the deceased or his or her survivors, which are often expressed through the design of the stone. Some memorials are specifically designed to commemorate the personal quirks and passions of the deceased.

Epitaphs and Inscriptions

Epitaphs and inscriptions on gravestones can express familiar, universal sentiments of love and loss—"Beloved Son"; "Devoted Mother." Others may paint a clearer picture. An inscription on the grave of a well-loved New Jersey raconteur, for instance, displays his favorite opening gambit: "That reminds me of a story ... "

Inscriptions on gravestones are often illegible, worn away by the effects of time and weather. If the burial is in a European churchyard, you may find some of the same information in the parish records. In the United States, cemetery offices hold supervisors' record books, which may contain some of the lost details.

Family Plots

Relatives often arrange to be buried under a single headstone. In private cemeteries, plots or vaults are often purchased in advance to make sure that everyone stays together. This practice benefits the family researcher, making it easy to find several people at one time. If your family comes

from a rural area in North America, or you hail from landed gentry in England, you may find previous generations interred in private burial plots on the family estate.

Searching for Lost Graveyards

Burial areas have always been subject to disinterment and transferral. In England and Wales, for instance, transcripts are often made of epitaphs before a churchyard is dismantled. These can be found in county records offices and local libraries.

This nineteenth-century gravestone in the coastal town of St. Ives, England, contains a wealth of information about four members of the same family. Without any prior knowledge, a complex process of deduction is required to figure out how the subjects were related. Can you work it out?

Not all burials take place in enclosed civic or religious graveyards. These Romanian stones lie in an open field set within rolling hills.

Probate Records

Governments have laws to assist in the administration of property belonging to deceased persons. Depending on the laws of the country and whether the deceased person wrote a will, an estate will be administered either by the court or a person appointed by the court. This distinction will affect the amount of information available to the genealogist.

Wills provide hard evidence about specific family members, such as their names and degrees of kinship to the individual who made the will. They are also rich sources of information about wealth, social attitudes, and religious beliefs. Intestate probate in the United States can provide as much information about the deceased as a will, since the courts directly settle the estates of those who die testate or intestate.

Official Sources for Probate Documents

By the turn of the twentieth century, most wills were typewritten. Ready-prepared templates, such as these English examples, became increasingly popular.

UNITED STATES AND CANADA

U.S. county courts publicly administer both testate and intestate estates, although procedures and records vary regionally.

Depending on the province, Canadian wills may be found in the court in which the estate was originally probated. For further details, contact the National Archives of Canada or log onto their website (http://www.archives.ca) under Services to the Public: Researcher Services: Genealogy Research.

GREAT BRITAIN

English and Welsh wills after 1858 are at First Avenue House, 48 High Holborn, London, or in district registries. Many earlier wills are at the Family Records Centre (London), the Borthwick Institute, the National Library of Wales, and county offices. Scottish testaments are in the National Archives of Scotland, Edinburgh. For intestate estates, probate registries usually only hold the name of the person appointed to administer the estate.

IRELAND

Most Irish Republic wills prior to 1922 were destroyed by fire, but the probate summaries 1858–1922 survive, along with some will abstracts. Wills before 1858 were administered by the church and these are indexed on a CD published by Eneclann (Trinity College, Dublin). Wills after 1922 are either in the National Archives of Ireland, Dublin, or the Public Records Office, Belfast. For intestate estates, courts only hold the administrator's names.

AUSTRALIA AND SOUTH AFRICA

Probate records are managed by individual states or territories. Refer to Public Records Offices or the National Archives for specific details relating to the time period you are researching.

Who's Who in a Will

THE TESTATOR

The person who has made the will.

THE BENEFICIARIES

The people named as the heirs to any part of the estate.

THE EXECUTORS

The people chosen by the testator to guarantee that the terms of the will are carried out. Often, executors are relatives or friends, but an executor or executrix can be anyone the testator considers trustworthy enough to undertake the task.

● Beneficiaries of a will are usually informed by a letter from an attorney; this document may be retained with other papers relating to the deceased person

● You may find ancestral wills among old family papers—this is one document that people tend to keep

● When requesting probate records, make sure you tell the clerk whether the deceased died testate or intestate

Viewing Checklist for Probate Records

THE LOCATION

The region, the name and whereabouts of the court or registry, the volume and page number where the will or probate record appears. Note whether you have seen the original or a copy.

PERSONAL DETAILS AND SIGNATURES

The name, address, occupation, and any other details of the testator. Record all the names that appear, exactly as they are written, even if the spelling is unfamiliar. Details of all signatures or marks, such as an X. Even recent wills may have been made by people unable to write.

BENEFITS, GIFTS, AND NON-BENEFICIAL PROVISIONS

Look for details relating to every sum of money, piece of property, and possession, with the recipient's name and his or her relationship to the testator. Gifts refer to charitable donations stated in the will, and non-beneficial provisions deal with the care of children, powers of the trustees, and professional charges.

DISPOSAL OF BODY AND WISHES

Funeral instructions and other details relating to religious beliefs. Wishes refer to sentiments directed to beneficiaries.

DATES

The date of the will and the date the case is presented in court for probate.

Family heirlooms passed down by a deceased relative will be noted on an itemized list of gifts. Such a list will detail every item bequeathed by the testator.

Working with Inheritance Documents

Until the late nineteenth century, a woman was not the automatic beneficiary of her late husband's estate. A man's will could place serious conditions on his widow's financial allowance. With the burden of children and minimal employment opportunities, many suffered because of these constraints.

of particular items. Much has been made, for instance, of William Shakespeare's bequest to his wife, Anne Hathaway, of his "second-best bed." Some scholars see this as the reflection of a less-than-happy relationship, while others speculate that someone in Shakespeare's social class would have reserved the best bed for guests, and that the "second-best" was the one in which their children had been lovingly conceived. Children are regularly left out of wills or testaments, especially if they were granted their inheritance while the deceased person was still alive.

Gender Issues

Women had few property rights in many parts of the world until the end of the nineteenth century. Property defaulted to male heirs, and would bypass widows or eldest daughters unless otherwise stated in a will. A devoted husband could guarantee his spouse's future financial security by

● Every death generates some kind of paperwork, even if the estate of the deceased is relatively small

Even if a deceased person did not make a will or owned little more than the blankets on the deathbed, there could be enough reason for survivors to dispute the estate. Every legal system has developed its own procedures for negotiating and recording the transfer of goods after a person's death. The result is a treasure trove of useful documents for the genealogist.

Precise Instructions

Most people who make wills are very precise about how their possessions should be distributed, and these instructions might provide an insight into the personal motives and status of the deceased. However, avoid jumping to any conclusions about the motives of the testator.

Gifts and Provisions

Gifts refer to the specific items earmarked for a particular heir, and may illuminate family relationships and the perceived value

Professional Hint

Inventories literally "open the door" into a person's home or workplace, and provide significant clues as to the lifestyle of the deceased. Even wealthy households in earlier periods had fewer possessions than their modern counterparts. Look for the presence of imported or luxury goods, such as carpets or crystal, since these will indicate considerable prosperity. Also look for clues to the person's profession, such as tools or machinery.

Understanding Inventories

NAMES

An inventory made by order of a court contains the names, addresses, and occupations of the people who compiled it. These may have been family members or neighbors, or an official appraiser hired to complete the task.

PROFESSIONAL CLUES

Look for mention of any tools or articles that give you a clue to occupations. A collection of chisels, saws, hammers, for instance, may reveal that the deceased was a carpenter by trade. But remember that many households, especially in rural areas, had to be almost entirely self-sufficient: The presence of a modest supply of needles, thread, and bolts of cloth, for instance, may signify a thrifty housewife rather than a professional dressmaker.

CLUES TO EDUCATION

The presence of a book collection will indicate the level of education attained by the deceased. Any mention of specific titles or subject matters may indicate religious beliefs, political views, vocations, or personal hobbies.

● Executors are often creditors of the deceased

● Very few people dispose of their personal estate under such general blanket statements as "all my worldly goods"

making specific provisions for her in his will. Equally, a man could use his will to control his wife from beyond the grave. It was not unknown for wills in Europe, North America, Australia, and elsewhere to state that a widow would have access to her inheritance only during her widowhood, losing rights to the estate if she remarried.

Inventories

When wills or testaments were settled, or if no will existed, it was sometimes the practice to make a list, or inventory, of the movable items belonging to the deceased. Inventories can paint a colorful and vivid picture of what life was like in the past, although they became increasingly uncommon after the end of the eighteenth century. They can also give us valuable clues about the personality, taste, and profession of the deceased person.

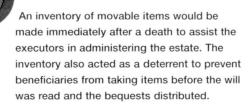

An inventory of movable items would be made immediately after a death to assist the executors in administering the estate. The inventory also acted as a deterrent to prevent beneficiaries from taking items before the will was read and the bequests distributed.

Family Bibles and Bound Memoirs

Before civic bodies collected vital records, many people recorded landmark dates, events, and names in their family Bible. Such an heirloom is a valuable research tool. Although the accuracy of the data cannot be guaranteed, the book is a tangible link with earlier generations. Bound family memoirs, written histories, and diaries are equally illuminating and provide extra background detail.

marriage, were inscribed on one of the endpapers or in the midsection, to be followed, in due course, by notations of births, marriages, deaths, and other life-cycle events. Some family Bibles came with the endpapers or center section ready-prepared for this purpose.

Individuals often had different ideas about what to put in. A straightforward sequence of names and dates may occasionally be enlivened by some intriguing detail, such as a note of a daughter's elopement or a reference to a soldier son buried on a distant battlefield.

The family Bible may provide the only written record of children who died at birth or in infancy. Even when official birth registration was in force, vital details of these abbreviated lives often remained unrecorded except in the family Bible.

A Homegrown Register

A family Bible was often bestowed as a wedding gift, to mark the sprouting of a fresh branch on the family tree. The names of the bride and groom, with the date of the

Bibles were often handed down as a legacy from one generation to the next, with new entries appended to the ancestral records by different family members. Not surprisingly, these volumes are often found in a rather dilapidated condition.

Assessing and Using a Family Bible

UP-FRONT DETAILS	Check the title page for the date and place of publication. Some of the family details may be earlier than the year the Bible was printed because records from an old family Bible were copied into a new one. When this happened, names and dates may have been transferred incorrectly.
CHECKING FOR ACCURACY	Unless the family Bible is your only available source of information, check for accuracy by comparing details with those you have found in other documents. Entries for events up to half a century after the printing date are those most likely to be correct, since they were probably written by someone who witnessed the recorded events.
VISUAL CLUES	Keep an eye out for changes in handwriting styles, different inks, or details about long-dead relatives that were clearly added later. These additions are not necessarily wrong, but—like those copied from an older Bible to a new one—they may indicate secondhand information, which might contain errors of transmission.

● Steer clear of commercial publications advertising themselves as the "family history" of your surname

Recording Family Bible Entries

PHOTOCOPYING	If you want to photocopy endpapers, make sure the volume is sturdy enough to stand up to the photocopying process. Use only those machines designed to take open books without putting pressure on their spines.
PHOTOGRAPHING	It is always worth photographing the endpapers as a visual record. If you are not able to take a good-quality photograph yourself, ask for help from a more experienced photographer.
TRANSCRIBING	You may want to copy the entries by hand. If you do so, be sure not to make transcription errors of your own.
PRINTING DETAILS	Always note where and when the family Bible was printed, plus any information about its past and present owners. If you are making a photocopy or taking a photograph of the family entries, be sure to copy the title page and any other page that displays the year and place of printing.

● When you are studying a family Bible, cross-reference the publication date with the entered data to assess whether the information has been transcribed from an earlier volume

● Family records may also be recorded in other religious volumes, such as a prayer book or hymn book

Memoirs and Letters

Personal memoirs and letters provide an atmospheric insight into an earlier era and offer a sense of continuity and personality to one person's life story. However, such sources cannot be regarded as factually reliable, since they are written from a subjective point of view.

All dates, locations, and names must be verified by official records before they can be taken as fact. Always follow up references, but do not be surprised if official records do not tally with the information offered by the author.

Bound letters and memoirs (right) are notoriously subjective documents, but provide illuminating details about the experiences and attitudes of your ancestors. Some personal memoirs may also include a photograph or drawing of the author.

When there was no more room on the endpapers of a Bible to enter family details, the information was often rewritten on a fresh sheet of paper (left) and kept separately.

Photographs

As a genealogist, you will quickly appreciate how much truth lies in the old saying that a picture is worth a thousand words. The shoebox full of vacation snapshots, the class photograph of grinning six-year-olds, the dusty album in an attic, or an array of brides on an elderly relative's mantelpiece—these documents are as illuminating as any record stored in a government archive.

Since the popularization of photographic technology, images have been displayed in professional or home-made albums. These often contain vital captions detailing names of the subjects and the date and place where the photo was taken.

For the genealogist, the most valuable photographs are those that were labeled by a knowledgeable individual soon after they were taken, recording names of the subjects, the date, the place, and the occasion.

For unidentified photographs, ask older relatives to help you identify the subjects, date, and location of the picture: Even a small amount of information can offer valuable clues to follow up. For very old images, look out for physical resemblances between different generations, since these may help you guess the relationships between individuals.

Set an Example

If you are tantalized by unidentified pictures, learn from other people's omissions. From now on, be meticulous about labeling your own photographs. Genealogists of future generations will thank you for it.

Up until the 1930s, formal studio photography was the primary source of photographic records. The artistic styling of these images changed as frequently as the fashions worn by the subjects.

Learning From Photographs

FAMILY RESEMBLANCES

Set out pictures of yourself and your relatives, generation by generation, as far back as you can go. Study the physical traits. Does the chin above that stiff Victorian collar reappear later down the line? Does the cap-and-gowned graduate from the class of 2000 have the same dimpled chin as that 1920s' flapper?

MOTIVATION AND CONTEXT

If not immediately obvious, try to imagine the motivation behind the photograph. A naked baby on a hearth rug may be intended to illustrate that this new sprig on the family tree was healthy and happy. The man in his best suit standing before an American flag might have informed kinfolk that the immigrant had finally become a citizen.

Hairstyles, clothing, cars, and even houses all reflect changing fashions. Most libraries have illustrated books showing the alterations in design that can help you date your photographs.

PHOTOGRAPHER DETAILS

Many photographers stamped their name and address on the back of their work. The town where a picture was taken may indicate the places where earlier generations lived and where records might be found.

SCHOOL PHOTOGRAPHS

Class photos can help track the migration of mobile families, especially if they include a pupil holding up a board that identifies the school, the year, the class, and the name of the teacher.

SOLDIERS AND SAILORS

Uniforms can be easily dated, and a magnifying glass can be used to inspect badges, insignia, and medals. These details may lead you to your relative's service records.

● Take note of photos that have been strategically cut up, since the missing part of the image may have included a relative or friend who fell out of favor

Studio prints often have the name and address of the photographer printed on the front or back of the image. This can be used to locate the subject in a particular town and could be a valuable clue in tracking their vital records.

● It is possible to roughly date a picture by identifying the technology used to capture and reproduce the image

Photographic Technology

Daguerrotypes appear to change from a positive to negative image when tilted slightly.

As with other black-and-white formats, ambrotypes were often hand-tinted.

Even after the invention of color prints, tinted black-and-white images remained popular.

DAGUERROTYPES

This first method produced images on silver-plated copper. A slow exposure meant sitters had to keep still for long periods, often causing pictures to blur. Used *c*.1839–1860.

TINTYPES AND AMBROTYPES

Also known as ferrotypes, tintypes were made on enameled iron, then varnished, with sitters always seen against a dark background. Ambrotypes were produced on glass instead of metal, and finished with a black backing. The lighter parts of the print may look gray, while the darker areas can turn transparent. Subjects may appear more relaxed, since exposure times were shorter. Used *c*.1850–1900.

ALBUMEN PRINTS

These prints were made on paper treated with silver nitrate and albumen, then mounted on cardstock. Small prints were known as *cartes-de-visite*, after the tokens exchanged by socialites, and often bound into albums. Larger prints were known as *cabinet cards*. In use *c*.1855–1910.

PLATINUM PRINTS

These matt images were often hand-tinted with artistic chalks to create an early version of a color photograph.

MODERN PRINTS

Color prints became popular and affordable in the 1950s, and eventually replaced black-and-white. In more recent times, digital photography has eliminated the need for both negatives and prints, and has revolutionized visual archiving for genealogists.

RESEARCH NOTES

FAMILY RESEARCHER *Cindy O'Brien*
FOCUS OF INQUIRY *Hereditary Similarities*

Old family photographs allow you to meet your ancestors face to face. When Canadian Cindy O'Brien and her seven siblings study their family photographs—of their great-grandfather Timothy O'Brien, who emigrated to Canada from Ireland, and his sons, William and their own father, Francis— they see strong resemblances between themselves, their own children, and their paternal ancestors.

"We're all very tall," explains Cindy. "My brothers are all 6' 5" or 6' 6". We all have strong, heavy, dark eyebrows and lots of dark hair. All of us look a lot like my dad, Francis, and the resemblance continues down through his grandchildren. And though some of my nephews started blond, they all grew into tall, dark, hairy men."

The resemblances extend beyond the physical traits. Common to all generations is a strong streak of practicality, a talent for fixing things, and a penchant for working with materials and machines: Timothy built houses, William mined coal, and Francis— enjoying new social and educational opportunities denied to his ancestors— became a civil engineer.

The O'Briens through the ages. Clockwise from the top: Timothy, William, and Francis (at his wedding to Iris Doreen Mottram). Below right: Young Cindy and brother Michael, looking remarkably like grandfather William. Below left: Cindy and her siblings with their parents, Francis and Iris.

Photographs

Census Records

By the mid-eighteenth century, most Western countries employed a basic system for taking census surveys. However, as populations began to grow and migrate in the nineteenth century, authorities gathered more detailed data to help them meet future population needs. As a result, many census returns provide profiles on every individual, and a wealth of clues for genealogists.

Birthplaces of children and parents recorded on different census forms are a useful source of information as to the different towns and countries in which a family lived.

Census Development

The United States is a perfect example of how government census policy adapted to its changing population. The first U.S. census in 1790 names only the heads of households and numbers all others by age and sex only. It excludes slaves and Native Americans living outside towns.

The 1850 census reveals more detailed information on all household residents, including the occupations of males over the age of 15 and individual levels of education. The 1850 census also details the names of slave-owners, the numbers of slaves owned, and the number previously set free. Returns from the 1920 U.S. census provide even more comprehensive data, although millions of urban and rural residents were still missed by this important enumeration.

Other Trails

Census returns provide other pointers back into the past. Ownership of real estate may, for instance, start you on the search for a property deed, while employment details may point you to a city's trade directories to discover where your ancestor worked.

Census returns are often stored on microfilm for viewing on a special reader and screen. If the country you are investigating does not store census data in this form, you may need to order an original or printed copy from the holding archive.

Census Restrictions

UNITED STATES AND CANADA	U.S. information for individual households is released after 72 years. Unfortunately, a fire in 1921 incinerated nearly all records from the count in 1890. The latest Canadian returns, as of 2000, are for 1901.
GREAT BRITAIN AND IRELAND	Access to returns is granted after 100 years. In Ireland in 1922, a conflagration at the Public Records Office in Dublin wiped out most records from 1821 to 1851, while the government destroyed those from 1861 and 1871.
AUSTRALIA	The law requires the destruction of census returns after the statistics have been processed. However, convict returns can be used in a similar way and run from 1788–1837. Refer to regional archive libraries for details.
SOUTH AFRICA	The only records available are the ones taken in the Cape in 1865 for tax purposes. All other records are destroyed after the statistical information is extracted.

- To protect citizens' privacy, governments restrict the availability of census records either permanently or until long after the count

- Most U.S. census data is available on CD or the Internet

- The switch to detailed census questionnaires took place at a similar period in many countries: England, Scotland, and Wales in 1841; Canada in 1850

- In countries with a colonial past, census data relating to the indigenous population may be less detailed than that for the rest of the community until relatively recent times.

- The massive English, Scottish, and Welsh census index of 1881 is a key resource for researchers with British links

The comprehensive census of 1900 and federal enumerations thereafter also provide an indication of how many years an immigrant has been resident in the U.S., and whether the individual is an alien or a naturalized citizen. With this data, the researcher can search for naturalization documents and passenger lists which provide details of national origin.

Full-scale censuses were periodically supplemented by local population surveys. In 1885, for instance, the states of Colorado, Nebraska, and Florida, and the territories of New Mexico and Dakota took additional surveys to monitor the rapid growth in population in newly settled areas.

Even meticulous census recorders could misspell a name or confuse a date. Returns were only as accurate as the information supplied: Those being interviewed might accidentally or deliberately give false data.

Accessing Census Records

The census records of many countries are stored on microfilm rolls and indexed in printed books. To find the right roll, simply look up the index for the chosen year through the relevant local archive center or library. Census indexes are generally divided by region, such as state or county. Listed by surname, the indexes indicate the location of each household's records, the Enumeration District, the number of the census sheet and microfilm roll. The Family History Library of the Church of the Latter-day Saints has microfilmed the census details of many countries and these are available worldwide. Their catalog is shown on-line at http://www.familysearch.org.

The U.S. Soundex Code

After 1880, U.S. returns for families with children aged ten and under were indexed using a code called Soundex (see right), rather than their original name. The Family History Library has also completed a name-based index for the 1880 census, making it possible to bypass the Soundex system.

Before census returns were put onto microfilm, records were filed in their original volumes. Although some countries still have their data in this form, others, such as the United States, have digitized their records and made them available on-line through websites such as Ancestry.com.

Key Stages in Census Searches

LIST NAMES AND IDENTIFY SOUNDEX

List all the names for which you are searching. Include any spelling variations, and be prepared to search these variations. Earlier generations were frequently inconsistent about spellings. A German-born householder named *Schwartz*, for instance, might have one son who preferred the spelling *Swarts* and another who translated it into the language of his new country, such as *Black*.

For the U.S. census, work out the Soundex versions of each name you are seeking (see right).

EXTRA DETAILS

Alongside each family name, write down any location details. You can start searching even if you only have a surname and a regional area, but the more details you know, the easier it will be to find the household you want.

UNDERSTANDING CENSUS ENTRIES

Records are indexed by head of household. Some archives store both the Soundex and regular census indexes, while others have one or the other. In the U.S., the Soundex name code is followed by the first name and possibly an initial.

When you find the listing for the names you are seeking, the index will identify the volume number and microfilm roll holding the forms. You will also find the Enumeration District (E.D.) and the Supervisor's District where the census took place. When you reach the complete record, make an copy of all the data, including any reference numbers.

Converting a Name into Soundex

SURNAME AND FIRST LETTER

Soundex codes consist of an initial letter followed by a three digit number. First, write down the surname, for example, the name *Adamson*. Keep the first letter as it is, in this case, A.

CROSS OUT KEY LETTERS

Cross out any of the following letters—apart from the first letter of the name: A, E, H, I, O, U, W, and Y. For this example, you will be left with the letters *A-d-m-s-n*. Retain the initial letter and the three that follow it. Delete the remaining letters. For this example, you will be left with the letters *A-d-m-s*.

REPLACE KEY LETTERS

Replace each of the last three letters that remain with the appropriate number, according to this list:
For the letters *B, F, P,* and *V*—use the number 1
For the letters *C, G, J, K, Q, S, X,* and *Z*—use the number 2
For the letters *D* and T—use the number 3
For the letter *L*—use the number 4
For the letters *M* and *N*—use the number 5
For the letter *R*—use the number 6
For the Adamson example, the Soundex code is A352.

SOLUTIONS FOR SHORT NAMES

If the surname has fewer than three letters left after the initial—or none at all—after you have made the deletions indicated above, form the necessary initial letter plus three-number code by replacing each blank space with the number 0. For example, the surname *Lal* becomes L400; the surname *Rae* becomes R000.

SOLUTIONS FOR DOUBLE LETTERS

If the surname includes two or more consecutive letters that take the same code number, the whole set is coded as if it were one single letter. For example, the letters *mn* in *Bremner* is represented by 5, not 55.

If the name includes a double letter, the two are represented by a single number, not by the same number written twice. For example, the letters *tt* in *Spinetti* would be coded as 3, not as 33.

SOLUTIONS FOR PREFIXES

Surname prefixes, such as *Le, De, O',
Mac,* or *Van,* may be coded either as part of the name or not. Search the Soundex code for both versions.

● Traditionally, the "head of household" was a man, but you can also look under a wife's, widow's, or eldest son's name

● You might find that entries for the same surname in the same locality refer to related households

● When recording details, always write down the index, microfilm, and volume numbers so you can return to the same place at a later date

Computer advances during the 1960s allowed analysts to process census data more rapidly and to use the information to plan social and economic policies.

Census Records

Geographic and Real Estate Records

Whether your ancestors lived in the heart of a bustling city or deep in the countryside, there is a wealth of evidence to help you locate them in space as well as time. There are a variety of documents you may come across in the course of your research, each providing a useful insight into the social and economic status of your ancestors.

From the days when cameras first became available, amateur and professional photographers have captured the buildings, street life, and rural landscape of their hometowns. Today, many of these images survive in libraries and museums, and you may be lucky enough to find your family's home preserved in a photographic archive.

● If you have trouble deciphering a title deed or other property document, an experienced real estate agent or attorney may be able to help you

Deeds are legal documents evidencing ownership and changes in ownership of land or buildings. They are especially useful if your family research concerns New World countries during the nineteenth and twentieth centuries, since many land transactions took place during this period. As well as detailing the location, size, and type of property, deeds indicate the names of old and new owners, and may also refer to family relationships: For instance, stating that the seller of the property was Mrs. X, surviving daughter and sole heir of farmer Mr. Y.

Since the transferral of property involves a contract between individuals, original deeds are usually held by the signatories to

Deeds are usually held by the signatories to the transaction

the transaction, or by their respective attorneys. If there is a mortgage or loan agreement, deeds will be held by the financial lender. Current deeds are usually held by regional courthouses or by land registry offices. Land registries do not usually keep records of past deeds, so you may have to continue your research at legal or historical archives.

Taxation Records

Your ancestors might not have enjoyed paying their property taxes, but the tax collectors of years gone by can turn out to be good friends to an aspiring family genealogist. Records of taxes paid on any property can identify names of owners or tenants responsible for payment, the description and financial value of the property at any given time—and, by extension, can give you a clue to the economic circumstances of its owners. Owners of multiple properties will be listed more than once in the tax records.

Property taxes are indexed by street or location rather than by name of the taxpayer. However, if you know the address where your ancestor resided, and can look at the tax records extending over a period of years, you may be able to verify the dates when your family arrived at or departed from that location. Not all communities preserve these records: In some U.S. districts, county courthouses may only keep tax rolls for a few decades, while some English county record offices retain books of rates—the British form of local property tax—going back many centuries.

City Directories and Town Plans

The modern telephone book—even in its on-line and CD version—is only the latest in a long line of public directories. For generations, published listings of the names and addresses of local merchants, artisans, professionals, and private residents have been compiled for the use of locals and visitors alike. One of the earliest of these directories was the City of London directory for 1677. By the nineteenth century, the practice had spread to Boston, New York, Baltimore, and other international cities.

In some cases, these early city directories included data for the towns and villages within easy reach of the metropolitan area. As these satellite communities developed, they began to publish their own directories. City directories offer insights into the economic life of your ancestors' hometown. If you find a series of directories covering

Title and mortgage deeds (right) traditionally included the personal red wax seal of the signatories. Deeds were usually validated by the payment of a property tax, in this English example shown by a blue square. For rural areas, deeds would often include a map reference: This can be cross-referenced to maps from the same era to check locations.

Professional Hint

Use old maps and town plans to pinpoint those farms, villages, and roads long vanished from the landscape, abandoned due to depopulation, or swallowed up by other developments. Reproductions of historic maps, such as the Ordnance Survey series covering Great Britain or the maps published by the U.S. Geological Survey, are available from public libraries and specialty bookstores.

a span of years, you may be able to find out, from the dates in which entries appear and disappear, when your relatives first settled in that community, and when they left. Collections of directories are held by public libraries, historical societies, municipal archives, and are also republished.

Urban street plans displaying the names of thoroughfares, public buildings, and prominent private houses have a venerable pedigree. Illustrated guides were created for London in the 1600s, and the map collection of the Library of Congress, some of which is available on the Internet, includes a Manhattan map of 1639 and the 1752 Scull and Heap map of Philadelphia.

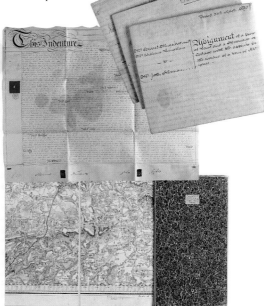

- The central registration of title deeds did not become standard until the twentieth century

- As populations increased in the nineteenth century, so did the need for residential and commercial directories

- Commercial directories can help you find the places your relatives lived and worked, and may also provide names of other people working at the same address

Immigration Records

As worldwide migration increased in the nineteenth century, so too did the bureaucratic machinery for processing new arrivals. Your foreign-born ancestors, stumbling down a gangplank after weeks on the ocean, may have struggled under a barrage of questions and official forms.

If your ancestor—like 12 million others—entered the United States between 1892 and 1954 via the New York reception center on Ellis Island (right), his or her records will appear on a database that is available on the Internet and CD.

Key Documents

There are two key documents to use when researching immigrant history. First, passenger lists show that a person was on board a particular ship and accounted for by the shipping line. Upon arrival, these lists were handed to customs or immigration officials, who would grant or deny entry to each arrival. Second, naturalization records, which are filed after arrival, document the immigrant's request for a new nationality.

Start by questioning relatives and check vital records to gain details about the countries from which your relatives came, when they arrived, their ports of entry, and the first neighborhoods in which they settled.

Passenger Records

Since the rapid growth in international migration from the seventeenth century onward, most ships have compiled passenger lists for every journey. These usually include the name of the ship, the captain's name, the port and date of departure and arrival, and varying degrees of data on all registered passengers. Hundreds of passenger lists are available in various formats for the United States and other countries. Be aware that the "country of origin" may be the country from which the ship sailed, not the one from which your ancestors came. For instance, Poles who sailed from the German port of Hamburg, may have Germany given as their country of origin.

By the twentieth century, federal authorities in countries experiencing increases in immigration responded with more detailed entry forms. These included the applicant's name, age, birthplace, trade, and a physical description. Immigrants were required to supply details of the relatives they were joining, and some later forms also noted the next-of-kin in the native country.

Later forms also noted the next-of-kin in the native country

Naturalization Records

The first step in acquiring new citizenship was for an immigrant to declare his or her wish to do so. In the United States, an immigrant completed a "first paper," or Declaration of Intent. This expressed a wish for citizenship and officially renounced allegiance to his or her native country. Before 1906, these declarations could be filed with any U.S.

● The more immigration details you start with, the more leads you are likely to obtain

Home Office No. 387,937
(A.) Certificate No. 6905

British Nationality and Status of Aliens Act, 1914.

CERTIFICATE OF NATURALIZATION.

Whereas Meier Rotimberg, known as Maurice Charles Roth,

has applied for a Certificate of Naturalization, alleging with respect to himself the particulars set out below, and has satisfied me that the conditions laid down in the above-mentioned Act for the grant of a Certificate of Naturalization are fulfilled in his case:

Now, therefore, in pursuance of the powers conferred on me by the said Act, I grant to the said Meier Rotimberg, this Certificate of Naturalization, and declare that upon taking the Oath of Allegiance within the time and in the manner required by the regulations made in that behalf he shall, subject to the provisions of the said Act, be entitled to all political and other rights, powers and privileges, and be subject to all obligations duties and liabilities, to which a natural-born British subject is entitled or subject, and have to all intents and purposes the status of a natural-born British subject.

In witness whereof I have hereto subscribed my name this 26th day of July, 1920.

Home Office,
London.

One of His Majesty's Principal Secretaries of State.

PARTICULARS RELATING TO APPLICANT.

Full Name — Meier Rotimberg, known as Maurice Charles Roth.
Address — 42, Victoria Park Road, in the County of London.
Trade or occupation — Manager of a Clothing Factory.
Place and date of birth — Roman near Bucharest, Roumania, 13th June, 1892.
Nationality — Roumanian.
Marital, single, or widower [colon] — Single.
Names of wife —
Names and nationality of parents — Cune and Seina Sima Rotimberg, known as Cune and Seina Sima Rothenberg. Roumanian.

(For Oath
see overleaf.)

This naturalization certificate contains a standard Declaration of Intent and also the personal details of the applicant.

— Birth name and known name, if different

— Declaration of Intent

— Address at time of application; in this case the applicant lived in London, England

— Date and place of birth

— Birth name and known name of applicant's parents, plus place of residence

● Your search for passenger and arrivals lists will be easier if you know the name of the ship on which your relative traveled

● If you know the port and likely year of arrival, a ship-by-ship search may be worth the effort

court. Once the applicant fulfilled the legal requirements, he or she could go to any court—not necessarily the same one—to file for naturalization and be granted citizenship. After 1906, the process was centralized under the federal Immigration and Naturalization Service. It is interesting to note that only a relatively small percentage of immigrants to the United States were fully naturalized.

Immigration Details to Record

NAMES

The full names, including any middle names, of the individuals you are seeking. Bear in mind that the spelling you are familiar with may not be the one that your relatives used at the time, or the one that the official wrote down, so be prepared to search for likely alternative versions.

ARRIVAL DATE

The closer you can get to the exact date, the easier your search will be. If you do not know the year, you may be able to obtain it from other official records. The 1920 United States census, for instance, specifically asked for immigrants' date of arrival; if the family was resident in the U.S. at that time, the year should appear on the household's census return.

PORT OF ENTRY

This is relevant for a number of reasons. Before governments centralized the control of immigration on a national basis, individual ports kept records, which may be available in local archives, or on CD or the Internet.

Sourcing Arrival Lists and Documents

● Back issues of ethnic newspapers covering the period when your ancestors lived within an immigrant community may contain reports or announcements relating to them

● Passenger boat lists and port arrival records are constantly being updated, both in printed indexes and on-line

Passenger List Indexes

Passenger list indexes for many countries are available from national archive organizations, genealogical libraries and publishers, and also the Internet. If you are researching immigrants arriving in the United States or Canada, for instance, one useful source is the annually updated *Passenger and Immigration List Index: A Guide to Published Arrival Records*, edited by P. William Filby and published by Gale Research, Detroit, covering the period between the 1600s and 1900s. This book is also available on CD from GPC, Baltimore.

Naturalization Documents

Depending on the country, naturalization documents may be split between national and local archive organizations. However, helpful indexes and references on specific ethnic groups are widely available from genealogical libraries and on the Internet. Most information is recorded on microfilm.

For the United States, naturalization documents can be hard to locate, since they could have been lodged in any local, county, state, or federal court. However, the Immigration and Naturalization Service has duplicate copies of most naturalizations filed after 1906. Other countries, such as Australia, keep naturalization documents in regional offices.

Professional Hint

If you do not have an exact address for your immigrant ancestors' first home, research the historical archives concerning the neighborhood in which they settled. New immigrants often gravitated to areas inhabited by their countrymen. In the United States, for instance, Scottish industrial workers moved to the New Jersey town of Kearney, while, back in Scotland, Glasgow became home to thousands of Irish immigrants.

Exploring Your Immigrant Heritage

As you trace your immigrant ancestors, you

Some coastal towns in Massachusetts, such as New Bedford and Provincetown, attracted Portuguese fishing families. This church in Provincetown was a communal focal point and a source of local immigrant knowledge.

Before the age of affordable airline travel, large passenger ships were the main method of international travel and took millions of migrants across the ocean to their new homeland.

can learn more about their lives by exploring the reasons they immigrated and the communities they joined on arrival. Seek out history books focusing on the region from which your ancestors came and find out what important events were taking place there prior to their departure.

Throughout history, people have migrated for economic reasons, but also to escape war, famine, revolution, and religious and racial persecution. By matching the dates of your family's migration with any traumatic events, political, or economic upheavals in their homeland, you will gain an insight into the problems, preoccupations, hopes, and fears of your ancestors.

A Piece of Home

Most immigrants first settled in their ports of entry or the nearest town. Their neighborhoods often still exist, preserving a cultural flavor even after immigrant communities have moved on. Revisit your roots with a trip to one of these areas. You may find the restaurants serving your ancestors' favorite dishes, houses of worship preserving their faith, or specialty music stores selling music from the old country. While you are there, drop into the public library or arrange a visit to the local historical society, since these will hold local histories and municipal records. Also, you may like to view back issues of local newspapers, magazines, and periodicals from the era when your relatives lived or worked in the neighborhood.

Until the mid-nineteenth century, only a tiny proportion of the world's population held passports. With an increase in global migration, governments slowly standardized their passport formats and made them more durable. This English passport from the mid-nineteenth century comprises just one sheet of paper on which international customs officials would record their stamp of arrival and departure.

Specialized Searches

● When searching for archives in your ancestors' country of origin, you may get more initial help from members of the diaspora community who have already undertaken such research

● If you do not speak your ancestors' mother tongue, ask a native speaker to translate your questions and conduct your research by mail or E-mail

The quality and consistency of vital records varies across the world and over time. Changing social and economic conditions through the ages provide modern-day genealogists with many difficult challenges in sourcing information. But even if your foreign-born ancestors turned their backs on their past when they stepped onto a ship or crossed a border, you may still be able to recover something of their history.

Genealogy Without Frontiers

Thanks to modern technology, the scope of genealogical research has expanded beyond the wildest dreams of previous generations. Specialized help and data for an ever-increasing number of countries and ethnic groups is available both in print and on-line. The end of the Cold War and the breaking down of international barriers means that some formerly inaccessible

records are now available to outside researchers. For the first time in over half a century, it has become feasible for the descendants of central and eastern European immigrants to visit their ancestral homelands.

Accessing Research Services

Genealogical societies have been organized by descendants of many ethnic groups. A public library, historical society, or general genealogical society should be able to point you in the right direction.

Libraries and bookstores stock an ever-growing number of handbooks concerned with ethnic research. Public genealogical conferences often feature seminars and lectures by ethnic specialists, as do organizations dedicated to those particular communities. Check the programs of events taking place in your area. If your ancestors

RESEARCH NOTES

FAMILY RESEARCHER *Ian Hancock*
FOCUS OF INQUIRY *Romani Heritage*

Ian Hancock, a professor of Romani Studies at the University of Texas, began tracing his Romani heritage after the death of his grandfather, Reg Hancock, in 1956.

Working under the stage name, Marko, Reg had earned his living as a musical entertainer, clown, sheet-music peddler, race-track tipster, and also a rat-catcher. Ian carefully collected archive material relating to Marko and also taped his elderly relatives' recollections. From his research, Ian learned that his Romani kinfolk still ran a carnival in Hungary and the London branch of the family had settled among the closely knit Notting Hill Romani community during the late nineteenth century. SEARCH TIP Ian says, "Speak to your oldest relatives. Get them on tape!" Appreciate your oral heritage; otherwise, it will be lost forever.

Romani legend Reg Hancock during one of his clown shows on the streets of London's Notting Hill in the late 1940s.

For genealogists of Japanese descent, the *koseki*, or family registry, is a vital document. For each family, the registry details births, deaths, parents' details, marriage, and emigration. Most local ward offices in Japan hold copies of *koseki*, but access is limited depending on the area. Consult your local Japanese society or search on-line genealogy links for specialist advice.

belonged to an ethnic group with a strong religious affiliation, churches or other religious bodies may have useful resources in their own libraries. Jewish institutions in the United States, such as the YIVO Institute in New York City, hold material on European Jewish communities.

Settlers often established economic and welfare support associations for their kinfolk, such as the Chinese Family Associations in San Francisco, London, and elsewhere. Libraries and historical societies in districts where immigrants settled can direct you to these friendship societies.

Disappearing Homelands

Since civilization began, vast empires have vanished and national borders have shifted. Towns and cities have changed their names, populations have been uprooted, new nations—such as Italy—have been created from smaller regions, while other sovereign states have been totally erased from the international map.

Poland, for instance, was divided up at the end of the eighteenth century and absorbed into the territories of Russia, Prussia, and the Austrian Empire. Only in 1918 did it regain its autonomy. If your ancestors emigrated from Polish lands during the 1800s and early 1900s, they may not be identified as Poles on their documents. For example, a Pole from the ancient national capital of Krakow may be described as "Austrian." In these cases, church records can provide more continuity than national archives. The Roman Catholic church in Poland has maintained vital records since 1809: Data for Polish forebears from some Russian- or Prussian-held areas are still held by the church, while those from regions under Austrian control are likely to be found in municipal archives.

Chinese Records

According to tradition, the people of China first acquired surnames in obedience to an order by the emperor Fu Hi, who ruled around 2800 B.C. Their purpose was to identify individual families and prevent intermarriage. Since the veneration of ancestors was an essential aspect of Chinese culture and social control, many families kept detailed records of their lineages. These compilations, known as Jia Pu or *Book of Generations*, contained information about the family's origins, mapped lines of descent, and held the vital records for the males of each passing generation.

Other cultures with a strong sense of social lineage also keep written records of their ancestors, especially if there is a caste system or social hierarchy which families wish to preserve for future generations.

● For on-line website resources on specific ethnic and religious groups, refer to Chapter Five

Immigration Records

African Heritage

Migrants from the South helped develop a vibrant new culture and economy in the cities where they settled. This 1941 photograph illustrates the exciting atmosphere of children waiting in line at a Chicago movie theater, and would be an ideal starting point for researching the lifestyles of previous generations.

● Coax elderly relatives to offer their memories about the family's hometowns, farms, jobs, and the names of migrating relatives

The last decades of the twentieth century saw an explosion of interest in African-American genealogy. The result has been a wealth of new historical discoveries, resources, and research techniques.

In the case of African-American families, especially those who joined the mass migrations between 1914 and 1920, oral history may provide the first clues as to where to search and what to look for. If you are lucky enough to belong to a family that hands down its memories as treasured heirlooms, you may unearth recollections of long-vanished childhoods or narratives of courage and social change preserved since the days of slavery.

Working Your Way Backward

Since African-Americans were not officially considered United States citizens until the 14th Amendment was ratified in 1868, pre-Civil War records of African-American ancestors can be hard to find. Even post-war records may be sketchy, especially in Southern states where segregation laws kept public records separated. The 1870 census was the first to include African-American residents. In previous censuses, slaves were registered under the name of the slave-owner, recording each individual's age and sex, but not his or her name.

Once you have found the localities your ancestors came from, cast your research net

Church ministers were a focal point of the African-American social infrastructure and a good source of information for genealogists. Taken in 1966, this snapshot shows a young Alabama minister speaking with his elderly congregants.

wider to include funeral home, church, and cemetery records. These are a rich mine of information, but they can often be hard to find, particularly for rural congregations or churches that no longer exist. However, if you can trace the whereabouts of the most recent church officials, they may be able to help you source the relevant records.

Digging Deeper

There are many books and Internet sites relating to African-American genealogy to guide you back into the period of slavery. Documents from the Reconstruction period are stored in the U.S. National Archives, and include land grants, labor contracts, and statements made by freed slaves trying to trace lost family members. Records such as the U.S. Colored Troops database contain the names of African-Americans who served in the Civil War.

Do not assume that all African-American ancestors were slaves. Since the beginning of colonial times, people of African descent have lived in North America as free settlers and citizens, especially in the long-established cities of the eastern seaboard. And even individuals who arrived as slaves,

or were born into slavery, found ways to obtain their freedom. Be alert for any references to ancestors whose presence in the United States predates the twentieth century migrations and those whose histories date back to before the Civil War.

For British residents of African-Caribbean descent, the ship *Empire Windrush* symbolized a turning point in their migration history. The *Windrush* brought the first of many settlers to the United Kingdom in the 1950s, signaling a wave of migration and a change in Britain's cultural make-up.

RESEARCH NOTES

SOCIAL RESEARCHER *U.S. Works Progress Administration (W.P.A.)* FOCUS OF INQUIRY *Oral History*

For African-Americans, oral history is vital for recording family history. Although oral history is now generally collected by relatives, official records are also extremely useful. Thousands of first-hand accounts of former slaves were compiled by the United States Works Progress Administration (W.P.A.) in the 1930s.

One interviewee, Nathan Beauchamp, offered to tell the W.P.A. recorder "a story of my mammy an' pappy," as he sat by the cabin in which he lived for over fifty years in Eufaula, Alabama. Nathan told the story of his father who was a slave in Alabama to Mr. Green

Beauchamp. Nathan recounted the first time his father saw his mother—a Native American woman from St. Francis Village—as he drove a wagon into Eufaula to get supplies. He recalled how his father went to Master Green to ask permission to marry the woman, Mimi. Such stories provide priceless data. From a few quotes, the genealogist learns names, a time frame, and locations related to Nathan's life. These elements allow the researcher to identify information that may lead to more vital records.

The language of the individual is also captured by interviews, offering far more than impersonal vital records. In his statement, Nathan Beauchamp said, "My mammy died 'bout five year atter freedom, but I can remembers dat she had long black hair, end I remembers the way de sun sparkle on her teeth when she smile."

● Until recently, some Southern states kept African-American vital records separated from those of white citizens

Specialist Searches

Between the sixteenth and nineteenth centuries, Spain, Great Britain, and other European nations settled the resource-rich lands of the New World and southern hemisphere. If you are descended from the indigenous peoples of colonial lands, such as North America, South America, or Australasia, there is a variety of specialized resources to trace your roots.

European culture had a deep impact on Native Americans, as with the cultures of other colonized nations. The perceived social advantages of European dress are all too evident in this early twentieth-century portrait of an Ute man.

North American Sources

The United States National Archives have large document collections, especially at the regional branch in Fort Worth. University libraries with local Native American histories are also a good resource, such as the Western History collection at the University of Oklahoma. Public libraries with Native American collections, such as the Newberry Library in Chicago, are also helpful. If you know your ancestors' tribe, look for specialized sources about that particular community. The Cherokee tribe, for instance, is well-served by *Cherokee Roots*, a two-volume compendium of Eastern Cherokee tribal rolls for 1817–1924 and Western Cherokee rolls for 1851–1909.

For Native Americans, census returns are also a vital resource, especially the 1880 Indian Census. The Bureau of Indian Affairs (B.I.A.), and the National Archives and Records Administration (N.A.R.A.) also hold similar data. The Internet also provides extensive resources on individual tribal histories and family heritage.

RESEARCH NOTES

FAMILY RESEARCHER *Joe Williams*
FOCUS OF INQUIRY *Native Ancestry*

Raised in Chicago, Joe Williams grew up with little knowledge of his Native American history. He began researching when he discovered he was eligible for a business grant if he could prove his minority status. Joe needed the names of his great-grandparents and their address or the tribe to which they belonged. Sadly, the relatives who knew this information had already passed away.

Joe first read through old letters belonging to his late grandmother. From these, he discovered various places in Wisconsin where his family had lived. Using the 1920 census returns from these places, Joe confirmed that his mother's family had lived on a reservation. Using the Chicago branch of the National Archives, Joe was referred to the records of Lac du Flambeau, a Chippewa reservation. After several days reading through unindexed records, his patience was rewarded with conclusive proof that his grandfather and his great-grandmother were members of the Chippewa tribe. From the records of 1922, he found a photograph and description of their house, and a brief profile of each occupant. The records noted that the family made "maple sugar, syrup, moccasins, and bead work. They pick, can, and dry wild berries. Both sisters are industrious and competent but lean to old Indian customs and morals."

SEARCH TIP At every stage of his research, Joe asked the advice of the experienced staff at archive and document repositories.

The home of Joe Williams' ancestors, as photographed by an agent of the Bureau of Indian Affairs in 1922.

Australian Convict Records

TRANSPORTATION REGISTERS	These give dates of ship departures, names of convicts on board, and the dates and details of their sentences.
FAMILY PETITIONS	Applications by wives and children to travel with, or follow, transported husbands and fathers to the penal colonies.
CENSUS RETURNS	These date from the early 1800s covering mainly Tasmania and New South Wales. The 1828 census asked whether each person in a household was of Australian birth or foreign-born, and whether they had come as free settlers or convicts.
PRINT AND INTERNET	Books, magazines, and databases include transportee lists from specific British or Irish towns and counties.

Focus on Forced Settlers

Some settlers to the New World were forced, rather than free, colonizers. For example, between 1787 and 1870, the British government sent more than 160,000 men, women, and children to penal colonies in Australia. Present-day Australians of British and Irish descent take pride in their convict ancestors, and there are various archives in Great Britain, Ireland, and Australia that hold details of these settlers.

Spanish Inheritance

If your ancestors came from former Spanish or Portuguese colonies, such as Mexico or Cuba, your research will vary according to when your relatives left their country. For those arriving in the United States in the nineteenth or twentieth centuries, start with vital records, census returns, and church records. Also look in libraries and historical societies in neighborhoods with large Central or South American communities.

- There are an increasing number of Internet sites for Central America and Cuba, providing links to societies, parish registers, and village censuses

- Genealogy magazines feature articles on the indigenous communities of colonized nations, and also on their early European settlers

- The Internet is an essential resource for Native American history, since it provides data on tribal histories and family heritage

- Be sure to check the LDS Family History Library, with its network of branches worldwide, for native and colonial information

For early settlers of North and South America, records exist in the colonial archives of the mother countries, such as Spain and England. This print shows the first settler ships to arrive in Jamestown, Virginia, in 1607: the *Godspeed*, *Discovery*, and *Susan Constant*.

Military Service Records

You can gain a vast range of data from military records. The details available, even for distant ancestors, go beyond basic names and dates of service. They provide a wealth of material about servicemen or servicewomen, their parents, spouses, and children.

● The individual parts of the armed forces—air force, army, and navy—hold their archives separately

● Local veterans associations may have records relating to your ancestor after he or she retired from the armed forces

Depending on the country in which your ancestor served in the armed forces, military files are held in either national or local archives at various levels. Records kept in national archives are usually those of key historical or administrative importance. Besides the individual service records, there are also records relating to every aspect of a soldier's life and career, from enlistment as a young volunteer to injury or death on the battlefield or at home.

Military Service Files

To find a military service file, you will need to know a soldier's full name, the war in which he served, or the period of service. Individual armed forces may require extra information: In the United States, for instance, you must know the state from which the soldier came. It also helps to know whether that individual was in the enlisted ranks or was an officer. For the Civil War, you must know if the soldier served in the Union or Confederate forces, since these records are kept separately.

Military service files are only made available years after the service period has elapsed—United States records, for example, are released after 75 years.

When searching through military indexes for references to individual files, you should be sure to make an exact copy of all serial numbers, names and numbers of units, and dates and references of applications made or certificates issued. This type of information is vital if your ancestor had a common surname or given

A professional soldier will have a host of memorabilia relating to his or her career. The archive of this British officer includes an informal photograph sent from the French front in December 1915 (below left), dispatches signed by Winston Churchill in 1916 (below center), postcards sent from Germany, where he was held as a prisoner of war in World War II, and a 1960s local newspaper clipping reproducing an old photograph of the Allied officers held in that same camp.

If you do not know when or where your ancestor served in the armed forces, make a rough timeline of his life from birth to death. From this, you will be able to discover when he became eligible for voluntary service or the draft, and in which conflicts he may have served.

Always ask archive centers if you can order military information through the mail to save you visiting the center in person.

name. Consider the number of "John Smiths," for instance, drafted to serve their country: Make sure you do not waste time ordering the wrong file.

Depth and Detail

Military service files contain useful biographical details, including name, number, period of service, place and date of birth, and details of marriage and death. Some service files offer a physical description, such as hair and eye color, height and weight.

Occasionally, files record a place of origin, since some units were recruited from the same geographic area.

However, this system deteriorated as internal migration increased—in Scotland, the Highland Light Infantry battalion of World War I was composed of transportation workers from the lowland city of Glasgow.

Military service files also include details of rank, promotion, wounds, capture, acts of heroism, commendations, court records, and location of grave.

Land Grants and Pension Records

As a reward for service, soldiers were sometimes given bounty-land. In the United States, records of land grants are kept in federal or state archives.

Pensions awarded to service personnel or their survivors may include financial details, records of disabilities incurred in action, and the personal circumstances of veterans or their dependents.

Family Records

In some national forces, such as the British army, professional soldiers and sailors—as opposed to drafted civilians—live with their spouses and children on military bases. Since these families are supervised by military authorities, their vital records may be kept in military rather than civilian registers. For example, the Family Records Centre, London, has indexes of Regimental Registers of Births and Baptisms 1761–1924, and registrations of births, baptisms, marriages, and deaths back to 1796.

Cemeteries and War Graves

If you are seeking details on those who died in action, you may find indexes in your national archive or records office—such as lists of British soldiers who died in combat in South Africa between 1899 and 1902. There are also war grave records, including the American Battle Monuments Commission and the Commonwealth War Graves Commission, with indexes available on the Internet.

Some service files offer a physical description

● Military pension applications may include affidavits describing the specific hardships or state of health of applicants

● Many military databases and lists are available over the Internet and on CD—these may be able to confirm any facts you have already learned and lead you to further archive sources

The events of war, whether it is officers returning home from the front or the tragic deaths of young recruits, are never forgotten by relatives. Personal effects and mementoes, such as a tag or diary, are often kept by surviving relatives and may provide useful sources for genealogists.

Educational and Occupational Records

Educational, vocational, and professional records provide intriguing insights into the lives, personalities, and relationships of earlier generations. They may also provide concrete information about birth dates, migrations, and social aspirations. Records may be both visual and documentary, both of a primary and secondary nature.

● Even yearbooks dating from the early twentieth century may contain photographs of pupils, notes on their academic and sporting prowess, participation in school clubs, nicknames, and ambitions

School report cards (above left) often indicate the personality of the child—this one requests the child to attend church more often. Portraits taken to record a new qualification (above right) also provide an emotional context—you can clearly see the pride of this young nurse.

Most school systems restrict the access to transcripts, reports, and other material contained within students' personal files. Restrictions usually apply to age groups still likely to be living, so it may be possible to obtain records that go back three or more generations. Even if the educational authority refuses access to your great-grandmother's report card, there is plenty of data available from other municipal, county, or state archives, such as school registers and log books.

School and College Documents

School registers record essential personal information for each pupil on the school roll: Birth date, names of parents, address, previous schools, and the dates the pupil arrived and left. Reasons for early departure may be noted, such as the family moving to another town, expulsion, or even the child's death.

Records also exist from orphanages and charitable schools set up to house and educate paupers, homeless children, and other young people in need.

Yearbooks are an accessible and less formal source of information. School archives and local libraries generally store these volumes, but you may well find them lurking in the attics of your older relatives.

Academic transcripts are not usually available for recent generations without the written request of the subject or a written request from a close relative accompanied by the subject's death certificate. Other documents, such as unclassified enrollment records, may provide similar information. College and university libraries are rich sources of material, such as yearbooks, student newspapers and journals, and copies of dissertations.

Apprenticeships

An apprentice is a trainee learning a trade under the personal supervision of an expert master or mistress in that field. For centuries, apprenticeships were the most common form of vocational training, and the first step to employment. They usually

Occupational ID cards will not only tell you what your ancestor did for a living, but may also include a photograph. This card is for a traveling salesman to use on British railroads.

Equipment or uniforms owned by your ancestors may provide clues as to their profession. Historical archives relating to these professions may help you date any such items that you uncover.

They may turn up in family papers, or the employer's company records.

Some apprenticeship agreements have found their way into public archives. In Great Britain, for instance, trade regulatory bodies, known as Guilds, hold records that date back to medieval times. Since the Guilds were an integral part of the establishment, their records are often found in city archives.

Professional Associations

Professional bodies, especially those that give accreditation in fields such as medicine or law, are good sources of information on the date that an individual formally entered his or her profession. They may also help you to establish dates of death or retirement. Individual members of professional associations will usually keep their certificates of admission or qualification, since these are likely to have been required as proof of qualification.

As well as formal membership registers, professional archives hold newsletters giving notices of new entrants into the profession. Legal and medical associations confer the right to practice, and there are also trade bodies that regulate teaching, architecture, nursing, and engineering. Directories of professional organizations can be found in most reference libraries.

began with a formal agreement between the specialist and the young person, or his or her parents or legal guardians. The agreement set out the obligations of both parties: The amount of time the apprentice would be required to serve and the form of payment or subsistence that would be provided. Since they were private contracts, apprenticeship documents, commonly known as indentures, are often hard to find.

Genealogical Organizations

The old saying that "many hands make light work" holds true in genealogy. People searching for their ancestral roots generally find they have much in common with others engaged in the same quest. Never underestimate the practical help you can get by joining a genealogical society.

● **Many societies run courses and conferences, giving you opportunities to network and to learn from other people's expertise**

● **Magazines published by family history societies include useful research tips, historical background, and classified sections for queries**

Genealogical societies provide a host of services; some of these are free of charge, while others impose a fee. National or regional genealogical societies have extensive reference libraries and databases that can save you time, effort, and even money. By gaining access to these collections, you can consult a variety of indexes that would otherwise require visiting different repositories.

Upon joining a genealogical society, you will probably be asked to provide vital details of your own family history in order to expand the society's own records and provide possible links with other members. You will be able to improve your research techniques by drawing upon the experience of other members, who may have come across similar challenges. Many societies hold seminars and lectures on particular research problems relevant to its members.

Although many genealogists exchange information and ideas via E-mail and the Internet, it is important to remember that some extremely experienced researchers are not on-line: Genealogical societies can give you access to the advice and specialized knowledge of such experts.

Family History Societies

Family history societies focus on the genealogy of a single region, community, or family. Depending on their size and age, many diaspora communities sport at least one genealogical society. They are usually

Based in New York City, the American Irish Historical Society records the story of the Irish in the United States from the earliest settlement to the present day. With a rousing motto, "That the World May Know," its mission is to remind Irish Americans of their heritage. Its extensive library includes records covering both Irish and American-Irish genealogy.

run by the descendants of immigrants belonging to a particular cultural group and are motivated by a wish to understand their heritage and revisit their roots. These specialized groups often hold records that are unavailable elsewhere.

Ethnic genealogical societies offer tips on researching both your ancestor's country of origin and the locality where they settled on arriving in their new country. Whether the organization is based around the Greek community in Melbourne, Australia, the Swiss community in Wisconsin, U.S.A., or

Sporting its own coat of arms, the Society of Genealogists in London has one of the largest collections of documents from before 1837: Its resources include parish registers, census names, vital records, tombstone inscriptions, and trade directories.

the Italian community in Wales, members will have a shared sense of cultural identity. Such groups may also sponsor collective research projects, such as the compilation of a database on cemeteries, or a study on some aspect of local social history. If you are researching a family with connections to a particular place, you may find it worthwhile to join a local genealogical society in order to make contacts, receive publications, and gain access to their resources, especially if you live far away from the area you are researching.

Focusing on the Name

Surname societies research individuals with a particular surname, or those with connections to specific family groups. Some societies are well-established, while others are short-lived or only sporadically active, depending on the enthusiasm of members. Some genealogical directories publish lists of family associations and surname societies, and these groups may also advertise in family history magazines. Many now maintain their own Internet websites, or they can be accessed by searching a general genealogy site on the Internet. For more information on Internet skills, refer to Chapter Five.

Using the Local Press

If you are researching relatives who lived in a particular town, you can place a classified advertisement in the local newspaper, asking for information. Even if the last surviving family member died some time ago, you may find an elderly neighbor who

When submitting a letter or classified advertisement to a genealogical magazine, choose the publication very carefully in order to maximize the possibility of a response. Consider whether the readers will be interested in your areas of research.

still remembers them, or someone with a knowledge of local history who recognizes the name. Some newspapers even have genealogy columnists who may be willing to publish your inquiry; others may print an inquiry on the regular Letters page.

When writing, keep your letter short and to the point. Ask only one or two short questions. Explain that you are a family member seeking information specifically for genealogical research.

Give the name of the person or family you are researching, plus the likely dates of their residence in the town, and any street address or neighborhood if you know it. Briefly mention other details that might trigger someone's memory, such as, "Mr. X was a widower bringing up four children alone …" Include a a photograph of the person after whom you are inquiring.

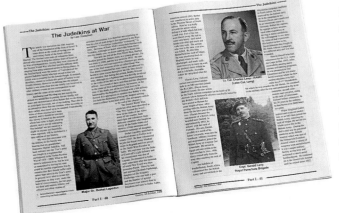

Larger family history societies publish regular newsletters or pamphlets, develop databases, share research, store documents and memorabilia, and put members in touch with each other.

CHAPTER FOUR

PRESERVING YOUR FINDS

As you begin exploring your family history, you will probably find that your workstation starts to stack up with family memorabilia, photographs, research notes, and documents that took time and effort to obtain. Now is the time to get organized.

Documents and other archive items are precious, many of them irreplaceable. Even your research notes—the fruits of your labors—are not only vital resources for you but a wonderful legacy for future generations. However, all these things are perishable. Heat, humidity, light, the moisture on your hands, and even the materials from which your documents are made are all potential enemies that can damage or even destroy them.

In terms of administration, it is vital that you keep your data well-ordered and easily accessible. Storing information in a chaotic way can lead to its temporary disappearance or permanent loss or damage. Fortunately, there are methods you can employ to store your acquisitions correctly, and measures you can take to protect them against damage

You will, no doubt, collect a range of historical items to preserve—from photos and cuttings, to damaged albums and scrapbooks. Each item may require your special care and attention, depending on its composition and future usage.

caused by environmental conditions and the passage of time. In some cases, if you act quickly enough, it may even be possible to reverse or mitigate some of the harm caused by earlier neglect.

The first step in safeguarding family treasures is to understand the factors that can cause harm, then take measures to protect them. This chapter shows you safe, affordable, and user-friendly ways to protect, store, and display your archive material. You will learn the best way to preserve your genealogical collection, including paper documents, family mementoes, old photographs, home-movie reels, and audiotapes.

A helpful overview of information technology explains how computer and digital technology can be used to preserve and enhance your original archive material and assist in the administration of your research. You will receive useful advice on selecting appropriate hardware, software, and peripheral hardware for your individual needs.

Storing Paper

Anyone trying to protect and preserve documents, books, and other items made from fragile and perishable paper or card stock, soon realizes that time—contrary to the old adage—is not a great healer. However, a few simple measures can protect family treasures, whether you are storing for the first time or preventing damage to an item already showing signs of deterioration.

● **When handling documents, do not expose them to light for any longer than absolutely necessary**

When handling documents and books, be sure your hands are perfectly clean, dry, and free of ink, grease, or oily residues. Even the natural oils in your skin can pose a threat to old paper, so it is best to wear thin cotton gloves when handling any items. These are widely available from suppliers of medical equipment and also retailers of archival products.

When writing or making notes in the vicinity of any document, use only a soft lead pencil rather than any kind of pen. Keep food and drink far away. Spilled coffee or water, a buttery bread crumb, a stray droplet of juice from an apple, or ink from a carelessly held pen will permanently mark paper and speed up deterioration.

Light, Humidity, and Heat
Light, whether from electric bulbs or from the sun, causes yellowing on paper and the fading or disappearance of its text. Damage to documents is cumulative, and the worst effects are caused by the ultraviolet light of fluorescent lightbulbs and the sun's rays.

An excessively damp atmosphere can cause problems, encouraging the growth of mold on paper or causing the emergence of small brown spots, known as foxing.

This United States title deed from May 1860 has been kept folded while in storage. As a result, the folded parts of the paper have deteriorated slightly. Luckily, the main horizontal fold does not run over any text.

Protect archive family postcards in acid-free storage boxes. For extra protection from dust and fingerprints, put the postcards into plastic sleeves before storing.

Always store your papers and books in the driest part of your home: Avoid damp basements and areas exposed to the moist air of a bathroom or a utility room where a washing machine or dryer are in frequent operation. Shelves or storage areas are likely to be driest if they lie against an inside, rather than an exterior wall. Ideally, the humidity of the room should be no more than 35–40 percent.

Heat also encourages deterioration. Archivists consider 55° F (13° C) the most suitable temperature for documents, but this is likely to be colder than most homes. Attics, despite their convenience, are not

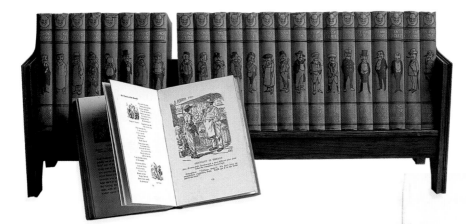

Books that are kept out on display are susceptible to damage from moisture, pests, light, and also fire.

recommended, since they are liable to become far too hot, especially in summer. And many experts consider a steady temperature just as important as a cool one. Extreme variations can do as much harm as excessive warmth. Choose a storage place in the living area of your home, with a temperature that remains stable all year round and never exceeds 72° F (22° C).

Acidic Contamination

The paper on which documents are printed, the envelopes or folders that hold them, and even the cardboard boxes in which they are stored contain natural acids that seep out over time, causing deterioration to the item and to anything else with which it comes into contact. Newsprint and telegram paper are highly acidic and particularly prone to leaching.

Use widely available acid-free folders and scrapbooks, both to protect the documents themselves and to prevent their own acidity from contaminating other papers. Folders made of transparent materials, such as plastic film, make it easy to see your stored papers and documents, without subjecting them to wear and tear

through removal from their storage containers. It is also possible to purchase special boxes made of acid-free, alkaline-buffered materials to hold documents stored in acid-free sleeves.

Animal Pests

Mice love to eat most types of paper products; so do bookworms, book lice, and silverfish. The various waste products excreted by these insects can do as much damage as their voracious appetites. The best protection against rodent and insect raiders is constant vigilance, and a scrupulously clean and dust-free environment. Remember that a cardboard box also makes an attractive snack for a hungry mouse. If you keep documents in a room prone to vermin, use archive-quality metal or plastic boxes.

Preserving Damaged Documents

To prolong the life of a document that is already damaged, make a photocopy of the original, using alkaline-buffered, acid-free paper. Use the copy for reference; keep the original, stored in a clear, acid-free sleeve in a cool, dry, and dark place.

Official Publication of the Cleethorpes Urban District Council.

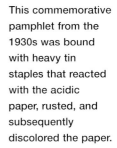

This commemorative pamphlet from the 1930s was bound with heavy tin staples that reacted with the acidic paper, rusted, and subsequently discolored the paper.

Archive-quality dry cleaning pads are ideal for removing surface dirt from paper documents. Carefully read the manufacturer's instructions before using.

Storing Photographs

Family pictures are priceless treasures, but the chemicals used to produce these images, and the nature of the materials on which they are printed, make photographs particularly vulnerable documents. With care, though, there are many different ways to protect, preserve, and reproduce these visual records for yourself, your relatives, and for future generations.

● Color film processing methods were designed to create vivid images, but not necessarily lasting ones

Photographs are processed with strong chemicals and almost always printed on some kind of paper or card stock. They are exposed to the same dangers experienced by any other paper or card document.

Environmental and Chemical Risks

The environmental and chemical dangers to your old photographs include light, dust, dampness, extremes of temperature, insect larvae, hungry vermin and insects, and acidic contamination by the materials from which they are made or those in which they are stored. Exposure to strong fumes, such as paint or solvent, can also trigger deterioration; even the natural oils in human skin, passed on in a mere thumbprint, can pose a serious threat.

In terms of damage, the printed image contained on the surface of a photograph may fade, blacken, or otherwise discolor; the paper itself may crumble or crack or become mottled. Unframed pictures may

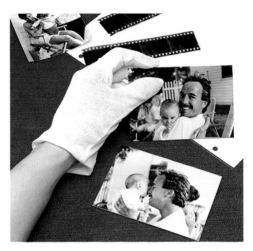

Professional archivists wear thin cotton gloves when handling documentation. These are widely available from retailers or archive storage catalogs and also drugstores.

curl and fray around the edges. Be aware that modern photographs are just as vulnerable as those from an earlier era.

Photographic viewsheets are an ideal way to store and file prints, and are available in a variety of sizes.

When you search through photographs belonging to your relatives, you will invariably find many kept loose and in unsatisfactory conditions. Unless the owner was an avid recorder of family details, do not be surprised if many of them are unnamed and undated.

Choosing Photo Albums

Albums are intended to protect your pictures. But there is a risk that they may, over time, damage them instead: Unless they are made from archive-quality, acid-free materials, the pages on which photographs are mounted, any mounts or paper corners used to hold them in place, and even overlay sheets and dividers can cause chemical contamination leached from the plastics used in their manufacture. Depending on the format, photographs can be damaged during the process of placing the print in the album itself, especially if it includes built-in cardboard mounts, adhesive pages, or requires the use of photo corners.

Avoid albums or scrapbooks with plastic covers and pockets, or with pages treated with adhesive or magnetic backing. When purchasing albums, reject any that do not bear a label guaranteeing them as "archival-quality," "PVC-emission-free," or "acid-free." Question the sales staff closely to reassure yourself before you buy.

Making Copies

To limit the risk of damage or loss, the best thing you can do to protect a photographic heirloom is to make a copy—or several copies—of the original image. Once you have done this, the precious original can be stored in a safe place while its duplicates are available for display or sharing with relatives elsewhere. Depending on the type of photograph you want to duplicate and the amount of money you are able to spend, there are various options available. If your budget allows, make multiple copies to distribute to interested family members.

Of course, if you have a valued set of photographs displayed in their original old album, you must weigh the risks of removing the prints from their original setting in order to copy them or store them in a more protective environment. Consider the storage and restoration requirements of your albums so they can be preserved in the best environment and delay any damage to the photographs they contain.

This cardboard picture mount shows signs of "foxing," a common condition characterized by dark spots over the paper. It is usually caused by storage in a damp atmosphere.

Storing Photographs

79

Taking Action

● Processing old photographs is more specialized and expensive than developing your latest set of snapshots

● Never use an express developer, drugstore, or department store to process archive photographs

Using Photo Labs

Photo labs can make negatives from old photographs, so you can create as many duplicate prints as you like. Technology has made it possible to produce digital copies of photographs with a scanner, producing replicas that retain the original quality.

Photo labs can also produce touched-up copies of old photographs. The original print is scanned in, then improved digitally using image manipulation software, such as Adobe Photoshop. A high level of training is used to complete this procedure successfully, so always ask to see an example of the lab's work before commissioning them to do the same on your photographs.

Many firms can transfer photographs to CD for viewing on a home computer. However, scanners are relatively cheap, so you may prefer to buy the relevant hardware and software yourself so you can digitally archive your material at home.

If you are on a tight budget, start by surveying your collection of photographs. If you could only afford to rescue a handful of them from any hypothetical disaster, which ones would you choose? Duplicate the most precious items first, saving the remainder until you have sufficient money and time to complete the project.

Professional Hint

Before you entrust your photographs to a photographic shop or commercial laboratory—even one that comes well recommended—ask the lab about their precise methods for processing your photographs and safeguarding the items. If pictures are sent off the premises, what steps do they take to make sure nothing is lost or damaged in transit? Ask about the level of training given to staff, since any errors made during processing may damage your property forever. Before you order copies, make sure you have some idea of the costs involved.

Lamination and Tinting

Never laminate a photograph, either with a do-it-yourself kit or through a commercial outlet. You risk causing irreparable damage to the photo. Never attempt to tint original black-and-white photographs, since this should only be done by professionals.

Photocopying

Making photocopies of family pictures has its pros and cons. A high-quality color photocopy—even of a black-and-white or sepia image—can produce a reasonable

Digital tinting produces impressive results and lets you keep black-and-white images in their original condition.

Digital retouching of this photograph has successfully removed the overall mottling, creases, and dirt.

• Always discuss your requirements with photo lab staff before handing over any pictures for copying

• Duplicate photographic prints lose color quality and sharpness if the original image is enlarged more than ten percent

version of the image. Although antique photographs will not benefit from the strong light emitted by the photocopier, the exposure time is short, and constant handling will not do them much good either. If you want a copy for frequent study or display and cannot afford the services of a photo lab, this method may be your safest and most economical option. Make sure to use a high specification, up-to-date machine. These are available at print and reprographic shops, or office supply stores. Libraries—especially those with manuscript collections—may also offer these services.

Storing Negatives

Store negatives away from the prints, and make sure they are kept in acid-free, archival-quality materials. Color film is less durable than black-and-white, so you might like to order black-and-white negatives of color images for archive purposes only.

Rescue and Repair

DIRT AND MOISTURE

To remove surface dirt from photographs, clean them gently with a soft, dry brush or an air spray. If you are framing a photograph under glass, make sure the glass and the surrounding frame are clean, dust-free, and bone-dry. Just one tiny drop of moisture or grease can cause mold or decay.

TEARS AND DAMAGE

Avoid the temptation to mend a torn picture with adhesive tape or glue. Always refer to a professional restorer or conservation expert, since these technicians are trained to flatten wrinkled surfaces and curled edges, and to fill in scratches by the application of special oils.

To find reliable specialists, consult libraries, museums, or galleries that use such services. Alternatively, take advice from photographers' studios or photographic supply houses. If you belong to a genealogical society, its reference library or your fellow members may be able to give you recommendations based on their own experience.

An air spray is a convenient way to remove dust from slides, prints, or negatives.

Storage Options

There are many options for storing your collection of family papers, photographs, and other heirlooms. Ask yourself how you intend to use them, since this will affect your storage methods. Do you simply want to store your treasures for future generations, or do you feel that your images deserve to be seen as often as possible?

If you inherit a scrapbook or photograph album that is damaged or deteriorating, you will need to consider whether to move the contents to a safer environment or keep them in their original setting, which itself will be a treasured family heirloom.

Ideally, your archive materials should be stored in a fireproof location, such as a safe-deposit box or bank vault. However, family documents are more likely to be kept in your home. But even if a quiet corner is the most secure storage space you can provide, there are still ways to keep this documentary legacy in good condition.

Storage Boxes

Archive storage boxes provide the safest housing for original photographic prints, especially if you insert an acid-free sheet between each item. Photographic and office supply firms are good sources of these items. You will find advertisements in genealogical publications and on the Internet for firms specializing in conservation materials. File boxes are available in a variety of materials and sizes. However, be sure that the boxes—as well as any dividers, folders, sleeves, or pockets—are guaranteed "archival quality" to avoid acidic contamination.

If your collection includes deeds and wills, these are likely to be printed on legal paper, which is larger than regular paper. Select boxes, folders, document pockets, and dividers that can hold your largest documents lying flat. Never store your documents folded, since prolonged or repeated creasing will render lines of text illegible or tear brittle paper.

Archive-quality storage boxes are available for larger documents, such as art prints, and avoid the need to fold items.

Professional Hint

A storage system is only as good as the way in which it is organized. You can arrange the elements in any way that you find comfortable and easy to keep track of—by family branch, type of document, historical period, or source of information. Label each drawer or box, and each item within it, with a summary of its contents. Keep an up-to-date index of your archive material at the front of each box or drawer for reference, and note how much material you have. If a section of your archive is about to burst, find a logical way to divide the material. You may find the need to adjust your system as you develop your own personal methods of research.

Scrapbooks

Archive-quality scrapbooks and notebook-style ring binders are also available. Use archive-quality transparent sleeves with pre-punched margin holes. Never punch holes in original documents. Before placing a document in a sleeve, carefully remove any clips or staples, which can rust and eat into the paper. If either has been used to append an explanatory note or another relevant document, store the attachment in an adjacent sleeve, and label the outside of each holder with a note explaining the connection between them.

Filing Cabinets

Consider the space you have available, as well as the variety of materials you want to store. As your interest in genealogy increases, you will find that your collection of archive material also grows.

A regular filing cabinet with hanging inserts is an efficient use of floor space, but horizontal files, not lateral, are more accessible for larger documents. As with file boxes, filing cabinets are usually designed to accommodate either large legal-sized or smaller letter-sized files. If your budget

allows, the legal size, although more expensive, is a better option, making it unnecessary to fold larger documents. When buying, look for drawers that roll smoothly to their full length and a stable overall structure. As a safety feature, most cabinets allow only one drawer to open at a time, which prevents it from tipping over.

Secondhand furniture suppliers are a good source of high-quality filing cabinets at a fraction of the new price. However, if you buy a secondhand filing cabinet, be aware that internal fixtures may be broken and the overall structure may not be safe. Inspect all the drawers and runners before you purchase, and be sure you can obtain suitable fixtures and files. These pieces may not represent the cutting edge of design, but they make up in affordability what they lack in aesthetic appeal.

Fireproof Cabinets

If you are storing highly prized and irreplaceable material, a fireproof cabinet may be a wise investment. Be aware, though, that none are entirely invulnerable, and there are differences in the degree of protection afforded—ranging from the simply "fire-resistant" to those guaranteed to shield their contents from heat and flame for a specified period of time, generally no more than two hours.

● Never overfill a filing cabinet or storage box, since this may damage your archive material

Keeping your most valuable documents in a fireproof safe will give them the best chance of survival in a fire. Be aware that the length of time a safe can survive in extreme heat conditions may vary.

Display Ideas

Genealogy is not just an entertaining pastime, but an act of generosity in sharing your knowledge. After many hours spent in record offices or scrutinizing genealogical websites, other relatives will most likely be appreciative recipients of your findings. Fortunately, there are ways to display your memorabilia without subjecting items to unwelcome wear and tear.

● All sorts of mementoes can find a place in a scrapbook—old photographs, party invitations, newspaper clippings, birthday cards, graduation programs, exotic postcards, letters, journal extracts, family recipes, or even grocery lists

Rather than locking all your cherished discoveries away in your files, you may want to compile some of the highlights of your research for an accessible tour of the family's past. There are a host of different ways to do this.

Scrapbook of Mementoes

Creating a family scrapbook is a rewarding task for a genealogist and also makes an ideal gift for relatives.

Even if you only use copies of documents, rather than the originals, remember that this simple scrapbook may turn out to be an heirloom for future generations. Be sure that all the materials you use—the labels, adhesives, and the pages themselves—are of archival quality. You can purchase these materials from stationery suppliers, catalogs that specialize in genealogical products, and reputable Internet dealers.

Framing

For best results, commission a professional framer to frame your chosen items. A professional will be able to advise you on the best frame and mount, and is trained to handle delicate documents with care. Be

This framed display of wartime medals and a military commendation brings together two landmark aspects of a soldier's career.

aware that long-term exposure to artificial light and natural sunlight will speed the decay of paper and photographs. If possible, only display duplicate material, since a well-framed, good-quality photocopy can look just as effective as an original. Always choose mounts and frames that are sympathetic to the items and enhance the heirloom feel of the overall display. Ask like-minded genealogists how they have displayed their own finds: They are sure to offer helpful ideas.

Nineteenth- and twentieth-century scrapbooks and albums are often beautifully finished and decorated. Use the mounts, details, and decorative devices as inspiration for your own keepsake projects.

Professional Hint

If you possess an heirloom Bible, ancestor's memoir, or one of the oversized photograph albums beloved of past generations, do not strain its spine by standing it upright on a shelf. These volumes are best allowed to lie flat on a flat surface, with nothing on top of them. Do not despair if one of these books has a damaged binding. It is a sound investment to have its binding repaired or replaced by an expert. Consult with your local library, genealogical society, or museum for recommended bookbinders, or ask an antiquarian bookseller or antiques dealer for names of binders whose work they can recommend.

Archive material is best displayed in its original setting so, where possible, have damaged albums and scrapbooks professionally restored. With a broken spine and flaking leather, this antique photo album was extremely fragile (top left). Restoration involved treatment of the leather and the application of an inexpensive canvas spine (bottom left).

Textiles and Collectibles

Textiles such as needlework samplers and heirloom knits are a pleasure to frame or hang. However, they must be placed in a dark room away from sunlight to slow the process of deterioration. Cover the frame with thick fabric when it is not on show.

Box-style frames are ideal for small mementoes and collectibles; they are available in a variety of colors and are easy to assemble at home. By combining two or more items in a display, you can tell a story relating to your family history. Consider the documents, heirlooms, and records you have collected through your research and how they reflect the personal experiences and personalities of your ancestors.

You may want to select a photograph of your parents or grandparents when they were young adults and set it in a pretty frame with a good-quality photocopy of their marriage certificate. Alternatively, use a suitable box frame to show a selection of an ancestor's collectibles, accompanied by a duplicate photograph of the original owner and a copy of his or her signature.

A well-chosen picture frame, such as this antique-gold style, can transform an old photograph into a stylish home accessory and provide an emotive focus for any room.

Audio, Video, and Movie Archives

Documents and photographs are not the only archive material worth storing. Old home movies, videos, and audiotapes—those containing your recorded interviews, stories, and even music—are heirlooms in their own right. Without attention, such material can deteriorate, but fortunately there are many ways to preserve it, for your own enjoyment and as a legacy for the future.

If you inherit home movies on video-tape, be sure to make a copy for your archive or transfer them to another format, such as CD or DVD. Be aware that the quality of a digital conversion will only be as good as the original.

Storage and retrieval of audio- and video-tapes and home movies is much easier if you keep a catalog of your collection. Write a small file card for each item giving—if available—the contents, date, source, and names of those people producing and participating. Make sure to label every reel or tape, along with its container, to make sure it is not taped over by accident. To prevent audiotapes from being recorded over, use the end of a pen to break off the two plastic flaps on the back edge.

Home Movies

In the 1920s and 1930s home movie-making was a pleasure enjoyed only by the very wealthy. Movies were silent and shot in black-and-white on narrow gauge "safety" stock, identified by its 8mm, 9.5mm, or 16mm width. By the 1960s, equipment for amateur use was more affordable and available, encouraging the filming of every aspect of domestic life, from babies' first steps to rain-soaked family picnics. The mid-1960s saw the invention of Super 8mm movie stock, which made this pastime more affordable than ever before.

To protect the original movie reels, store them in non-corrosive metal containers, in cool, dry conditions, away from exposure to light, dust, and changes in humidity.

The safest way to view archive movies is to transfer them to regular videotape or even DVD or CD format. There are many companies that offer this service, allowing you to create compilations for transmission through your video player or home computer without the need for projectors, screens, and extra peripherals. There is software available for converting Super 8mm movies to video using a home computer. If considering this option, make sure you have the correct equipment: variable speed projector, camcorder, screen and/or transfer box, tripod, and enough capacity on your computer hard drive. Be sure to take advice from an archive movie society or a multimedia software specialist

Until the 1960s, movie cameras, film stock, and processing were prohibitively expensive. As a result, home movies up to this time did not generally record the trivial or ordinary aspects of life. Chosen topics reflected more "important" events, such as vacations, state occasions, and key events in the subject's life.

before attempting this task. Alternatively, you can play old movies through an original projector. Reconditioned secondhand projectors are available from electronic and camera retailers, and also Internet outlets.

Color stock is far more perishable than black-and-white because of the chemicals in its composition. If your priority is simply to preserve the contents of the movie, you can have a duplicate made in black-and-white. If you wish to retain the color—and are not concerned about cost—it is possible to separate the colors on the original and make negatives for later reproduction.

Professional Hint

Prior to 1951, some home movies were produced on nitrate stock, a highly combustible material. It can be identified by the word *nitrate* or by an explosion symbol on the edge of the reel. If the film is not nitrate but safety film, the word *safety* will be printed on the reel instead. If you come across any old movie reels that you suspect may be nitrate stock, immediately consult an official film archive for guidance. To locate your nearest archive consultant, check the telephone directory or ask at your local library.

Video- and Audiotapes

Although videotapes are less fragile than movie stock, they, too, will last longer when stored in optimum conditions. Exposure to excessive heat and light—such as a radiator or direct sunlight—will damage the cases and tape. Never store video- or audiotapes above television sets or stereo equipment and speakers. Take care to play your archive video- and audiotapes on good-quality equipment, since an old or low-quality machine may damage your tapes.

Very early movies should be handled by a professional film archivist. This stereoscopic film required an original projector and a skilled technician to convert it to a modern format.

- For all video and audio material, keep a master list that can be easily updated

- If you lend any part of your archive collection, note the details of the borrower and the date taken, as if you were a librarian lending books

- Film archives are always on the lookout for old home movies and videotapes of earlier decades

RESEARCH NOTES

FAMILY RESEARCHER *Michael Nyberg*
FOCUS OF INQUIRY *Home Movies*

California-based movie enthusiast, Michael Nyberg, was asked by his cousin Sara Brewer to convert 35 rolls of 8mm film to video. The rolls were shot by Sara's mother, Lynn, between 1962 and 1966. Sara had little interest in the reels and thought only of having a quick look at the old days. However, when Michael finished transferring the rolls, they reviewed a small excerpt together and became excited about the prospect of sharing these wonderful family memories. When transferring the reels, Michael carefully removed the poorly exposed scenes and those frames where there was no apparent subject.

The edited reels were shown at the next family Christmas party, prompting a combination of shock, delight, laughter, and also a few sad memories from their relatives. SEARCH TIP Archive movie reels can bring the whole family together, so always try to convert to a more modern format.

Using Information Technology

There was a time when genealogists would struggle under a mountain of paper and files. Now, however, every facet of genealogy—from the storage and retrieval of words and pictures to the creation of family trees—has been made faster and more flexible by information technology. You can choose from a range of genealogy-tailored software, reference materials, historical information, and vital records available on CD and over the Internet.

Administrative Benefits

Use information technology to enhance your overall genealogical experience and maximize the information you have found. When considering which computer, software, and peripherals to buy, ask advice from other genealogists.

FILING

Genealogical software allows you to create your own computer database for collating information and storing it in an organized and accessible manner, including names, dates, addresses, relationships, anecdotes, recipes, sources and records, diaries, and lists of tasks to be done.

RESEARCH ASSISTANCE

Never forgetting that the first commandment of genealogical research is to cite the sources for every fact you obtain, many packages provide easy-to-use systems for recording and accessing these details.

DATA FLEXIBILITY

Software packages can organize and summarize your data in different ways. Once you have entered names and vital details, you can ask the software to prepare individual summaries or charts showing selected family information and relationships. Such reports show you what information you possess and what gaps you need to fill.

Pull-down screen menus offer you many options for structuring data: You can, for example, create a breakdown of one ancestor's entire line of direct descendants, track surname holders through several generations, or survey the details for all members of a selected family group.

CHARTS AND DIAGRAMS

Unless you have a flair for drawing or a passion for compiling charts by hand, you are likely to appreciate the facility to design, create, and update different styles and formats of family trees and charts, ranging from simple documents to poster-sized full-color artwork handsome enough to frame. Most software allows you to fit the chart to the paper size on which you need to print and adapt the given template to your own requirements.

Access Benefits

● Using a computer to organize your research requires a systematic approach to filing and data processing

MULTIMEDIA OPTIONS

Multimedia programs allow you bring together images, sounds, and words relating to your family history. With the right hardware and software, you can create your own interactive scrapbook, inserting and editing photographs, sounds, and video footage. You may want to create a slide-show tour of your ancestral hometown, a photo album of living relatives including recordings of their voices, or a video diary from a recent family wedding.

SEND AND RECEIVE DATA

If you plan to purchase a computer for genealogical research, make sure you arrange access to the Internet at the same time. From the Internet, you can download a vast pool of reference material and exchange information with your family members and other researchers.

PUBLISHING OPPORTUNITIES

Some software packages include a self-publishing program that allows you to create a personal genealogical website, or design and print a traditional volume on your family's history. If you are on-line, look up other personal genealogical websites to give you an idea of how these work.

DATA ACCESS

Most software programs also have search capabilities to help you retrieve details. They vary in sophistication: The most efficient have the capacity to search for more than one category at a time, according to detailed criteria. If, for instance, you plan to visit a cemetery, you can pull out the names of relatives buried in that parish during a specific period so you know whose tombstones to look for.

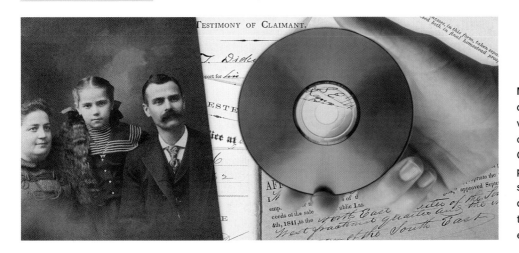

Masses of documentary and visual information can be stored on CD, including photographic scans, scans of original documents, and transcripts of epitaphs and letters.

Using Information Technology

89

Hardware and Software

● GEDCOM software can save data in a format that can be read by other computer programs, making it an essential tool for genealogists

Before investing in any new computer hardware or software, ask yourself what you realistically wish to gain from such technology and how you intend using it. If, for example, you have no intention of creating a website, do not choose a software product with this feature. It is also essential to check that your computer system has enough memory and power to run your chosen software package.

Hardware Essentials

Software packages are re-released onto the market as frequently as every six months, and each new edition often requires higher specification hardware than the previous version. Your home computer will need a sufficiently fast and powerful processor and a compatible operating system. You will need to check that you have adequate RAM (Random-Access Memory) and enough free space available on your hard drive. Most new computers have a built-in CD drive.

For convenience and portability, you may prefer to choose a laptop computer, rather than a regular PC. These can be battery-charged for use away from home and can be equipped with the same speed and memory specifications. They are ideal for the genealogical traveler.

Professional Hint

In addition to helpful general reference materials, such as encyclopedias, atlases, and museum tours, CDs provide a broad range of genealogical tools. These include indexes to the records held by major archives; documentary sources, such as nineteenth-century city directories; military muster rolls for the American Revolution and later wars; and English parish registers.

Read the Review

Many genealogy websites and magazines regularly produce up-to-date advice on suitable hardware and software programs, objectively reviewing their strengths and weaknesses, and identifying the ones best suited to your individual needs. Study these articles in advance, to brief yourself on everything about a program's design, efficiency, ease of use, and special features.

If you are a novice genealogist, start with a simple package that helps you organize your information, make records of your sources, and produce a small but useful selection of charts. As your interest deepens and your database begins to swell, you can replace or supplement your software by investing in a more sophisticated package.

A key factor of digital genealogy is the opportunity to exchange information. This is only possible if your hardware and software are compatible with others. You may decide to choose bestselling products for the simple reason that other researchers have the same.

Software-buyer's Checklist

CAPACITY

Always read the specifications on the software packaging or sales material, since requirements vary. Do not be seduced by lavish extras if they force you to either upgrade your existing computer or buy an entirely new system—unless you are looking for an excuse to do so!

EASE OF USE

How user-friendly is the software you are considering? If you are new to computers, choose a software package with clear instructions and a generous amount of guidance, rather than one with a plethora of advanced features and less assistance. For instance, does the package contain a printed manual written in simple language? Does the manufacturer offer technical support by telephone or on-line? If support by telephone, is the number toll-free? If there is only on-line support, and you are not connected to the Internet, the product is unsuitable.

Always make an external backup of your documents on a floppy disk, CD, or other storage medium. Not even the best computer is immune from electrical power failure, virus, or corruption.

EXTRAS

With so many competing software packages, it is common for manufacturers to include a selection of supplementary materials, ranging from the U.S. Social Security Death Index and printed atlases to family reunion party-planners and genealogical reference libraries. Study these special offers; you may find something of benefit.

Many companies offer free demonstration software over the Internet which can be downloaded and used for a limited time. Be aware that these samples occasionally contain bugs that can conflict with your hard drive. However, if you are new to genealogical software, you may want to try out one of these offers to see how the software works.

The Church of Jesus Christ of Latter-day Saints also offers a free on-line Personal Ancestral File including many of the same features as other packages.

COMPATIBILITY

Choose a package that is interactive with other researchers. Extra help comes from Gedcom, a software created especially for genealogical research. It stores data in a format that is accessible to other programs, whether it is in an Apple Macintosh or Microsoft Windows format. It is a standard tool for exchanging data via E-mail or external disk.

IT Peripherals

● Make sure you use the correct type of paper for your printer; otherwise, you may damage the printer mechanism

● CDs are an attractive storage option since blank disks are so economical

The development of relatively inexpensive and user-friendly computer peripherals has taken some of the hard work out of genealogical research. Scanners can speed transcribing and note-taking. Miniature palm-size computers mean that hard-working researchers no longer have to court back trouble as they stagger from archive to archive with a swollen satchel of notes. Digital cameras, sound cards, and video caption boards have made it possible to explore, record, and edit the actual sights and sounds of your family's history.

Scanners

A scanner is a useful copying device that reads text and visual images from a printed source and transfers them, in digital form, to your computer. Different types of scanners with new modifications are introduced all the time.

Flatbed scanners are the most common home scanning device. Documents and other printed and visual matter are placed on the scanner bed and copied to a computer file. If you intend to scan slides or transparencies, you will need a special transparency hood.

Sheetfed and snapshot scanners are not ideal since documents or photographs may become damaged when they are fed into

If you are scanning negatives, slides, or transparencies with a flatbed scanner, you will need to use a transparency hood.

the machine. Although these scanners can often be converted into hand-held devices, you will achieve a higher-quality image with a digital camera.

Film scanners are ideal if you record your images on 35mm slides or have inherited a large number of negatives. They offer high-resolution settings and are able to pick up very fine details.

Digital Cameras

Digital cameras allow you to import the pictures you shoot directly into your computer. They are as easy to use as any traditional camera, but allow a variety of options for editing, enlargement, and

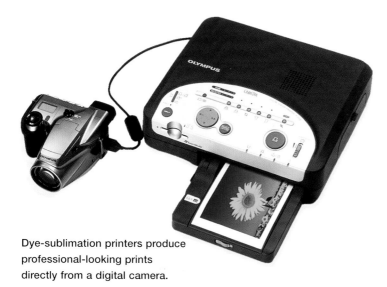

Dye-sublimation printers produce professional-looking prints directly from a digital camera.

Professional Hint

Before you purchase any computer peripherals, make sure you know the specifications of your computer system. Compare these details with the information provided on the package to make sure your hardware has enough capacity. Also, check that you have the necessary software to utilize the devices.

printing. The camera does not use regular film, but stores the images in its internal memory and/or on removable memory devices, such as memory cards. The images are transferred to the computer hard drive using a connecting cable.

Dye-sublimation Printers
Dye-sublimation printers produce high-quality photographic prints from a digital camera. Although expensive, they are useful for printing large numbers of digital photographs, rather than sending images via E-mail or the Internet.

Sound Cards
Most home computers are now routinely equipped with sound rendering devices. As long as your system includes speakers and the appropriate software, you can play, record, and download audio material from your own stereo system, radio broadcasts, video sound tracks, or the Internet.

Video Capture Boards
These handle video images in the same way that sound cards process audio. Unlike sound cards, they are not usually built into computers as a standard feature, but can be purchased as peripherals. Check the system requirements before buying.

External Backup Devices
There are many types of backup devices, and your choice should depend on the digital size of your documents. Although some computers do not include a floppy disk drive, these are still a popular choice. Since floppy disks only hold 1.4MB, they are best for text documents and small databases, rather than pictures and sound. Other storage formats include Zip disks, (up to 250MB) and CDs (up to 650MB), and DVDs (up to 17GB), all of which require a separate drive or writer. When choosing an external storage facility, be aware that such peripherals are constantly superseded by technical innovations and may have to be upgraded after about five years. Ask fellow genealogists to advise you on the most suitable device for your needs.

Palmtop Computers
Also known as personal digital assistants, these miniature computers are a portable note-taking tool. They run on electricity or batteries and can be linked to your computer to download information. Information is entered via a touch-sensitive screen and a stylus, and some also recognize handwritten characters. They also function as address books, calculators, and calendars, with E-mail and Internet access, too.

Inkjet printers (far left) produce high-quality printouts and are relatively inexpensive. Film scanners (near left) are capable of a higher resolution than most flatbed scanners, but this capability results in very large files.

CHAPTER FIVE

INTERNET SEARCHES

The Internet is a communication network that connects computers and allows for the transmission of data between them. Since the quantity of available information is so vast, the Internet has become a vital tool for genealogists.

The most popular parts of the Internet are the World Wide Web, electronic mail (E-mail), and mailing lists and newsgroups. The World Wide Web opens up a whole new world of research: international records; federal, state, and county records; collections of genealogical societies; on-line search facilities; and vast quantities of general reference material. The Web is a window on the world: At the press of a button, you can see the catalog of a library, explore the records of your ancestors, and view the findings of other genealogists.

Plan of Action

Where you begin your Internet search depends on what you are looking for. Assess what data you have before you go on a wild surfing spree. If you wander around search engines aimlessly, you may be disappointed.

The Internet allows the genealogist to access and analyze data, view on-line family trees and reference material, and share information with others, when at home or while traveling.

Set specific on-line goals: Once you have decided what you are looking for, the next steps will be clearer.

Internet searches mean you must be as organized as you'd be with regular inquiries. Although your discoveries may turn up facts beyond your original brief, do not alter your goals according to your finds. Note any websites that may be useful in the future, but do not abandon your plans until you have found the data for which you were searching.

Constraints

The Internet cannot replace all traditional research methods. Although on-line databases will save you hours visiting archive centers, there are no facilities for conducting face-to-face interviews with elderly relatives, transcribing Bible entries, or identifying the subjects of old photos. However, on-line resources can help you follow up, verify, and build on your field work. This chapter guides you through the choices available on-line so you can access relevant data and contact other researchers.

Getting Started

The World Wide Web can be compared to a huge electronic library, and the books in that library are called websites. Websites are viewed in software programs called browsers, and each website may contain many pages. Just as you need to know the correct shelf before locating a library book, so you need to select the right part of the Web in order to extract the data you need.

Anatomy of a Website Address

Each website page has a unique address or URL (Uniform Resource Locator), and a typical URL might look like this:

http://www.mydomain.com/main.htm

Each section of the URL represents a different part of the address (similar to the parts of a mailing address). http:// is the protocol. The letters *http* stand for Hyper Text Transfer Protocol, which is the format commonly used on websites. The letters *ftp* (File Transfer Protocol) is another format that you may run across. The first part of the URL, *www.mydomain.com*, is the domain name, which identifies the address of the site. The suffix *.com* tells what type of organization it is. In this case, the *.com* indicates that *mydomain* is a commercial business. Other common suffixes include:

.edu—educational institution
.gov—government agency
.mil—military site
.net—network
.org—nonprofit organization

International Indicators and Links

Website addresses originating in countries outside the United States usually have an additional suffix denoting the country in which the site is based. Examples include *.au* for Australia, *.ca* for Canada, *.ie* for

Located at http://cpl.lib.uic.edu/, Chicago Public Library's Central Library is a perfect example of large public organization with user-friendly on-line catalogs, details of opening hours, and locations.

Ireland, *.uk* for the United Kingdom, and *.za* for South Africa. Many web pages also contain links, known as hyperlinks, that allow visitors to jump to other related websites by simply clicking on the hyperlinked text. Hyperlinks are often represented by underlined sections of text, underlined website addresses, or visual icons. Hyperlinks occasionally break down, and they need constant updating.

Search Engines

Search engines are the general navigational tools that help locate information in the vast expanses of cyberspace. Your choice of search engine should depend on the capabilities you require. Ask fellow genealogists which search engines they favor, since some are more successful with genealogical inquiries. New search engines are coming onto the Web all the time, often using innovative methods of finding sites.

Internet cafés are public access points for accessing the Internet and E-mail. They are especially useful if you are traveling around and need to follow up field work or check your E-mail.

Mastering the Search Window

ADVANCED SEARCHES

Take the opportunity to refine your search with the advanced search options. For example, ask for your chosen subject to be found only in the URL address, rather than the entire body text of the site. Or, specify the country and language in which to search. Some search engines use Boolean operators, or "quick keys," to perform advanced searches. These sites offer a tutorial section to help you refine your search.

SEARCH FOR ANY WORDS

With this setting, a search for the phrase *Minnesota naturalization records* will turn up any site it finds containing the words *Minnesota*, *naturalization*, or *records*. You are unlikely to reap a successful hit on the first page of sites found.

SEARCH FOR ALL OF THE WORDS

With this setting, a search for the phrase *Minnesota naturalization records* will turn up any site with all three words in any order. This may be more successful, but may not be specific enough for your purposes.

SEARCH FOR THE EXACT PHRASE

With this setting, a search for *Minnesota naturalization records* will turn up sites with the exact phrase only. This may be the best route to a direct hit. If you are unsuccessful, try a different search engine, a general genealogical site, or a regional society.

REWORD AND RE-PHRASE

By trying variations of the same terms, you can often find other resources that may have been otherwise overlooked. Try both singular and plural versions of the same words, such as *naturalization* and *naturalizations*. Check also for abbreviations. For example, *Minnesota* may be abbreviated to the letters *MN*. Search engines can find documents from all over the world, so you may find yourself browsing the pages of a library site halfway around the globe. Some major search engines also have different versions for various countries, and here you may find more location-specific results.

FINDING LINKS

Another way to find genealogy pages on the Web is to visit sites that offer links. Cyndi's List is a popular example: Created by Cyndi Howells, it contains over 80,000 links to genealogy-related sites, categorized and cross-indexed by topic. There are sites for various ethnic backgrounds, geographic locations, surnames, record types, organizations, repositories, and much more.

● If a general search offers more than 20 possible sites, you should define your search more closely

● When searching for a website, it is essential to type the address correctly

Although the mouse is a vital component of your computer, use keyboard commands where possible, since this will reduce the possibility of hand and wrist strain.

Surname Searches

Websites devoted to specific surnames can help you focus your search and find leads regarding a particular ancestor. You will, no doubt, find other genealogists researching the same name, and some of them may be looking in the same geographic location or time frame that interests you. By utilizing the right surname sites, you can find a surprising number of new leads.

● When looking for relevant surname sites, narrow your search by specifying the location where you believe your ancestors lived

● For more information on surnames, refer to pages 128–129

Searching for common surnames can result in a large number of Internet hits that may not offer actual links with your own ancestors. This can be especially frustrating if you do not have any other leads on the people bearing the name, such as a geographic location. By searching for less common names, you are more likely to find a hit that relates to your ancestors.

Surname searches can also be useful for finding out about family lines for which you already have a significant amount of information, since you will be able to offer more details up front and find more direct correlations with details offered on-line.

The formation of surnames varies according to ethnic origin. Hispanic tradition, for instance, assigns a double surname to each person, with the paternal family name followed by the mother's, as typified by the name of Miguel de Cervantes Saavedra, the author of the Spanish classic *Don Quixote de la Mancha*.

If you are researching Chinese or other Asian ancestors, remember that the family name traditionally precedes the first name, but some immigrants to western countries reversed this tradition to ease assimilation.

Spelling Variations

Surname spellings can vary greatly, especially those surnames belonging to people who have migrated across national boundaries. Always search for a variety of spellings. There are websites specifically designed to suggest surname variations. In larger countries such as the United States, there are also websites that display name distribution maps based on census returns and telephone directories. These are particularly useful for locating the geographic core of your ancestry. Find these sites through main genealogy websites and links sites.

The Roots Surname List

The Roots Surname List (http://www.rootsweb.com) is simply a list of surnames and contact information for the person who placed the name on the list. The format of each entry starts with the surname. This is followed by the earliest known date for which you have information on the name, locations through which the family has passed, and a name tag for the submitter. Look up the Roots Surname List to check out how other genealogists have formatted their entries.

Asking the Right Questions

Most surname websites give you the opportunity to ask questions of fellow researchers and also to read those posted by others. First, check that your query is relevant to the site, since some sites have specific geographic, historical, or cultural criteria. Also, analyze how the majority of queries have been formatted and phrased so the site maintainer can process the information quickly—in the simplest terms, you can just enter the surname and/or region you are researching. Type surnames in capital letters, since this makes them

Types of Surname Websites

PERSONAL SITES

Personal sites are set up by individuals or families who wish to publicize findings on one or more family lines to which they are related. These pages are dependent on the people responsible for maintaining them—they can range from a few listed surnames to entire databases, personal recollections, and family trees in different formats. You will also notice a great variation in presentation and usability, and in the length of time they take to download. Most personal sites include an E-mail address so you can contact them directly. If you find a useful site, note down the E-mail address and contact details immediately, in case the person responsible changes his or her service provider or has to discontinue the project on-line.

Since women in many cultures abandoned their maiden names when they married, the female line of descent can be hard to follow. Make a special effort to research female names, since they will lead to surname sites relating to these ancestors.

ONE-NAME SITES

These offer a range of information on a particular surname, irrespective of regional or national location. Even if they do not offer details on your own family, they may help with geographic origins and variations in surname spellings. Advanced one-name sites may offer a choice of display languages, reflecting the national origins of the family.

Family associations and organizations also offer similar types of sites, but may have more focused goals and a more structured administration.

LOCATION- OR EVENT-RELATED SURNAME SITES

Since some families are known to have settled in the same area for many generations, some local genealogical societies offer information on those families. This can be useful if you know the areas where your ancestors originated or lived for a significant period. Similarly, there are names associated with particular events, such as the early arrival of European settlers in Mexico.

Kentish Cherries

easier to read. Keep the query short and to the point, and make sure you mention who you are looking for, what information you want about that person, when and where they were born, lived, and died, and how you can be contacted. You may also wish to include spouse and offspring names.

There are surname sites associated with specific events in history, such as the settlers who were on the first European ships to land in North and South America.

Databases

A genealogical database is a collection of information arranged and formatted for quick search and retrieval. There are thousands of on-line databases that offer a range of information—from government vital records to minor county records. There may only be one or two databases relevant to your research, but they could put you on a path to finding concrete information.

On-line databases must be regarded as a secondary source, and any facts gathered from them will need verifying using a primary source. Use on-line data as a guide to locating original records, rather than proof of any date, name, or place. This is particularly true of lineage-linked databases and data without cited sources.

Databases should be treated with a measure of skepticism. They are typically transcriptions, indexes, or abstracts, and are thus subject to a margin of human error. In addition, by finding the original documents instead, you may find useful information that was omitted from the database.

On-line data should be accompanied by full source information. This should state where the cited records were found, since you may have to contact an archive center or library for original documents.

Scanned Originals

Scanned images of vital records are a more reliable source, since they show the original document. However, you will need to assess the validity of the record itself from the

The records of many local churches have been transcribed and made available over the Internet in the form of GEDCOM databases. You may be lucky and find data relating to your ancestors.

person or organization that posted the document, and be sure that it has not been altered during scanning. Remember that even original records can contain errors.

The Family History Library

The Family History Library in Salt Lake City, Utah, is home to the world's largest genealogical collection and contains vital information on millions of names. Its website, located at http://www.FamilySearch.org, houses a vast array of records. Included

Selected high school and college attendance lists can be found on general genealogical websites and also through alumni websites, such as http://www.highschoolalumni.com/.

Professional Hint

GEDCOM (GEnealogical Data COMmunications) is a file format that allows genealogical databases and charts, to be read by different software programs. Information can be downloaded from the Internet and also posted for others to access. Submitting your GEDCOM databases and other files to genealogical websites, such as the Ancestry World Tree, is a great way to make contact with family historians researching the same lines. GEDCOM is sold separately and also included with most genealogical software packages. Follow the manual for creating and transferring GEDCOM files. When sending GEDCOM data to genealogists, find out what software they use so you can customize the file correctly.

● All information gained from on-line databases must be verified with primary sources and official records

● Databases can be accessed directly or via a links site, such as Cyndi's List, which can be found at http://www.cyndislist.com

in this database is the International Genealogical Index (IGI), a collection of birth, christening, and marriage data about persons of many nationalities and cultures, who are now deceased. The catalog of the Family History Library's holdings is on the website, and users can browse it at Family History Centers all over the world. Also included in its database is the Ancestral File, which is a special lineage-linked database submitted by family historians worldwide.

Commercial Databases

Commercial sites offer huge amounts of data from around the world. Ancestry.com is one of the most popular of these sites. While some records are available only to subscribers, other databases, such as the U.S. Social Security Death Index (SSDI), the Ancestry World Tree, and European and U.S. telephone listings are all free. All databases can be searched simultaneously by using the Global Search template. Ancestry.com also offers international databases, including a number from Canada, France, Germany, Ireland, and Great Britain.

Other websites from all over the world are posting new databases at an increasing pace. The Danish Emigration Archives in Aalborg, Denmark, maintains a database of

Information on births, marriages, and deaths for many countries and regions is available through general genealogical websites, official archive websites, and the Family History Library at http://www.FamilySearch.org.

emigration lists compiled by the Copenhagen police 1869–1940, which it has made available on its site. The National Archives of Canada has an index to the 1871 Census of Ontario on-line, as well as other databases and finding aids. The General Records Office for Scotland has posted a variety of indexes to vital records and census returns at http://www.origins.net/GRO. By performing a search on a search engine, you will find similar sites for your area.

Lineage Databases

There are several on-line lineage databases. The Ancestry World Tree is composed of pedigree files submitted by site visitors and is the largest collection of its kind. RootsWeb sponsors the WorldConnect Project, a similar project that forges connections between researchers working on the same family lines. You are welcome to post your own GEDCOM databases on such sites.

Databases

101

Making the Most of On-line Databases

Genealogical websites, such as Ancestry.com, offer recollections and narratives about family life from days gone by. Although they may not offer concrete information they may provide clues about your ancestors' lifestyles.

You will find on-line databases devoted to a wide range of local subject matter—from cemetery records to military draft lists and school records

An important thing to remember when searching databases is that most databases will only give hits on exact matches. When too much information is included in a search, you risk eliminating a hit in cases where names have been abbreviated or misspelled, where variations exist, or when information is missing. When specifying a date, try including only the month and/or year, as opposed to the full date. One of the most extensive collections of databases is the GENDEX website. Searching with surnames and given names, you can access millions of personal histories and also find out which vital records were used to submit the data. GENDEX is most appropriate for information on individuals, rather than general surname searches.

Consider the Cost

Although many on-line databases are free of charge, such as those located at http://www.searches.rootsweb.com, others require payment through an on-line subscription. Consider if this payment is worth the investment in terms of the unique databases to which you will gain access.

RESEARCH NOTES

FAMILY RESEARCHER *Loretto Szucs*
FOCUS OF INQUIRY *Using Internet Directories*

"In 1997, I wrote my first family history article, *Somewhere in France*, for *Ancestry* magazine. It was based on letters that my mother had, which her uncle Edwin had written to his American father and sister while fighting in World War I.

As the article was being written, my mother and I talked about finding Uncle Edwin's grandchildren, as these letters surely belonged to them. We put a note in the article asking anyone that knew of Edwin Dyer's descendants to contact the magazine. About this time, my mother found an old letter tucked inside a storage file at home. Written by her aunt, the letter gave the married name of Edwin's daughter and mentioned 'New Jersey—three boys.'

"We searched the New Jersey on-line telephone directories for the married name. My mother began calling the numbers and got lucky first time. A cautious-sounding woman answered our questions about the possibility of being a relative. She said, 'You definitely have the right family, but my husband is the one you should have talked to, and he died just a few weeks ago.' The woman was Edwin's second wife. She said that her stepson, one of the boys mentioned in the letter, might like to speak with us, since he was interested in family history. She said she would call and ask him if he wished to get in touch.

"After ten minutes, the telephone rang. On the line was a man saying that 'Ghosts were surely swirling around,' and the hair on his neck was standing on end. It was Edwin's grandson, Bob Lazell, calling from New York. His mother died when he was a boy, his father remarried, and contact with his mother's family was lost. He was amazed to find that his grandfather had sisters and that he had cousins. He now has the letters, and we have found a kindred spirit."

Database Search Tips

KEEP A LOG

With the immense array of resources available on-line (and new sites going up every day), it can be difficult to keep track of where you have searched, when, and for what. Do not rely on the "favorites" option offered by your Internet software. Keep a research log of sites visited, searches performed, and results, since this will help you plan which sites you use and avoid returning to the same sites time and again. With websites that are constantly being updated and/or added to, you may want to go back every so often to re-check them. Use your log to tell you when you last checked a site.

CITATIONS AND SOURCES

When you find a piece of information, be sure to include the full bibliographic citation. Include the original source of the data, name of the database, the URL of the site on which you found it, and the name of the site (very important in the on-line environment where URLs can change.) You will be grateful for this information farther down the research road.

FOLLOW UP OFF-LINE

While the Internet has put a wealth of information at our fingertips, traditional sources should not be overlooked. On-line data needs to be verified with original or primary source documents. The exception to this would be scanned original documents that have been posted on-line, but in these cases, the method of indexing these documents may contain errors, causing you to miss the document you search for.

SAVE TIME WITH OFF-LINE RESEARCH

When you are planning a trip to an off-line facility, such as an archive center, check to see if its catalog is available on-line before venturing out. This can save you unnecessary trips in cases where the facility either does not have the materials you need for your research or is closed for one reason or another. Contact the facility in advance to make sure that the collections you seek will be available (the phone number and/or E-mail address will be available on the site). This checking procedure will save you valuable time at the facility itself, since you will have already searched the catalog before making your trip.

Despite the Internet, you may still have to travel during the course of your research to verify records in person. However, by researching on-line in advance, you will be better prepared and save time while you are there. Refer to Chapter Eight for more details on genealogical travel.

USING ADVANCED SEARCHES

General genealogy websites offer advanced search tips that allow you to specify a particular geographic region, date range, keyword, or proximity. Use these facilities wherever possible.

Databases

Utilizing E-mail

E-mails are messages sent through the Internet using special E-mail software. Messages can be sent to one individual or many individuals simultaneously. Messages can include attachments, such as Microsoft Word documents, scanned photographs, GEDCOM files, and more. When you sign up with an Internet service provider, you will get an E-mail account and an E-mail address.

● Do not respond to provocative messages, known as flames

● Check to whom you are sending your E-mails; make sure you are not writing to an entire group rather than one person

● Never use uppercase letters, since these indicate shouting; the exception is for surnames, which should be written in all uppercase

The first part of an E-mail address identifies you personally. For this part, customers choose their name or a nickname as an identifier. It is followed by @, meaning *at*, and then the domain name of the E-mail service you have chosen. A typical address might look like this:

jpublic@mydomain.com

The way in which you view your E-mail depends upon the service to which you subscribe. There are a number of providers, such as Microsoft Outlook, Eudora, and Netscape Mail. America Online (AOL) has an E-mail program built into its interface. There are also increasing numbers of companies offering free Web-based E-mail, such as Hotmail, Juno, and MyFamily.com.

E-mail Services

There are various free newsletters (E-zines) that bring information to your inbox. The *Ancestry Daily News* is one newsletter that goes to over half a million subscribers. It contains helpful articles from columnists to guide you in your research and introduce you to new genealogical resources. E-zines also contain news from the genealogical community, both on-line and off-line, as well as readers' tips.

Controlling the Flow of E-mail

Once you become active in the on-line community, you may find that your inbox is overflowing with E-mails. E-mail software allows users to sort E-mail into folders. For instance, all mail coming from an Australian genealogy mailing list could be labeled *Australian Genealogy*. Or, you can label folders according to family lines. The messages can be filtered by sender, recipient, subject line, or content. Check the Help function on your software to learn

Many Internet and E-mail service providers give you more than one address for a single account. This allows all members of the family to have their own E-mail address and allows for more efficient processing of messages.

how to create folders. Messages can also be copied and saved into your regular computer word-processing software.

E-mailing Strangers

As you search the Web, you may find others researching the same family lines as you. These contacts may have had some of your family information passed down to them, such as treasured stories, tangible papers, or even inherited heirlooms. Since they share the same origins, their data can be extremely helpful. However, while it is great to make contact with fellow researchers,

Popular E-mail Symbols

:-) Happy, smiling

;-) Winking, ironic

:-> Sarcastic

8-) Wearing glasses

:-(Unhappy, sad

:-< Disappointed

:-o Surprised

:-() Mustache

The time a message takes to reach its destination—which can be as short as a few seconds—depends on how fast the Internet hardware is working.

1 The sender types a message, attaches any files, specifies the E-mail address(es) of the recipients, then sends.

2 Client software, such as Simple Mail Transfer Protocol, encodes the message for transmission over a network.

3 The mail server, located at the Internet Service Provider or other server, sends the message to the E-mail address.

4 The Internet carries the encoded E-mail message to a server, located at the domain address of the recipient.

5 The server converts the message into a form that can be read by the recipient's software and puts it in the mailbox.

6 The recipient logs onto the server, and new mail messages are delivered into his or her inbox, along with attachments.

remember that they are strangers to you, and you are a stranger to them. They may resent the inquiry, and many may look at it as an invasion of privacy. Do not be surprised if they think that you are trying to take advantage of their research.

E-mail Etiquette

Begin your contact by sharing data that may be of interest or scanned photos of shared ancestors. Be patient, too. After your letter of introduction, wait a while for a response. After some time, follow up with a gentle reminder, but do not be pushy. Remember that they are not obliged to answer. Do not send information on living people. Tread with caution until you know someone better. Verify any data you receive and check sources before you incorporate that information into your files. Incorrect leads will waste both time and money. Use information as a guide, rather than fact.

E-mail etiquette (known as netiquette) and common sense dictate that you should get permission before submitting someone else's data. However, this does not always happen. If you are going to send out GEDCOM files or any other data, be aware that it may be passed on to other on-line and off-line contacts without permission.

Take precautions by removing the names of living people. In the same vein, if you plan to submit data you have received, even if you are footnoting the source, obtain permission first and omit all living persons. Clarify with your contact in advance where you both want to submit your shared data.

On-line Mailing Lists and Newsgroups

Mailing lists allow you to request data to be E-mailed to you. When joining a list, choose *digest* mode, since this will collate multiple messages before sending them. Newsgroups offer a similar service, but data is posted on a news server rather than being E-mailed. Server access is arranged though Internet Service Providers, websites, or mailing lists.

Before posting messages to a newsgroup, first clarify which groups are relevant to your area of research and how messages should be formatted.

Remember that all E-mails are potentially public, so do not write anything that may offend. Do not violate copyright laws by distributing excerpts of published works.

General Reference Sites

If you are unsure where to find the vital records or essential documents you are seeking—whether on-line or off-line—you may like to try one of the growing number of general genealogical reference sites that can help source this information for you.

- Log on to the government website of the country you are currently researching to discover what mapping data is available on-line

- An independent mapping site, such as http://www.mapquest.com, offers general map data

- For information on the European archive mapping scheme, log on to http://www.ria.ie/IHTAtlas.html

General reference sites offer a range of services: World GenWeb has message boards for visitors to post queries about ancestors from particular regions, while Ancestry.com offers articles on a variety of topics, and an E-mail newsletter.

GenWeb

The WorldGenWeb Project was created in 1996 by Dale Schneider to answer the needs of on-line genealogists. The goal was to have every country represented by a website hosted by researchers in each country or by those who were familiar with that country's resources. In 1997, the site came under the authority of RootsWeb.com, which allowed it to grow and continue to provide helpful information around the world.

The WorldGenWeb Project is now divided into 11 World Regions. Each region is divided up by country, and then by states, counties or provinces. The sites offer information about records in the area and contain hyperlinks to websites of record repositories and databases.

The MyFamily.com Group

MyFamily.com, Ancestry.com, and also FamilyHistory.com are leading websites for families and genealogists. MyFamily.com enables families to communicate through free secure websites. Visitors can offer news, create family photo albums, hold live voice and text chats, and maintain a calendar of family events. MyFamily.com also offers free on-line family history software that enables multiple family members to update their family trees.

Ancestry.com offers thousands of data-bases on hundreds of millions of individuals and a range of reference material, including facilities such as the U.S. State Resource Guides found in the Search by Locality section of their site. The FamilySearch page has a series of Research Helps, offering research outlines, maps, descriptions of sources, worksheets, records schedules, and

Many historical societies will answer on-line queries about social, economic, or geographic issues, which may shed light on your treasured family heirlooms, photos, and oral histories.

letter-writing tools. The Research Guidance section also offers guidance on locating vital records. The third website in the group, FamilyHistory.com, provides free family history message boards allowing family researchers to exchange data on surnames, regions, and specific topics.

Peripheral Reference Material

Genealogical websites and general search engines can be used to access a range of contemporary and archive information to help with your research. For most regions, up-to-date Yellow Pages are available through general search engines, while Ancestry.com offers free access to U.S., Canadian, British, and Irish residential telephone directories via its own surname search facility. Some larger historical and genealogical societies also offer on-line information on selected domestic and trade

WorldGenWeb
Connecting The World Through Genealogy

Ancestry.com

RESEARCH NOTES

FAMILY RESEARCHER *Patrick Carpenter*
FOCUS OF INQUIRY *Unidentified Photograph*

If you inherit a photograph and only know where it was taken, the Internet can help you find out more about the subject and your ancestors' relationship with the place. Patrick Carpenter followed this route to find out more about a photo identified by the words *Orkney Isles*.

Patrick's first port of call was a general genealogy site—he chose Ancestry.com. From the home page, Patrick chose the *Learn* option, then keyed in the word *Scotland*.

From the direct hits, Patrick chose *Scottish Links and Resources*, since this suggested a range of links. From there, he chose *Gateway to Scotland*, since this also suggested a general access point for Scottish information. Luckily, *Gateway to Scotland* turned out to be a helpful gazetteer sponsored by a variety of educational groups.

Patrick searched the gazetteer by choosing the *Place* in order to focus his search geographically, *Historic Building* in order to match the type of attraction in the photograph, then *Orkney*, to indicate the place more specifically. With this search, the gazetteer offered a range of historic places in Orkney. One appeared to be the building in the photo.

By looking at the image, Patrick saw the cross on the facade and knew that the building was a place of worship. Using his knowledge of architectural ornament, he guessed that the building was decorated in an Italianate style—quite un-Scottish, he thought. Using this information, Patrick chose the *Italian Chapel* option on the list of sites offered by the gazetteer. As if by magic, he was presented with an illustrated biography of the building and a starting point for research on why this photo is part of his family archive.

The Italian Chapel in Orkney, Scotland—the focus of Patrick's on-line search.

---

directories, and these can be helpful in researching households and workplaces.

Similarly, indexes of new and old newspapers are available on-line, and can direct you to libraries that hold the original archives. Some sites contain actual transcriptions of articles, or entire issues.

Many historical societies have their own websites and are easy to access via location-based searches on general or genealogical search engines. If you are unable to visit the society in person, you may be able to E-mail the administrator with your query.

Geographic Material
Use general search engines or genealogical links sites to access on-line gazetteers, such as the U.S. Geological Survey's Geographic Names Information System (GNIS) located at http://www.mapping.usgs.gov/www/gnis. This site offers a search facility for place names, which is useful if you do not know the state in which a town is situated. Other

mapping agencies that offer this facility are based in Great Britain, at http://www.ordsvy.gov.uk, and Australia, at http://www.auslig.gov.au/search.htm. The British mapping agency, Ordnance Survey, displays a range of archive maps that can be downloaded from their website: These are particularly useful if you are studying a location that has changed radically over the last hundred years or wish to view your ancestral landscape as it was in the past.

To find out about your treasured heirlooms, log onto one of the many antique auction sites, such as http://www.antiquesamerica.com, http://www.icon20.com, or http://www.qxl.com.

Government and Other Official Records

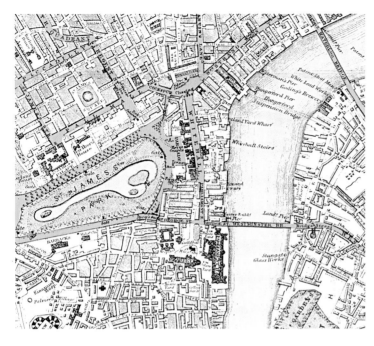

Since the status of buildings and land is subject to constant change, old street maps can help you understand archive land and tax records. Genealogists often post historical timelines on general genealogical websites relating to the particular buildings or land plots they have studied. If you find one that relates to the place or time you are studying, look for new leads to advance your research.

If you wish to order copies of records from government agencies, churches, or other repositories, check to see if the organization has a website. The website will offer the most up-to-date information on what records are available, practical details such as fees, opening hours of records centers or repositories, and access restrictions.

The extent and quality of government and other official websites varies between countries and federal departments. Some are extremely user-friendly and geared toward public services, while others are merely a reference point for internal policy. Some official websites offer downloadable request forms that can be printed or submitted on-line in order to apply for copy certificates, while others restrict themselves to contact details of repository offices.

Ask the Experts

Genealogical and historical societies also offer on-line assistance. In the U.S., many of these organizations can be found at the Federation of Genealogical Societies' Society Hall. For a reasonable fee, the staff will sometimes perform research for you on-site, or suggest researchers who are qualified to help you. These organizations will often have reference information available on the site to guide researchers.

Census Returns

Several general websites offer on-line census indexes listed by name. These sites can also direct you to the archive repositories in which the records are stored and from which copies can be ordered.

General search engines are useful ways of accessing census information for countries without genealogical websites. If you find one of your ancestors listed on a census index, write down all the details provided by the entry so you have the information to access the complete record.

For United States census records, the Family Finder Index is an extremely useful resource. It is produced by Brøderbund Software and is sold on a line of CDs. To find out which CDs contain the information on your particular ancestors, search the website list at http://www.familytreemaker.com/cdhome.html.

Immigration and Vital Records

There are increasing numbers of passenger lists and immigration and naturalization indexes available on-line through general and specialty websites. Some of these records are available free of charge. Some countries have made their emigration records available; for example, Norway has an excellent site located at http://www.sffarkiv.no/sffbasar/default.asp.

For on-line vital records, such as birth, marriage, and death certificates, there are many access points for indexes and instructions for ordering copy certificates.

● Official websites vary in terms of the services they offer and the degree to which they are geared toward public use

Professional Hint

In order to find out about your ancestors, you have to access more than a few on-line indexes of vital records. You need to understand why certain records were kept, what they contain, and where the originals are stored. You also need to learn the history and geography of the area you are researching, plus antiquated legal, medical, and foreign terminology, all of which can be found on-line with a general search engine. It is also important to evaluate your sources for accuracy. If the data you find is from a reputable source, it is more likely to be accurate than if it was found in an undocumented or casual on-line publication.

General genealogical websites are ideal places to start, since they will direct you to more specialized sites. Websites of official government registration offices and record centers indicate how you can apply for copy certificates. If possible, it is best to consult indexes before you apply, to confirm that a record exists for the person you are researching. Government websites vary in the amount of information they offer. A small selection of vital records has been transcribed, and these are best found through general genealogy sites. Access to adoption records is severely restricted over the Internet, as is the case with conventional records. However, adoption-related sites are accessible through general genealogical sites, and mailing lists are useful for seeking advice from other genealogists.

Land Records

Land records can help place your ancestors at a particular location and point in time, and these are generally administered by official government agencies. Consult general genealogical websites for links to sites for particular regions. Land record indexes are available over the Internet, and you may also find some transcriptions and scans of original documents. Property tax records are also worth searching for over the Internet through regional and federal archives, since they can shed light on inheritance and local taxation records.

Military Records

Access to on-line military records varies according to the country, location, and time frame that you are researching. Search through official government websites, general genealogical sites, general search engines, and military organizations.

● If official government websites do not appear to offer the information you need, consult a mainstream genealogical website for links

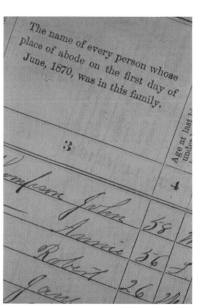

Most on-line transcriptions of original census returns relate to U.S. censuses. Transcribed records have not been made available in a particularly orderly fashion, but a couple of sites attempt to provide an overview of availability, including http://www.rootsweb.com/~usgenweb/census and http://www.censusonline.com/links/index.html.

Ethnic Records On-line

● The best advice will come from genealogists who have faced challenges similar to yours

● Newsgroups and mailing lists are ideal ways to access specialized advice on ethnic research

The effect of migration and population displacement has meant that records for people who have moved away from their homeland can be harder to find than for families who have lived in the same village for hundreds of years. Additionally, some cultures are more predisposed to keeping written vital records than others.

However, the dramatic increase in ethnic genealogical research has resulted in vast quantities of information being made available over the Internet, from opening times of specialty repositories to full transcriptions of migratory passenger lists. The same research techniques apply for other on-line genealogical research, except that your sources are more specific and your returns even more rewarding!

African-Americans

Prior to 1870, African-American records vary according to whether your ancestor was a slave or a free person. Log onto http://www.afrigeneas.com for helpful information on this area. This site offers limited transcriptions of U.S. Slave Manifests at the port of New Orleans and information on other slave documentation, such as bills of sale and slave owners, and mailing list and newsgroup facilities. Service records for men who served in the United States Colored Troops can be accessed in the same way as for other military files. Many records are also kept by the U.S. National Archives, including those from The Freedman's Bureau and the Freedman's Savings and Trust Bank. Another useful site is Christine's genealogy website at http://www.ccharity.com.

Native Americans

Oral family history is a vital starting point for Native American research, in order to establish the places in which your ancestors lived and settled, and the tribe to which they belonged. In addition to records held by the National Archives (http://www.nara.gov/publications/microfilm/amerindians/indians.html), there are also many websites you can access for general advice. Some sites

India does not have standardized vital records, so search via institutional records, such as ashrams, schools, temples, churches, and the armed forces. Try http://goidirectory.nic.in and http://www.gis.net/~rajiv/indgov.html for government information. Many other Asian links are also available through WorldGenWeb.

include transcribed marriage, cemetery, and census records. For clarification on tribal names, look at the tribal directory available at http://www.indians.org/tribes/tribes.html. To see what information is available for the region or tribe you are researching, log onto a general genealogy site and search under the appropriate sub-section for on-line records.

Hispanic Roots

For records relating to Latin America, access to roots will depend on when your ancestors landed in the New World. For nineteenth- and twentieth-century immigrants, look for clues within the family archive and oral tradition that indicate where your ancestors came from. For records before the nineteenth century, you may need to consult colonial records in the country of origin, i.e. Spain or Portugal. Apart from genealogical websites, there are also sites

There is a host of Italian-American genealogy sites, offering a wealth of information, from narrative recollections of life in New York's Little Italy (shown right), to passenger lists and details of vital records in Italy.

for Cuba, the Basque region of Spain, Argentina, Venezuela, Costa Rica, Mexico, Peru, Puerto Rico, the Dominican Republic, Spain, and Portugal.

Asia and the Pacific Rim

Asian cultures with the most established diaspora communities have the largest amount of genealogical data on-line. Japan, China, Vietnam, Korea, and the Philippines are the best served, and good links are provided by general websites, such as http://www.familytreemaker.com.

European Records

Many European records were destroyed during World War I, and native records in colonized countries were not standardized until the nineteenth century. There are websites devoted to most western and eastern European countries, with many of them based outside the country of origin. There are also organizations that research groups who cross international boundaries, such as Romanies, German-speakers, or French-speakers. Search through a general genealogical website first for links to the country or community you want to research.

Minority Religious Communities

Minority communities, religious sects, and fraternal orders keep separate records specific to their own traditions. Search general genealogical websites to find links to organizations such as Anabaptists, Roman Catholics, Huguenots, Hutterites, Jews, Lutherans, Mennonites, Methodists, Quakers, and other denominations.

The Rosicrucians are an ancient fraternal order that have many lodges throughout the world. Log onto http://www.amorc.org for links to various branches. As with other fraternal organizations, information on membership is confidential and restricted. However, individual lodges will usually accept written inquiries from genealogists who believe they have family links with the order.

Sharing Through the Internet

After investing so much time and effort in your research, it is natural to want to share your finds to help fellow genealogists. Home-produced GEDCOM files and databases are ideal candidates for posting on your own Internet website.

● **Try to give your site a unique focus; otherwise, it will not stand out among the thousands of others; if it is a surname-based site, focus on the name in one particular region**

There are various outlets for your research material. First, you can can submit your data to a genealogy forum run by an Internet Service Provider (ISP), such as America Online (AOL). Second, genealogical websites, such as Ancestry.com, welcome the submission of databases to join their existing on-line collection of information.

The third possibility is the creation of your own website. Web pages are no longer the exclusive domain of large organizations. Anyone can do it. Cyndi's List and America Online's Genealogy Forum are evidence of this, with thousands of personal home pages created by people just like yourself. Assure yourself that your research is at a suitable stage for uploading and that you have enough data to make your site useful; there is little point offering a database with only a couple of unconfirmed dates.

Creating a Website

For each page in a website, the developer creates an HTML (Hyper Text Mark-up Language) document. This contains text for the page, together with tags (codes), which define the layout, images, text, colors, and everything else about the page. Special web page creation software can be used for converting a developer's design into a tagged HTML document. Media files, such as images, are often referred to by the HTML document, but are not part of it.

The HTML document is the master file for any web page.

It contains text interspersed with tags (coding).

The website developer saves the files for each web page onto a separate folder on the hard disk.

Extra digital files are prepared for still images and sound and video elements, as necessary.

A web server is a computer with a permanent Internet connection. The website manager has access to the files on the server, so they can be updated.

As the person viewing a site moves from page to page, the browser sends signals (called GET requests) back to the web server, requesting the files.

To check how each page looks and works, the developer views it by opening its HTML document within a web browser. Pages are tested and modified many times during development. After testing, all the files for a website are transferred to a computer called a web server. It often resides at the offices of an Internet Service Provider.

Selecting Data for Your Website

● For more advice on HTML language and designing web pages, take a night class at your local college

● If setting up a website with your ISP, check what facilities they provide and how much data you will be able to post

LIVING PERSONS

Do not include any data on living persons. Some genealogical software can "privatize" this data, and there are also separate programs to do this job, such as GEDClean32 and GEDLiving. Do not include any personal comments that may be libelous.

LOCATIONS AND SOURCES

For all entries, check you have entered a city, county/parish, and state/county as necessary, and make sure the dates are accurate for each entry. Include references for all your data and use the correct citation style. Do not include any uncorroborated notes.

LINKS

Do not set up links to other websites until you have verified the quality of the information offered on those sites.

HOME PAGE AND CONTACT DETAILS

Always include a home page so that visitors have a starting point from which they can move to your databases. The home page should include a welcome message, contact information, and clarifications or disclaimers. Do not include your mailing address or telephone number as part of your contact information.

COLOR AND GRAPHICS

Use color and graphics with restraint. Too many bright colors and graphic elements make pages difficult to read and slow down the speed at which pages load onto visitors' computers. Waiting for a page to load is frustrating, and visitors will not wait more than a few seconds before they move on to another site.

UPLOADING

Loading procedures vary according to ISPs and hosting sites. Most use a simple File Transfer Protocol (FTP), while others allow you to download the relevant software. For more details, contact your ISP or follow the user instructions on your host site. Web browsers, such as Microsoft Internet Explorer and Netscape Navigator, interpret HTML documents differently and can alter the appearance of a site from its original layout. To avoid this problem, do not use tags unique to your browser. Test your site before posting it or use a testing service, such as the selection found at http://www.yahoo.com/Computers_and_Internet/ Information_and_Documentation/Data_Formats/HTML/ Validation_and_Checkers. Publicize your site via newsgroups or registration sites, such as genealogy.tbox.com/regis.htm.

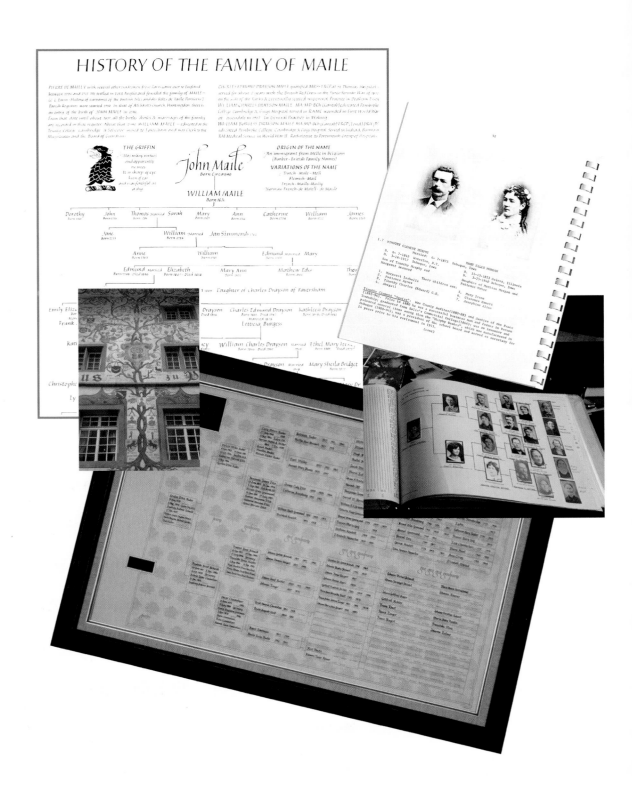

CHAPTER SIX

CREATING FAMILY TREES

The phrase "family tree" is familiar to most of us as a term for a collection of an individual's ancestors and connected kin. This chapter is designed to show you how to illustrate these connections in pictorial and narrative form.

As you delve into the world of genealogy, you will soon discover that, in order to represent the various relationships within a family, there are many different forms of family chart and tree. Some are working tools, used through every stage of your genealogical research, to help you assemble information and assess the gaps that need to be filled. Others represent the "finished product"—the fruits of your investigations, with all the members of previous generations laid out, as far back as can be traced, in graphic form.

Family trees can be illuminated with various decorative additions: Photographs, calligraphic lettering or borders, decoupage

Family trees can take various forms. Clockwise from top left: A traditional descendant chart dating from the seventeenth century to the present day; an illustrated family group sheet incorporated into a bound family history; a photographic pedigree chart; a handwritten pedigree chart; a traditional heraldic tree painted onto a house in Germany.

ephemera, and even examples of relatives' signatures. A professional-looking family tree makes an ideal gift for relatives and can decorate your own home, too.

Genealogical software programs allow you to create a range of family trees on your computer. You will find a variety of layout choices, allowing you to edit entries and incorporate scanned images as your research progresses. Computer-generated family trees can be creatively designed for black-and-white or color printing. If you intend to commission a decorative, handwritten version of your family tree, it is helpful to provide the calligrapher with the relevant information on a typed computer printout, since this will be easier to transcribe.

Writing a Family History

This chapter also provides hints for turning your genealogical facts and figures into a creative family history publication. Such a document is testament to your hard work and allows you to present your research in an accessible form.

Pedigree Charts

A pedigree chart, also called a lineage chart or ancestor chart, is a diagram setting out the direct ancestors of an individual. It is a vital tool, since it shows what data you possess, and what still needs to be gathered. Although many researchers use pre-prepared charts, drawing your own allows you to add data not included on regular templates and also style the chart decoratively.

Pedigree charts show the ancestry of one person through their maternal and paternal lines. The charts can be simply composed of names and vital details or brought to life using photographs. There is no limit to how many generations are shown on one chart, but five generations is a common standard.

Most pedigree charts work from left to right or from top to bottom. Full names are accompanied by the date of birth, date and place of marriage, date of death, and occupation. Five generations are usually shown on one chart, including the person for whom the pedigree is shown. Straight lines mark the relationship between entries, and sometimes the male line of ascent is highlighted in bold. Spouses may be written at the base of the chart and cross-referenced with the entries for ease of use.

● Men are always listed on the upper line of the pedigree stem and women on the lower line

● To save time, use ready-made pedigree charts, available from genealogical suppliers and included on genealogical software

Professional Hint

To avoid confusion in the recording of dates, note months by name—even if abbreviated—rather than number. In the case of unmarried partners, where no wedding date exists, replace the terms "husband" and "wife" with the more neutral "partner," and use "met" rather than "married" when dating the union. This approach is also useful on family group sheets (see pages 118–119) and other types of family trees dealing with same-sex partnerships, or unmarried male and female couples (the latter are traditionally known as "common-law" spouses.)

Drawing a Pedigree Chart

MATERIALS AND PLANNING

You will need a large sheet of blank or lined paper, pencil, eraser, and ruler. Typically, pedigree charts show five generations on a single page. This depends on how much information you have, and the size of paper available. You can use either a large single sheet or several smaller pages taped together.

VERTICAL ENTRIES

For a vertical chart, begin by writing your own name and vital details near the bottom of the paper. You may wish to allow some space below it for entering your own children and grandchildren. The next tier up is for your parents, the one above that for your two sets of grandparents, and so forth, working upward as you go farther back in time. Use a ruler to draw short lines linking each generation.

HORIZONTAL ENTRIES

If you prefer a horizontal chart, put your own entry near the left edge of the page, enter your parents' details next, and work from left to right as you track backwards through the generations. Be sure to include the maiden names—if you know them—for all married female relatives.

NUMBERING

As you fill out names on this chart, number each individual. The simplest system for a five-generation pedigree chart is to assign yourself, or the first person, the number 1. This applies whether you are male or female. However, for all previous generations, the convention is to assign odd numbers to females, even numbers to males.

As you accumulate more data, you will find it impossible to fit everyone on a single page. A numbering system allows you to cross-reference between different charts and view the same people in different contexts.

- When drafting a pedigree chart, always work in pencil until you have verified every name and date

- Only direct ancestors are listed on a pedigree chart; no aunts, uncles, or cousins

- When practicing drawing pedigree charts, start with your own pedigree

- It is customary to write all surnames in capital letters, since this avoids any confusion with given names

For clarity, you can write the name of each generation (in relation to the first entry) between the two branches of the tree, such as parents or grandparents.

Family Group Sheets

Family Group Sheets are detailed charts that record an individual family unit—consisting of a single couple and all their children. Each family unit in every generation is allocated a separate sheet of its own. If the pedigree chart forms the bones of your research, then the family group sheet adds the flesh and helps you keep track of your sources.

This first draft family group sheet shows an Irish-Jewish family. The details shown are taken from interviews with the children who were still alive in the year 2000. Shirley Samuelson, the researcher, will have to verify all data using vital records in Ireland, Israel, the U.K., Latvia, and the Ukraine. She will also have to cite all sources and fill gaps in the information.

FAMILY GROUP SHEET OF SAMUEL BROWN
Sheet No. 1

Samuel Brown
b. *? July, 1892, Gostine, Latvia*
m. *? ?, 1917, Liverpool, U.K.*
d. *24 March, 1965, Tivon, Israel*
Occupation: *clothing manufacturer*

Rachel Alexander
b. *? ?, 1898, Yarmolintsi, Ukraine*
m. *? ?, 1917, Liverpool, U.K.*
d. *4 November, 1983, Kibbutz Yasur, Israel*
Occupation: *homemaker*

1 **Sarah**
  b. *4 Jul. 1917, Liverpool, U.K*
  m. *David Summ, ? ? 1942, Dublin, Ireland*
  d. *12 Apr. 1998, Bat Yam, Israel*

2 **Emanuel**
  b. *? Jul. 1921*
  m1. *Felice Witztum, ? ? 1947, Dublin, Ireland*
  m2. *Tirza Bar Lev, ? ? 1955, Tel Aviv, Israel*
  m3. *Naomi Taylor, ? ? 1993, Tel Aviv, Israel*
  d. *3 Dec. 1997, Tel Aviv, Israel*

3 **Theodor**
  b. *? Aug. 1925, Dublin, Ireland*
  m. *Rita Meyer, ? ? 1954, London, U.K.*
  d. *9 Aug. 1974, Ramat Hasharon, Israel*

4 **Evelyn**
  b. *5 Feb. 1926, Dublin, Ireland*
  m. *Ludwig Weil, ? Sept. 1951, Dublin, Ireland*

5 **Rita**
  b. *18 Nov. 1929, Dublin, Ireland*
  m. *Benno Zell, ? ? 1952, ?, Israel*

6 **Malka Vera**
  b. *22 Apr. 1931, Dublin, Ireland*
  m. *David Meron, 4 Dec. 1955, London, U.K.*
  div. *4 Nov. 1961, Ashkelon, Israel*

7 **Shirley**
  b. *17 Nov. 1935, Dublin, Ireland*
  m. *Maurice Samuelson, 27 Mar. 1960, London, U.K.*

8 **Leslie Howard**
  b. *20 May 1940*
  m. *Elaine Goldwater, ? ? 1962 Dublin, Ireland*

This eighteenth-century Irish family group sheet records the two marriages and nine offspring of Mr. Nathanial Bang. Since two babies died at birth, they are only listed by gender.

Blank family group sheets are sold by genealogical societies and included on genealogical software. Alternatively, you can devise your own template to suit your needs. When filling in the sheet, some genealogists include the couple's parents to clarify their identity. If either of the couple was married more than once, that person will need another sheet for the second union.

When collating your sheets, give each one a number, starting with the generation

Essential Information for Family Group Sheets

HUSBAND AND WIFE

For the husband and wife, include the dates and places of birth and/or baptism, marriage, death and/or burial. There may be other dates, such as circumcision, confirmation, or divorce. Women should be entered with maiden names only.

You may like to include the names of the couple's parents, partners from previous or subsequent marriages, religion and nationality, occupation, and military service details. Pre-prepared family group sheets may allow space for other details than those listed, or omit specific entries that you feel are essential. Many templates provide a line for the man's occupation only, either assuming that women did not work outside the home or reflecting the fact that sources failed to record this information. Similarly, the assumption that only males have military service records is now out of date. For each fact, insert the reference number you have assigned for its source.

CHILDREN OF THIS MARRIAGE

Note the sex, name, date and location of birth, marriage or partnership, death, with the appropriate sources. Children are listed in order of birth. If any children had more than one spouse or life-partner, add these details as well.

SOURCES

Allocate a separate column or other identifiable section of the page to list the sources for all the information on the sheet, such as a copy of a death certificate. Give each source its own reference number, since this will be used to cross-reference to the entries. If necessary, continue the list on another sheet.

● Do not forget to check the details of stepchildren, since offspring from second marriages often use different surnames

● Always state the sex of each child, since the gender of modern names is not always obvious

● Do not be alarmed if you have many gaps on the first draft of your family group sheet—after all, this is the reason you are researching

closest to your own and working back in time. You may also want to add the number you assigned to entries on your original pedigree chart, noting this number next to the person's name (see pages 116–117). At the beginning of your research, this may seem unnecessary, but as your collection of data expands, you will find it helpful for keeping track of individual entries.

Understanding Gaps

If there is a long gap between the birth of children, this may indicate a miscarriage, stillbirth, infant death, that the mother suffered from poor health, or the couple were separated by war, work, or migration.

To add interest, illuminate your family group sheets with photographs of the featured couple.

Descendant and Drop Charts

Working backwards from the present generation into your family's past, you will eventually find a person who provides no leads to help you go back farther. Whether he or she is a medieval aristocrat or an immigrant from the 1920s, this person, in genealogical terms, can be credited as the "founder," or progenitor, of that particular family line. It is time to make a descendant chart.

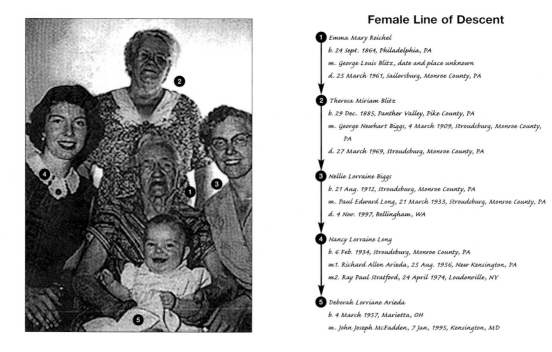

Female Line of Descent

1 *Emma Mary Reichel*
b. 24 Sept. 1864, Philadelphia, PA
m. George Louis Blitz, date and place unknown
d. 25 March 1961, Sailorsburg, Monroe County, PA

2 *Theresa Miriam Blitz*
b. 29 Dec. 1885, Panther Valley, Pike County, PA
m. George Newhart Biggs, 4 March 1909, Stroudsburg, Monroe County, PA
d. 27 March 1969, Stroudsburg, Monroe County, PA

3 *Nellie Lorraine Biggs*
b. 21 Aug. 1912, Stroudsburg, Monroe County, PA
m. Paul Edward Long, 21 March 1933, Stroudsburg, Monroe County, PA
d. 4 Nov. 1997, Bellingham, WA

4 *Nancy Lorraine Long*
b. 6 Feb. 1934, Stroudsburg, Monroe County, PA
m1. Richard Allen Arieda, 25 Aug. 1956, New Kensington, PA
m2. Ray Paul Stratford, 24 April 1974, Loudonville, NY

5 *Deborah Lorriane Arieda*
b. 4 March 1957, Marietta, OH
m. John Joseph McFadden, 7 Jan, 1995, Kensington, MD

This simple line of descent shows five generations of women through one family line.

● Where possible, accompany the entries on a descendant chart with vital birth, marriage, and death dates, and also names of spouses

A descendant chart begins with the name of the earliest direct ancestor for whom you have documentary proof of existence. This first person is entered with his or her date of birth, marriage, and death, if available, along with the details of any spouse.

The descendant chart moves down through the family line from the top of the page. Vital names and dates for each generation are carefully entered horizontally across the chart until the youngest generation in the family, which is placed at the base of the page. If you are tracing more than one ancestral line at a time, make a descendant chart for each individual progenitor. Names and details are entered on simple lines of text or in boxes of text. Each entry occupies its own line and indentations are used to indicate spouses and offspring.

Indentations are used to indicate spouses and offspring

Drop Charts

A drop chart, also called a box chart or drop-line pedigree, reads from top to bottom and from left to right. Generations are arranged in columns, and "drop" down from each other.

The first column on the top-left of the page shows the family's progenitor and spouse; this is the first generation. The second column includes the descendants and spouses from the first generation. The third and fourth columns show the direct descendants of the second and third generation.

In large families, it is not usually possible to fit an entire generation on one single page, so drop charts continue downward on separate pages until everyone in those four generations has been entered. At this point, if a person in the fourth generation

This four-generation drop chart shows that by the fourth generation, the genealogist found significantly more information on each person.

has a sibling, that person appears again as the first entry on a new chart and the process is repeated again. The base of each column should include a cross-reference to a new chart where that generation is continued. Each individual entry also requires a cross-reference if that person is featured as the first entry on another chart.

Variations on the Theme

For a special occasion, you can also make a pictorial descendant chart with photos or examples of the handwriting of the featured individuals. The names and vital dates of the progenitor and spouse may be highlighted in decorative boxes at the top of the chart or written in larger type.

- For multiple drop charts, make a note of the generations listed on each chart

- Don't forget to number all drop charts and cross-reference entries if they appear on more than one drop chart

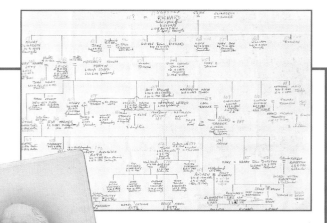

RESEARCH NOTES

FAMILY RESEARCHER *David Roth*
FOCUS OF INQUIRY *Overcoming Dead Ends*

In the course of 20 years' research, David Roth has overcome numerous obstacles: "Never," he urges, "accept the spelling of a name unless you are absolutely sure it is correct." Registry clerks, census-takers, and others responsible for records, he explains, often misheard what was said, or wrote it down incorrectly. "Do not," he adds, "accept places at face value either." Even knowledgeable people can be vague about geography.

David found this out the hard way when researching the birthplace of an English great-grandfather, John Spears Sladden. The census returns of 1851, 1861, and 1871 listed his birthplace as "Sandwich, Kent." But in Sandwich, there was no record of his birth. Fortunately, David's aunt knew that Sladden's sister had married a certain Dr. Jackson, practicing medicine in London's prestigious Wimpole Street. David checked the census returns for the years 1861, 1871, and 1881, and found the returns for the doctor's household. As he had hoped, the census noted not only the name of

John Spears Sladden, David Roth's great-great-grandfather and the pencil-drawn descendant chart David used during his research.

the doctor's wife, Jane, but her own place of birth—another Kentish town of St. Lawrence Thanet. When David followed up the parish records for this locality, he found not only Jane's entry, but that of her brother, John. David breathed a sigh of relief: He was back on the track, and able to trace the family through another generation.

SEARCH TIP If you run up against a brick wall when researching a direct line, make a sideways detour and seek details of the missing ancestor's siblings. This may help you correct errors of date, place, or naming, and lead you to the details of the previous generation.

Descendant and Drop Charts

121

Gifts and Displays

Once you have traced your roots back to your great-grandparents, or even earlier, you may like to create a decorative display of your finds. Many pre-printed or computer-generated templates are available, or you can design your own. Some templates are based on a tree motif, complete with foliage and branches, while others feature borders, boxes, and stylish typefaces.

A professionally drafted pedigree chart, mounted in a wood frame, can turn simple genealogical data into a treasured heirloom.

Family tree templates are advertised in genealogical magazines and mail-order catalogs. Most family tree software features templates for displaying your information, and there are many Internet sites offering free downloads. Decorative templates are also available from some bookstores and stationery suppliers.

Family trees are designed to show the names, vital dates, and the links between individuals, generation to generation. Some templates contain space to add other pieces of information, such as places and occupations, but they are essentially summaries of a group of ancestors and descendants.

You can arrange family tree details as you would for a pedigree chart, working backwards from your own generation to your earliest ancestors. Alternatively, you can use the descendant chart approach, starting with the progenitor or "founder" of the family and displaying the fullest possible extent of his or her descendants in the generations that follow. Finally, you can take the drop chart approach and display four selected generations.

Adding Photographs

You can also illustrate your family tree with photographs of past and present family members. Some pre-printed family trees are designed with spaces to attach these images, but the easiest and most flexible way of creating a pictorial tree is to use one of the widely available genealogical software programs

Illustrate your family tree with photographs of past and present relatives

● Refer to pages 92–93 for more information on scanning images and using digital photographs

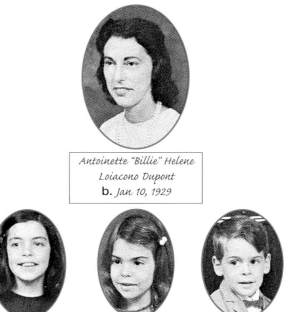

Antoinette "Billie" Helene
Loiacono Dupont
b. *Jan 10, 1929*

Ellen O'Neil Dupont
b. *Nov 11, 1955*

Antonia Chafee Dupont
b. *Dec 20, 1957*

William Albert Dupont
b. *Feb 7, 1960*

For an ideal gift, mount prints of archive family photographs on frame-style greeting cards, then stick a printed copy of a pedigree chart or descendant chart inside the card.

that allow you to scan in photographs on your home scanner, then crop and position as necessary.

Family Trees as Gifts

A family tree or other genealogical chart is an ideal heirloom gift for a new baby, elderly grandparents, or newly married couples. It also makes a fitting reward of all your hard work and a thoughtful way to display your heritage.

Family trees can be presented in a tree or chart format. If creating a family tree for an elderly relative, they may be particularly pleased to receive a descendant chart, possibly even with themselves in the "progenitor" position, decorated with photographs of their "clan."

For a baby, you can either produce a full pedigree chart or a simpler, but equally delightful, gift of two compact drop charts, showing the new arrival's direct line of descent for two or more generations on both mother's and father's sides. To share a family tree with several relatives—perhaps as a souvenir of a family reunion—color photocopy your finished tree onto large-size paper, then place in simple clip frames.

Use photographs to make family tree displays. With simple personal computer software, you can import scanned photographs into decorative picture boxes and caption them with the names and vital details of the people shown.

Professional Hint

To save yourself time, trouble, and expense, always make a rough draft of your planned tree, setting out the information in its intended location. A draft tree will help you make sure you know exactly what goes where and will also indicate how much detail fits comfortably on the page. If you are working on paper rather than on computer, the easiest way to do this is to make either a photocopy or a tracing-paper copy of the blank form, and sketch it out in pencil before you apply any ink or other form of lettering. If you are using a software-generated tree, you will be able to design, edit, and alter your contents on screen as often as you like before printing out the finished product. You will probably need to practice using the software a few times before you arrive at a satisfactory result.

Writing Your Family History

One of the most rewarding genealogy projects is writing and producing a family history. If you have the dedication to explore your own genealogy, you are perfectly qualified to share the knowledge and tell the story of your discoveries. You do not need to be an experienced writer or have any particular literary talent—all you need is enthusiasm.

● Make photocopies of old recipes, treasured letters, or other ephemera and use them to illustrate your family history

● Your family history will be more authentic if you footnote all information with an appropriate source

A written family history can be as short and simple, or as long and detailed, as you like. It can be nothing more than a series of photocopied family charts with captions, or an elaborate compilation of vital records, background data, anecdotes, extracts from personal diaries and letters, photographs, newspaper articles, primary documents, and maps. The choice is yours.

The Basics

The most fundamental feature of your family history is the compilation of the names, vital dates, and generational links that you have researched. You may find it helpful to include some or all of the following: A complete family tree, five-generation pedigree charts, family group sheets, a descendant chart, and drop charts for each branch of the family.

Organization

Many family history authors begin with an introductory note on whatever is known about the family's origins or the earliest-known ancestor. This can be followed by separate chapters on different branches of the family or themed elements of the

Professional Hint

Genealogical software can help you produce a surprisingly professional-looking family history, to print out as a booklet for distribution, or to post on the Internet. For a lasting heirloom, you may consider having your work professionally printed and bound. No matter what form your finished family history takes, remember that it is a valuable social document, not only for your relatives, but for the wider community. Public libraries and community museums are often very enthusiastic about receiving such documents for their own collections.

family's experience. If arranging the history by family branches, introduce each chapter with the appropriate pedigree chart, descendant chart, or family group sheet. Then, instead of having to list the names and dates repeatedly in your text, you can refer your readers to these charts and concentrate on your narrative.

Sources

Never underestimate the value of your own research, no matter how modest it seems. Your family history will be a valuable legacy for future generations, so always list sources for every piece of information, whether it is a census record, an aunt's recollections, or the faded inscription on a family tombstone. You do not have to interrupt your story to do this. Instead, use numerical

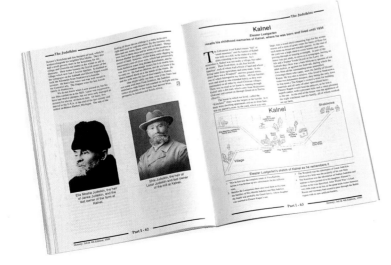

A family history publication can be formatted using the simplest personal computer software or genealogical software specially designed for this purpose.

Blank family history journals, available from genealogical suppliers, make it easy to create a bound volume of your family history. The easy-to-use format includes space for text and photographs.

footnotes on each page that clearly refer your reader to a separate documentation section at the back, or simply add an appendix, listing the source for each fact or detail. Check the reference shelves of your local library for guides to footnoting and citing sources. Most word processing programs include facilities for inserting and formatting footnotes.

Bringing History to Life

In order to bring your narrative to life, set the scene for your ancestors' story. Consult social, economic, and political history books to find out what was happening in their mother country, and in the world at large, during their childhoods and adult years. Think about your ancestors' experiences: Did historical events affect them directly? Did they immigrate because of racial or religious persecution? Did they fight in a war or suffer from a natural disaster or economic depression? Did they marvel at a new invention? You can weave these details into your narrative or list a selection to give a feel for each historical era. Retell any interesting family stories passed on by older relatives. Include newspaper articles that refer to ancestors, such as a hero of the school football team, or printed invitations and announcements. Carefully select extracts from personal letters and journals.

Geographical Information

In your family history, include details of the place where your ancestors lived or originated. Use maps, photographs, or other artwork to make reference to the ancestral homeland, hometown, or place of settlement after immigration. Look at atlases and encyclopedias to find out about their homeland. Was the land flat or mountainous? Was it an ancient city, a fishing village, or a frontier settlement? Did anything important happen there?

● Provide some historical context for your ancestors' lives

● Include group and individual photos in your family history, ranging from formal studio shots to casual vacation pictures

Janet Murphy Tabinski (circled), who was raised in California but now lives in England, treasures the chronicle of her Irish-American ancestors. She received her copy from her grandfather, Ray Murphy—who helped compile it—in 1968. It provides an account of her family's history, illustrated with charts, photographs, and details of her ancestors' achievements. Since having her own children, Janet became more appreciative of this volume: "Because I live so far away, I've been out on a limb of this family tree." But, thanks to the Murphy history, she has something to show to her children to remind them of their roots and connection to a flourishing clan.

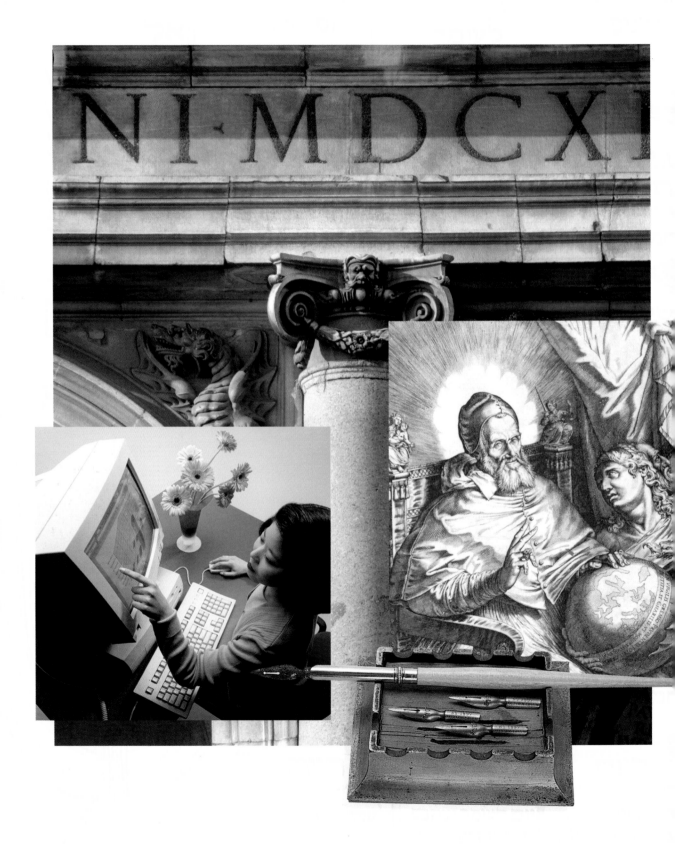

CHAPTER SEVEN

DECODING THE PAST

From inconsistent spellings to just plain bad handwriting, many barriers lie between you and your ancestors. Do not be discouraged, however, since these obstacles can often be overcome, and add to the excitement of ancestral research.

An English novelist once remarked: "the past is another country. They do things differently there'. Anyone who has ever struggled to decipher an old gravestone, puzzled over the function of an unusual but much-loved family heirloom, or wondered why three sons of the same ancestor have completely different last names, will appreciate this simple observation.

There will be occasions in your research when you puzzle over data that just does not make sense, or become frustrated by an illegible old letter or handwritten entry in a church register. Genealogists, historians and anyone else interested in exploring past times face these challenges sooner or later – but there is plenty of help at hand.

This chapter explains how customs for naming offspring may help you trace your family tree and how surnames – or even dates – may not always be what they seem. It will also give you tips for dealing with documents written in old-fashioned scripts, as well as a glossary of some unusual terms you may come up against as you delve deeper into your family's history.

Although we now live in an age of speed and convenience, our ancestors were also keen to save time wherever possible. As a result, they often abbreviated names and other key words when they recorded information. A basic understanding of these abbreviations can help you unravel mysterious handwritten scrawls.

Methods for measuring and recording dates vary according to historical time frame, culture and also geographic custom. This chapter offers tips on genealogical time puzzles and helps you put your family's records in context.

During the course of your research, you will encounter a host of genealogical puzzles. These may include Roman numerals to decipher, conflicting dates resulting from Pope Gregory XIII's calendar revisions in the sixteenth century, illegible lettering written in archaic scripts, and shifting international borders of your ancestral homelands.

Understanding Surnames

Our last names—signalling birth connections, shared ancestry, and marital unions—are used to identify us in numerous records. Over time, for many reasons, surnames change: Understanding the reasons for these changes can help you to overcome roadblocks in your research.

● Be aware of name changes and possible translations when researching your family tree, especially if you know you have immigrant roots

Consider how families got their names: In China, families have used inherited surnames for over 2,000 years. Half a world away, citizens of ancient Rome bore three names—a personal name, a family name, and an ancestral clan name. But after the fall of the Empire, the practice fell into disuse. In European societies, surnames have only been used in the last few hundred years, and their origins can provide clues about the person who first used the name. Where surnames do exist, they fall into basic categories (see the chart below).

Surnames also tell us about a family's earliest bearers. Some Swedish names, for instance, derive from the needs of Sweden's

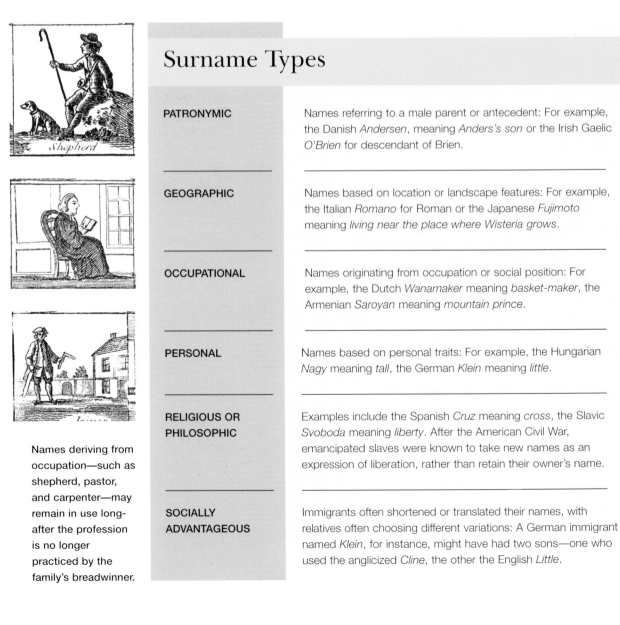

Surname Types

PATRONYMIC	Names referring to a male parent or antecedent: For example, the Danish *Andersen*, meaning *Anders's son* or the Irish Gaelic *O'Brien* for descendant of Brien.
GEOGRAPHIC	Names based on location or landscape features: For example, the Italian *Romano* for Roman or the Japanese *Fujimoto* meaning *living near the place where Wisteria grows*.
OCCUPATIONAL	Names originating from occupation or social position: For example, the Dutch *Wanamaker* meaning *basket-maker*, the Armenian *Saroyan* meaning *mountain prince*.
PERSONAL	Names based on personal traits: For example, the Hungarian *Nagy* meaning *tall*, the German *Klein* meaning *little*.
RELIGIOUS OR PHILOSOPHIC	Examples include the Spanish *Cruz* meaning *cross*, the Slavic *Svoboda* meaning *liberty*. After the American Civil War, emancipated slaves were known to take new names as an expression of liberation, rather than retain their owner's name.
SOCIALLY ADVANTAGEOUS	Immigrants often shortened or translated their names, with relatives often choosing different variations: A German immigrant named *Klein*, for instance, might have had two sons—one who used the anglicized *Cline*, the other the English *Little*.

Shepherd

Names deriving from occupation—such as shepherd, pastor, and carpenter—may remain in use long after the profession is no longer practiced by the family's breadwinner.

Variations in spelling can greatly increase the amount of time you spend searching vital records. When considering different spellings, ask someone else to speak the name, and write down all the ways it might be heard. Also, consider the way an immigrant's pronunciation might have sounded to an official. The name *Lazarow*, might have been noted as *Lazerow*, *Lazzaro*, or *Lazeroff.*

seventeenth-century army: Soldiers, who previously were known by their given name, were only required to adopt surnames for the convenience of their commanders, and these names often expressed some desirable trait: The name *Rapp*, for instance, meant *prompt*, *on time*, and *combat-ready.*

Variations in Spelling

Until recent times, there were few rules about the way a name was spelled. In English, for instance, spellings did not become fixed until the eighteenth century, when language scholars began to publish authoritative dictionaries. People spelled their names any way they liked, and were rarely consistent, even within families. As pronunciation evolved, so too did the way a name was written. Even if a name's owner stuck to one version, a census taker, parish clerk, or immigration official might well mis-hear or misspell it on the record.

Variations in Pronunciation

If you cannot find the name you are seeking under the spelling you know, try different versions. Different vowels may be used, or the letter *e* dropped or added at the end: the name *Smith*, for instance, might also be written *Smyth* or *Smythe*.

● Chinese names are passed down through the father, but women retain their names, even after marriage; although there are more than 3,050 surnames, over 80 percent use one of about 100 names

RESEARCH NOTES

FAMILY RESEARCHER *Lenny Yodaiken*
FOCUS OF INQUIRY *Origin of Family Surname*

With the help of his extended family and a variety of primary sources, genealogist Lenny Yodaiken has identified over 21 variations on his family surname. The name dates from the early eighteenth century when a Lithuanian nobleman granted Lenny's earliest-known ancestor part of his rural estate. The family adopted the family name, *Menaiken*, after the name of the nobleman's manor. Until that time, Lenny's ancestors, like other Jews, used only patronymic names or priestly names to identify themselves. During the eighteenth and nineteenth centuries, European rulers instructed Jewish and other citizens to identify themselves with given names and surnames. Governments often issued lists of approved names from which citizens could choose one to use.

This 1897 census return shows the entry for a branch of Lenny's family, with their surname listed as Jedeikin. *The family lived in Tukkum, in modern-day Latvia.*

Given Names

The names that parents give their children are some of the most valuable clues for tracing family roots. As you collect data on a particular family line, you may find certain names repeated again and again. In these repetitions, there may be patterns between the generations that help you identify individuals, establish connections, and work back toward more distant generations.

During the nineteenth and twentieth centuries, flowers were favorite names for girls, symbolizing natural beauty and vitality. Popular choices included Rose, Magnolia, Daisy, Violet, and Iris.

Examples of Naming Traditions

Naming traditions vary between different societies and also among families within single communities. Many old customs have now vanished or reflect modern times. For example, in Scotland until the 1950s, families named boys according to a fixed pattern—repeating the names of the father, male grandparents, and uncles in a set sequence. Girls followed a similar pattern or were named in honor of male relatives using a feminized name, such as Davidina.

Ashkenazi Jewish children were generally named after the closest deceased relative, unless someone else in the immediate family already had taken that name—this was usually a grandparent or a grandparent's sibling. However, highest priority went to the child's mother, if she died in childbirth, or the father if he had died before the baby was born. With the increase in assimilation in the nineteenth century, it became customary to give Jewish babies two names—a religious name following the traditions mentioned above, and also a secular given name.

A boy born into the Russian Orthodox tradition was generally named after the saint on whose day he was born. Girls were named Mary if they were the first daughter, Anna if they were the second, and Helen if they were the third. Subsequent daughters were named after deceased relatives.

A Matter of Taste

Many names are chosen according to the fashions of the day. As with clothing, naming fashions are prone to change. Every year, newspapers publish lists of the most popular names for girls and boys and it is often possible to date a name to the nearest decade. The name Wendy, for instance, was rarely seen before the publication of J.M. Barrie's *Peter Pan*, and the arc of a singer's or movie star's career can be tracked by the frequency with which his or her name appears in the birth announcements.

Nicknames

Nicknames have many origins. They are often derived from the individual's given name or surname. Alternatively, they are suggested by friends or family as a reflection of the individual's appearance or character. For the family researcher, problems arise when nicknames supersede given names used on official documents and vital records, or are informally replaced by new names altogether. To make matters worse, people may use more than one of these names in the course of a lifetime, switching according to whim or occasion. When seeking and studying given names on vital documents, you may avoid confusion if you allow for variations based on personal choice.

Errors can occur in the administration of given names. This baby's hospital nametag identifies him as Michael John Bebbington, although his given name was actually Graham John Bebbington. All other documentation relating to the child is correct, but this type of family heirloom could prove confusing for a future genealogist.

MICHAEL JOHN BEBBINGTON

In Christian countries, New Testament names, such as those of the apostles, have remained ever-popular for boys. Favorites include Peter, James, Thomas, Andrew, Paul, John, Philip, Bartholomew, Matthew, Simon, Jude, Francis, Joseph, and Jesus.

RESEARCH NOTES

FAMILY RESEARCHER *Frances and June Campbell*
FOCUS OF INQUIRY *Scottish Naming Traditions*

Mother and daughter genealogy team Frances Campbell and June Campbell used Scottish naming traditions to uncover the story behind one ancestor's name.

Frances and June knew that families named each child after a particular relative, according to the order of its birth. The first boy received the name of the paternal grandfather, the second son that of the maternal grandfather, the third his own father's name. On the female side, the first daughter was named after the mother's mother, the second after the father's mother, the third baby girl after her own mother. Later arrivals were named—according to gender and birth order—after uncles or aunts. Until recent times, large families were common, so there were plenty of names available. As Frances and June worked their way back in time, they saw the same names appearing on parish registers, tombstones, and census returns. "It's how I knew I was on the right track," June says.

Very large families may have to seek farther than aunts and uncles for names. Researching her paternal side, Frances and June found a nineteenth-century baby named Anne Mary Cushny Campbell. None of the three forenames

June Campbell outside the Scottish church where she confirmed the reason for her ancestor's given name.

matched any Campbell females. June researched the records from the Scottish parish where the child was born. She noticed that Cushing was the surname of the minister—and then discovered that he had a daughter called Anne Mary, in whose honor the baby was named in 1863. "I simply looked up the name and found the birth of someone of that name in the same parish, 15 years earlier. I followed up the census records, and she turned out to be the minister's daughter," June says.

SEARCH TIP Find out if there are any naming traditions that can help you identify links between ancestors.

Deciphering Handwriting and Printing

At first glance, original documents, such as personal letters or official entries in registers, often seem difficult to read. Like pronunciation and spelling, writing and printing styles have changed considerably over time. Interpreting penmanship may take a little practice, but it is a skill that is relatively easy to acquire, and well worth the effort for any aspiring genealogist.

● Look for books with handwriting transcription exercises, showing the "translations" printed alongside the original

● Capital letters written in old handwriting styles can look very similar: Some of the most confusing culprits are S, L, and T

To understand old handwriting and printing typefaces, you need to combine your detective work with some basic research. Ask at your local library for books showing handwriting and printing styles of the period you are researching.

Read it Over and Over

If you have a document which, at a glance, appears indecipherable, first cast your eye over it several times. It is unlikely that it is completely illegible. The letters and words which, at first, seem puzzling may gradually start to make sense. Consider what you already know about the subject of the document. What words would you expect to find in a passage of this kind? Do not be afraid to make wild guesses, and play with possible phrases or logical combinations of words.

Next, compare unclear words with those you can easily understand. Think about the way the writer shaped letters or linked them together. Once you have recognized a distinctive word or letter-shape, go through the document and see where else it appears.

> **Consider what you know already about the subject of the document**

Try it Yourself

Genealogists maintain that the best way to become familiar with old penmanship is to copy out the text by hand. This may seem daunting, but it is one of the most useful ways to acclimatize yourself to old-fashioned scripts. As you work, leave blank spaces for the letters, words, or phrases you cannot understand, or put down all the plausible alternatives. Once you have finished reading or copying, look over the passage again. The meaning of previously mysterious words may become obvious, once you know the context in which they appear.

If you get frustrated, take a break. Leave the task for a few hours, or even a few days. A rest may allow you to return to the problem with a fresh eye.

Names

Names are often harder to decipher than ordinary words. Even individuals whose handwriting faithfully reproduces the style of letter formation they learned at school tend to express themselves more freely

Throughout history, people have been taught, or have adopted, particular styles of handwriting. These styles reflected the gender, occupation, and social status of the writer, and the purpose of the document. The copperplate style, shown right, was widely used for legal documents.

The copperplate style was taught from the seventeenth century onward. Also known as English running hand, it was written with a narrow nib to imitate the fine lines made by the engraving tools used to create penmanship instruction manuals.

when it comes to signing their names. Lower-case letters, in old handwriting, tend to look more like their modern-day counterparts than capital letters, which have changed more radically over time.

Historical Anomalies

In eighteenth- and nineteenth-century documents, the first letter *s* in a word with a double *s*—as in the word *Confession*—was written with a long descending loop, as if it were the letter *f*, looking more like a word spelt *Confefsion*. This f-like character is known as the leading S. An odd-looking combination of letters may actually be an abbreviation of a regular word or name.

The letters *I* and *J* can also seem very similar. In Latin, they were, in fact, one letter. Scribes and printers treated them as the same character until the seventeenth century. Even after the difference was established, individual handwriting styles made the two hard to distinguish. You may find the name Iohanna that is actually the name Johanna.

Handwriting in some periods was particularly ornate, with a tendency to decorate individual letters and numbers with flourishes. Once you are aware of their existence, you may be able to see past these curves and elongated strokes to identify the letter beneath. Among numbers, it is easy to confuse the arabic numerals *6* and *8*.

Letters may be written in a variety of shapes, depending on historical convention and the personal style of the writer. To the modern eye, some letters are more easily decoded than others.

A	
B	
C	
D	
E	
F	
G	
H	
I, J	
K	
L	
M	
N	
O	
P	
Q	
R	
S	
T	
U, V	
W	
X	Y
Z	

Signs of the times: If a signature was required, illiterates often used a cross or wavy line to mark their name. Those who could write often abbreviated names to save time, omitting letters, using lines through or above letters, or dots and small letters at the end.

Deciphering Handwriting and Printing

Archaic Terms and Key Relationships

Sometimes genealogy seems to have a language all its own. As you delve deeper into your family history, you will come across unfamiliar terms and mysterious abbreviations. Wills, deeds, and other legal papers are sprinkled with Latin words and obscure terminology beloved by lawyers and bureaucrats, but which can cause problems for family researchers.

- Cousins are relations descended in a parallel family line from a common ancestor; first cousins share a same grandparent, second cousins share a great-grandparent, and third cousins share a great-great-grandparent

- Half brothers or half sisters have one natural parent in common

- A stepfather, stepmother, stepsister, or stepbrother is an individual who shares no blood tie with another person, but is connected to them through the marriage of a natural parent to an unrelated person

- In England, a stepson or step-daughter was often called a son- or daughter-in-law

Even everyday documents, such as personal letters or entries on parish registers, often contain odd turns of phrase and words that have fallen out of use. And generations of family historians, eager to cram as many details as possible onto a genealogical chart or tree, have resorted to all manner of abbreviations. The glossary on this page is a sample of the words and phrases that budding genealogists need to know. For a wider selection, consult a genealogical dictionary available in bookstores or on library reference shelves.

The Language of Latin

Latin is commonly used in legal documents and Roman Catholic sacramental registers

Until the twentieth century, illiteracy was common among women and the poor. Professional scribes were commissioned to write both official and personal documents.

Common Words and Phrases

DECEDENT	Person who has died.
DOWER	Share of a husband's real estate to which his widow is entitled.
ESTATE	The total property held by an individual, and available after death.
GRANTEE	Recipient of property, either by purchase, gift, or request.
GRANTOR	Individual who sells or gives property to another person.
IBID	Same location. Identifies a document that has already been quoted.
INFANT	A person below the age designated as the start of adulthood.
INTESTATE	Died without leaving a will.
ISSUE	Offspring.
NÉE	French for "born"; used to identify a woman's maiden name.
POSTHUMOUS	After death. A "posthumous" child is one born after its father has died.
PROXIMO	Latin for "next." Used in dates, referring to the following month.
RELICT	Widow of a particular individual.
SIC	"Thus!." Shows that an incorrect fact has been copied faithfully.

Common Abbreviations

For marriage terminology, see page 36; for will terminology, see pages 42 and 43

b. or bn.	Date of birth. Conventions vary for the use of *b.* (see next entry).
b. or bur.	Date of burial.
c.	Abbreviation of the Latin *circa*, meaning an approximate date or time.
d.	Date of death.
dsp	Abbreviation of the Latin *decissit sine prole*, meaning *died without issue*.
et. al.	Abbreviation of the Latin *et alia*, meaning *and others*. Indicates the presence of other names or items not listed individually on a document.
et. ux.	Abbreviation of the Latin words *et uxor*, which translates as *and spouse*.
fl.	Abbreviation of the Latin *floreat*, meaning *flourished*. Refers to the general time when a person was alive and used in the absence of precise dates.
inst./ultimo	*Inst.* is an abbreviation of the word *instant,* meaning the present month, as in *we have received your letter of the 12th inst*. *Ultimo* refers to the previous month and is used in letters and legal documents.
JP	Justice of the Peace.
m., m1, m2	Marriage date. Numbers indicate the first marriage, second marriage, etc.
nd	No date known.
N.S./O.S.	New Style/Old Style. Dates before and after the Gregorian calendar.
ob.	Abbreviation for the Latin word *obit*, meaning deceased.
otp	Of this parish.
Tutor	Guardian of an underage person or minor.
unm.	Unmarried.

until the mid-twentieth century. You may also see it used in academic and medical documents.

If you find yourself coming across documents written entirely in Latin, buy a small Latin dictionary to translate common words. Transcribe the document carefully, leaving a generous space between lines. Look up each word and write it below in the space allocated. If you have trouble with gender, nouns, tenses, or other elements relating to sentence structure, refer to an elementary school textbook, since these usually contain tables of word endings. Alternatively, ask someone with a greater understanding of the language to abstract the essential information, or consult a genealogical website.

Photographs of family weddings provide a chance to view relations from various generations. The age balance of the generations has changed over the last century: Although families have become smaller and couples have started families later in life, there has also been a dramatic increase in life expectancy.

Making Sense of Dates

Although time is something we often take for granted as a set and given concept, the way it has been measured through history has changed according to the level of scientific knowledge and cultural traditions of different societies. As a result, calendar dates can present certain inconsistencies for the genealogist.

● When requesting information from relatives or other sources, ask for dates to be spelled out in words, rather than with numerical abbreviations

● Some genealogical software packages include easy-to-use calculators for converting Julian, Gregorian, Hebrew, and Islamic dates

Dates are not as straightforward as they seem. For instance, a numerical day in a month—such as 5/7—can mean either the fifth day of July or the seventh day of May, depending on where and when it was written. Even years on tombstones should not be taken as read, since between the 1500s and 1700s, European countries and their colonies gradually converted from the Roman Julian calendar to the Gregorian calendar, which was more accurate.

The Gregorian Calendar
The calendar most of the world uses today only dates back to 1582. In that year, Pope Gregory XIII replaced the Roman Julian calendar, which began the new year on March 25, with one in which the new year begins on the first day of January.

Although Catholic countries accepted the innovation, Protestant countries took many years to agree to the change. Scotland adopted the new Gregorian calendar in

To calculate important dates, civil and religious authorities depended on astronomers to keep track of the solar and lunar cycles. This was especially important when European countries started using the Gregorian calendar.

1600, while England, Wales, Ireland and most British colonies did not fall into line until the year 1752.

For this reason, you may come across contradictory dates if you are researching records dating from the mid-eighteenth century. A document created in February 1749 of the new calendar may be dated February 1748 instead, if its author still considered February part of the old year. You may find copies of documents with the letters *O.S.* (for Old Style) or *N.S.* (for New Style) appended to the date, or assigned a double date, such as February 1748/9. If you can trace your family back to this era, there are handbooks to guide you through the maze and plenty of advice on the Internet.

Consistency and the Transatlantic Divide
When writing dates in numerical form, North Americans often use the sequence Month, Day, Year—as in 4/6/79 for April 6, 1979. In the rest of the world, however, the

order of the first two is reversed, with day coming before month, with the same date in April noted as 6/4/79. When you are copying dates from family records, avoid confusion by spelling out the name of the month, and use a universal form of date order—as in 6 April 1979. When you are drawing up a genealogical chart, use a consistent style of recording dates, especially if using a numerical form.

If you are copying dates noted numerically, and you cannot be sure which order of month and day the original writer used, the safest option is to write down both possibilities, with question marks attached next to your entry. Consider who wrote the dates and which order of days and months they would most likely have adopted.

Cultural Traditions

If you are researching non-Christian ancestors, you may encounter records dated according to different calendars. Once you are alerted to the possibilities, it is easy to recognize the variations and avoid mistakes.

The date assigned to the birth of Jesus Christ is the cornerstone of the western calendar. The years before Jesus' birth are identified as B.C. or B.C.E. (meaning before Christ or before the Common Era) and the years after are numbered as A.D. or C.E. (meaning *Anno Domini*, the Latin for Year of the Lord, or the Common Era).

Other cultures have their own modes of counting years. According to the traditional Jewish calendar, the beginning of time was

Advances in astronomy during the eighteenth century led to more accurate time keeping and navigation techniques. These improvements assisted European colonization and, subsequently, world population migration.

the Biblical date for the creation of the world, and years count forward from that point. In this system, the new year begins in the fall: The period 2000–2001 A.D., for instance, spans the Jewish years 5760–5761.

In the Islamic time frame, Year One comes much later in history, marking the date when the Prophet Mohammed and his followers moved from the Holy City of Mecca to Medina, in the year equivalent to the western calendar's 622 A.D.

The beautiful fountain of Acqua Paola in Rome was built in the year 1612. This closeup of the carved dedicatory inscription shows part of that year, MDCX.

Professional Hint

Old documents and building cornerstones often use Roman numerals to record dates. These are the numeric symbols:

M = 1000
D = 500
C = 100
L = 50
X = 10
V = 5
I = 1

To translate the date MDCCCLXXVI, work from left to right: M + D + CCC = 1800. L + XX + V + I = 76. Therefore, the full date, in common Arabic notation, is the year 1876.

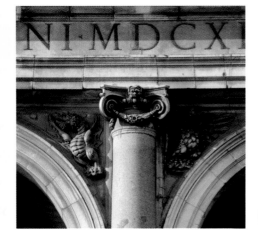

CHAPTER EIGHT

GENEALOGY ON THE MOVE

A trip to your ancestral homeland can bring your genealogical research to life. Whether you are visiting the next county or flying halfway around the world, you can unearth new information and find fresh historical trails.

Genealogy is not only about people but about places. A good genealogical trip can help you trace your ancestors' history farther into the past, and give you a taste for the landscapes that formed their world all those years ago.

Today, more than ever before, people are able to travel. Airfares have come down, and so too have many of the political barriers that kept the citizens of east and west apart. Parts of the world that were formerly off-limits are now open to anyone who has the time and the money to pay a visit.

Planning Ahead

Communities all over the world have begun to appreciate the value—economic and

A genealogy trip may uncover a host of sites. Clockwise from top left: The beautiful Italian city of Siena; memorial to education pioneer Thomas Haswell of North Shields, England, as photographed by his great-great-grand-daughter; soldier's gravestone from the U.S. Civil War; the Ellis Island immigrants' memorial.

cultural—of genealogical tourism. Many places now welcome roots-hunting guests, and do all they can to assist them in their explorations. However, it is essential to plan your trip and know what you wish to achieve in advance. Fellow genealogists who have also visited the area you are researching can provide invaluable advice at this early stage, not only with positive instructions of where to go and what to do, but also with warnings or advice on what *not* to do. Experience is the greatest teacher, and it is important you listen to any advice that is offered.

With a clear set of goals and serious research to undertake, planning a trip—national or international—is not the same as a regular vacation. Although there will be time to relax, your trip will involve more scheduled visits and bureaucratic challenges. This chapter will help you design and plan your journey effectively, show you how to make the most of what may be a once-in-a-lifetime adventure, and give you useful ideas for recording, preserving, and sharing your experiences.

Planning Your Trip

The secret of a successful genealogical trip is careful preparation. No matter where you are heading—to an ancestral hometown in the same country you live in now, or to a foreign land from which your forebears came—you will learn and enjoy it more if you plan in advance. When contemplating a journey to unfamiliar places, the anticipation becomes part of the adventure.

● Use a phrase book to familiarize yourself with the local language

● If you plan to rent a car, make sure you have an up-to-date driving license and road map of the area you are visiting

Once you have chosen your destination, find out as much as you can about the area. Study guidebooks and local maps, available from your local library or bookstore. Construct a realistic and relaxed itinerary that allows for the time you have available and the territory you hope to cover.

Are you planning to drive from place to place, or will you use internal flights, trains, buses, or taxis? If relying on public transportation, find out as much as possible ahead of time about the services to the places you want to see.

Are you hoping to make contact with any family members or potential informants still living in the area you are visiting? If so, and you know their whereabouts, a handwritten letter, phone call, or an E-mail in advance may guarantee a warmer welcome and prevent disappointment.

Bring a selection of photographs of relatives that might be of interest, a photocopy of a family tree or chart to establish your connections, and a small gift to show

appreciation. A handcrafted souvenir or specialty food from your hometown can help break the ice: Even farmers in the depths of Slovakia, for instance, have heard of the delights of Canadian maple syrup.

Tourist Information Centers
Contact the Visitors' Bureau or Tourist Information Center before traveling, either by telephone, fax, E-mail, or regular mail. They will, on request, supply tourist information, brochures, sightseeing advice, information on food and accommodation, and also local maps. They may be able to provide special advice for genealogical travelers in particular, steering you to local archives, historical societies, and other resources. Since family-history tourism is a growth area, an increasing number of communities are eager to welcome visitors in search of ancestral roots.

If you are heading for a foreign country where you do not speak the language, the Tourist Information office may be able to provide you with professional interpreters, reliable guides, or even volunteers—such as students of English—who are willing to help you in exchange for an opportunity to develop their language skills.

Even if you want to explore a place without any specific research aims, take time to consult maps and guidebooks. Once on the spot, you will be able to orientate yourself more quickly. You will then be free to soak up the atmosphere, appreciate the sights, and still take each day as it comes.

Before your trip, check any documents relating to the area you are visiting, such as land deeds, photographs, or even sketches drawn by elderly relatives. This will help you put the area in context when you arrive. Be sure to take copies of these documents with you.

Planning Checklist

KEY ANCESTORS	List the family members on whom you are seeking information, in order of priority, accompanied by a note of the information you hope to find for each person.
LOCATION AND LANGUAGE	Identify the locations—public archives, churches, cemeteries, libraries, and so forth—where the data you require is stored, along with access information and opening times. If you are visiting in foreign countries, be aware that not only place-names, but the official languages for recordkeeping may have changed over time. If your ancestors came from Poland, for instance, you may find that a single locality has been called, at different periods, by a Polish, Russian, or German name, with documents filed in any of those languages, according to the situation of the day. Consider your translation requirements in these situations.
NAMES	If researching foreign-born ancestors, make sure you know the given names and last names they used in their homeland. Without this information, you are unlikely to find their records.

● To avoid fruitless journeys, check the types of records kept by archive centers, plus the opening times and user restrictions

● Make sure your passport is fully up-to-date before you travel abroad

Archive Centers

If you are seeking vital records, find out as much as you can in advance about the archives where these are held. Make sure you have up-to-date details of location, opening times, access arrangements, any entry requirements or costs involved. If you have trouble finding out this information, ask fellow genealogists who have visited the same place if they can help.

International Borders

Even if your ancestors were born, lived, and died in the same place, remember that the official boundaries of their town, county, or country may have altered over time. Sometimes places are re-named, or may vanish from the map altogether after dramatic political events or wars in the region. Make sure you know where records are currently held for the people and time-periods you are researching. Check that these are not located in an archive far away from the place you will be staying.

Using the Internet

Since so much international data can be accessed on-line, do as much research as possible on your home computer or at a public library before you go. This will allow you to keep your valuable travel time free for research that can only be done on the spot. Refer to Chapter Five, Internet Searches, for more details on making the most of the Internet.

Do not underestimate the tiring effect of train, boat, and air travel. Leave plenty of time in your schedule for resting after each journey.

Equipment and Itinerary

Do not deny yourself the opportunity for casual sightseeing. You can learn a great deal by playing tourist for a day or two. Experience the beauty of the location, whether it be a seascape viewed from a Greek island (left) or the narrow streets of London's East End.

● Visit the Tourist Information center as soon as possible after your arrival

● Make sure you learn the words *hello*, *goodbye*, *please*, and *thank you* in the local language

To plan your localized itinerary, consult your map of the area and work out which sources are close together. Assess how much ground you can realistically cover before fatigue sets it. Allow plenty of time in your schedule for refreshment breaks, getting lost, and stopping to ask for directions.

Be realistic about how much you can achieve in one day. Allow yourself to be "human," and don't be disheartened if you lose time in your schedule unexpectedly. Remember that visits to official archives might take longer than you expect. Staff and systems are not equally efficient, or equally helpful, everywhere. However, if you are lucky, you might also find some new research lead that encourages you to change your priorities and stay in a particular place longer than planned. Be flexible.

Soak up the Atmosphere

If you know the district where your family lived, allow time to wander around it. Even if the actual street and original buildings have vanished, seek out locations that would have been known to your ancestors. Take time to investigate the local marketplaces, parks, bridges, farms, harbors, or even riverside promenades.

Look at surviving architecture from that period—or visit the local museum or library to study paintings or old photographs that depict the area as it was in the past. With a little imagination, you will be able to transport yourself back to the landscape or townscape of earlier generations. Seek out restaurants, bars, and cafés to sample traditional local dishes. Visit houses of worship belonging to the religion practiced by your ancestors. Even in a brand-new church, for instance, you may find clergy who know about the history of the local community or parish.

Meet the Locals

If possible, strike up a conversation with local residents to get a sense of what the place was like in days gone by. Explain the reason for your visit, and tell them what you know about your ancestors: You may find someone who remembers buying candy from your great-grandmother's store, or sat beside her to learn the alphabet in a one-room schoolhouse. The world is smaller than you think, and people are often eager to talk about their personal experiences.

Professional Hint

If you have no experience of foreign travel, or prefer not to embark on an independent research trip, take advantage of the opportunities offered by specialty travel companies. A growing number of firms organize genealogical tours of European countries and the Far East. Some firms supply tailor-made itineraries for small private groups and individuals; others concentrate on tour groups made up of people sharing a common cultural or religious heritage. You can find these services advertised in genealogical magazines, as well as on the Internet.

Genealogical Travel Kit

STATIONERY

Notebook, pens, and files or folders in which to keep your valuable documents, photographs, and local information.

DOCUMENTS

Copies (not originals) of vital records and other archival leads.

GEOGRAPHIC AIDS

Up-to-date road maps, street guides, and guidebooks.

TRAVEL DOCUMENTS

Passports, visas, driving licenses, traveler's checks, credit cards, local currency, and strong foreign currency, such as U.S. dollars or German marks.

INSURANCE POLICY

Check that all your belongings and documents are covered by your travel insurance policy and you have the original purchase receipts in the event of theft.

CAMERA, CAMCORDER, AND TAPE RECORDER

A camera—digital, if possible—and a good supply of film. Camera film may be hard to obtain or cost much more than you would normally pay. Check that your camera is suitable for photographing original documents close up and indoors, since this is an effective way of recording documents if you are not able to obtain a copy. Try photographing documents at home to make sure your camera is up to the job. Do not rely on photographs as a means of recording information on original documents: You will still need to transcribe or abstract the relevant information.

Video camcorders and audiotape recorders are useful for interviewing contacts and preserving your own experiences in the form of a diary.

CONTACT DETAILS

Names, addresses, and telephone numbers of your local contacts. You should also take a supply of cards or stickers containing your own name and address. You may meet people who will be able to find out information for you and send it to you after you return home.

PHRASE BOOK

Take a good phrase book and bilingual dictionary to help with the language. Do not assume everyone will speak your language.

● Worn-in, comfortable shoes are essential for genealogical trips, whether you are visiting foreign cities, cemeteries, farmland, cobbled streets, rural paths, or ancient church archives; do not be tempted to take a pair of new shoes, however stylish they look

Check that you have the right film for both indoor and outdoor photography. Be sure that your flash is working.

Creating a Travel Diary

The most valuable souvenirs you can bring back from a genealogical journey are memories, discoveries, fresh research leads, and new friendships. But without overloading your luggage, take the opportunity to collect some visual mementoes. Once you return, you can put the words and pictures together into an illustrated diary of your experiences.

● An aerial-view postcard is an extremely useful record, since it gives an overall image of a place

● Even if you are an experienced photographer, a professional postcard will often provide a better record of key landmarks

On your trip, take photos of the people you have met or who have some connection with your family. Arrange for a third party to take the picture, so you and your companions can appear in the photograph together. Immediately after processing, label the pictures with the names, addresses, date, and place of meeting.

While you are visiting, look for reproductions of early maps in libraries, bookstores, and museums. These are useful for understanding the historical era you are researching. Mark locations that have family connections. Copies of old photographs are also a useful addition to a travel diary, since it is fascinating to compare past and present images of the same location.

When you are composing a photographic travel diary, you might like to mount your images on archive-quality pages for storage in a ring notebook. This method provides more flexibility than a traditional album.

RESEARCH NOTES

FAMILY RESEARCHER *Malcolm Miller*
FOCUS OF INQUIRY *Finding a Scottish Barn*

For the past twenty years, New Jersey real-estate agent Malcolm Miller has been studying his Scottish roots and visiting the towns and villages where his Miller and MacLellan ancestors lived and died. He plans each trip as if it were a military campaign, studying detailed maps and drawing on the local knowledge of his Scottish relatives.

In 1996, Malcolm and his father made a genealogical pilgrimage together. They visited the ancient town of Dunfermline, where their ancestors lived at the time of the 1841 census, and the area of Dunbartonshire, where other farming ancestors were buried. They also visited the farm that had belonged to Malcolm's great-great-great-grandfather, George MacLellan, who was born in 1767. The present farmer showed them the stone lintel that he had removed when rebuilding the farm's ancient barn. An inscription on the lintel revealed that the barn was the handiwork of George MacLellan himself. Malcolm immediately asked the farmer's permission to ship the stone back to the United States. It took two years of negotiations with shipping agencies, but the 375-pound (170kg) lintel finally found a new home in the New Jersey yard of its maker's great-great-great-grandson.

SEARCH TIP When visiting a site connected to your family's history, introduce yourself to the present occupants of your ancestral homes and explain why you are there. You never know what information—or even memorabilia—you might go home with.

Wearing the traditional Scottish kilt, Malcolm stands with the lintel taken from his ancestral barn.

RESEARCH NOTES

FAMILY RESEARCHER *Andre Brummer*
FOCUS OF INQUIRY *Finding German Ancestors*

As a young man living in South Africa, Andre had seen his grandmother set aside every Monday to research her family history. From her research, and that of other relatives, he learned about a German ancestor named Johan Wichard Brummer, born in 1764 in Menslage, Hanover, Germany.

Andre knew that Johan and one of his brothers traveled to the Netherlands to join a ship of the Dutch East India Company that was due to sail to South Africa. Johan's

brother eventually returned to Germany and is said to have immigrated to the United States. However, Johan stayed in South Africa and became a part of the Afrikaans community of German, French, and Dutch immigrants.

Andre was told that his great-grandfather, Johannes Paulus Brummer, fought in the Boer War of 1899–1902 and that his grandfather, Andries Cornelius Brummer, was born on a ship in 1901 as his family was transported to a concentration camp. Brummer's grandfather was hidden in a box during the voyage so he would not be found and, as a result, was said to be shorter than his siblings.

These stories inspired Andre to visit Germany in 1987. With the help of an elderly lady who lived in the small town, Andre spent two whole days researching records in the 700-year-old church in Menslage, Hanover. Andre did not speak German, and the lady who was helping him did not speak a word of English. However, the two managed to communicate somehow, and she helped him find the right records. As a result of this trip, Andre collected the names of thousands of ancestors to add to his growing family tree.

Helped by a member of the local community, Andre researched his ancestral records in the village church.

If possible, take photographs, make photocopies, or order copies of documents that you find on your travels: A title deed, census return, or parish register bearing the signatures of an ancestral bride and groom, are as evocative as any photograph.

If you have jotted down notes in a hurry or tried to write while traveling, write up these notes at the end of each day, or you may find it difficult to decipher the information at a later date. Remember to update your files as soon as you get home.

• As a friendly gesture, mail a copy of your photographic prints to the other people shown in the photographs

RESEARCH LOG

RESEARCHER *STODDARD, Anthony*   LOCALITY *LITCHFIELD CO. LIBRARY, CT*
OBJECTIVES *Biographical Information of GOODENOUGH, ARTHUR*

DATE	SOURCE, REFERENCE, AND COMMENTS	DOC. REF.
1 Dec 1995	*Clergy of Litchfield County* *Biographical sketch on pp. 45–48* *Litchfield County Univ. Club, 1900*	*Photocopy* *A5001*
1 Dec 1995	*Clergy of Connecticut in Revolutionary Days* *History and biographical sketch pp. 1–6*	*Photocopy* *A5002¢*

Keep research logs on all the individuals you research and the places you visit. This entry from a visit to a Connecticut public library shows the biographical details found on one ancestor.

INTERNATIONAL DIRECTORY

Always consult the World GenWeb site for the country you are researching. This can be found at http://www.worldgenweb.org. Telephone and fax numbers are for national callers only. Consult your international operator for international dialing codes and up-to-date country dialing codes. Telephone numbers shown in brackets should be dropped by international dialers.

North America

For each U.S. state and Canadian territory, directory entries start with the contact addresses for vital records. This is followed by contact details for state archives, national archives (where appropriate), state and provincial libraries, genealogical and historical societies, and specialist libraries.

United States

ALABAMA

Alabama State Vital Records Office
Center for Health Statistics
Suite 1150
201 Monroe Street
Montgomery, AL 36104
Tel: 334 206 5418
Fax: 334 262 9563

Alabama Department of Archives
642 Washington Avenue
Montgomery, AL 36130 0100
Tel: 334 242 4435
Fax: 334 240 3433
http://www.archives.state.al.us/
index.html

Department of Archives and History
(records of births before 1908)
624 Washington Avenue
Montgomery, AL 36130
Tel: 334 242 4363

The Alabama Historical Commission
468 South Perry Street
Montgomery, AL 36130 0900
Tel: 334 242 3184
Fax: 334 240 3477
http://www.preserveala.org

Alabama Genealogical Society
P.O. Box 2296
Samford University Library
800 Lakeshore Drive
Birmingham, AL 35229
Tel: 205 726 2846
Fax: 205 726 4009

**Birmingham Public Library
(Southern History Library)**
2100 Park Place
Birmingham, AL 35203
Tel: 205 226 3665
Fax: 205 226 3764
http://www.bham.lib.al.us

ALASKA

Alaska State Vital Records Office
Bureau of Vital Statistics
350 Main Street, Room #114
P.O. Box 110675
Juneau, AK 99811 0675
Tel: 907 465 3392
Fax: 907 465 3618

Alaska State Archives
141 Willoughby Avenue
Juneau, AK 99801 1720
Tel: 907 465 2270
Fax: 907 465 2465
http://www.archives.state.ak.us

**National Archives and Records
Administration Pacific Alaska Region**
654 West Third Avenue
Anchorage, AK 99501 2145
Tel: 907 271 2441
Fax: 907 271 2442
E-mail: archives@alaska.nara.gov
http://www.nara.gov/regional/
anchorage.html

ARIZONA

Arizona State Vital Records Office
2727 W. Glendale
Phoenix, AZ 85051
Tel: 602 255 3260
Fax: 602 249 3040
http://www.hs.state.az.us/vitalrcd/
vitalrcd.htm

Arizona State Archives
Room 442, State Capitol
1700 W. Washington Street
Phoenix, AZ 85007
Tel: 602 542 4159
Fax: 602 542 4402
http://www.lib.az.us/archives

**Arizona Historical Society
Central Division**
1300 North College Avenue,
Tempe, AZ 85281
Tel: 480 929 0292
Fax: 480 967 5450
http://www.tempe.gov/ahs/frames.htm

**Arizona Historical Society
Northern Division**
2340 N. Fort Valley Road
Flagstaff, AZ 86001
Tel: 520 774 6272
http://www.tempe.gov/ahs/frames.htm

Arizona Historical Society
Rio Colorado Division
240 Madison Avenue
Yuma, AZ 85364
Tel: 520 782 1841
http://www.tempe.gov/ahs/frames.htm

Arizona Historical Society
Southern Division
949 E. Second Street
Tucson, AZ 85719
Tel: 520 628 5774
http://www.tempe.gov/ahs/frames.htm

ARKANSAS

Arkansas State Vital Records Office
4815 West Markham Street, Slot 44
Little Rock, AR 72205
Tel: 501 661 2726
Fax: 501 663 2832
http://www.healthyarkansas.com

Arkansas History Commission
One Capitol Mall
Little Rock, AR 72201
Tel: 501 682 6900
http://www.state.ar.us/ahc

Arkansas Genealogical Society
P.O. Box 908
Hot Springs, AR 71902 0908
http://www.rootsweb.com/~args

Hendrix College Library
1600 Washington Avenue
Conway, AR 72032
Tel: 501 450 1303
Fax: 501 450 3800
http://www.hendrix.edu/BaileyLibrary/
Default.htm

Texarkana Public Library
600 West 3rd Street
Texarkana, AR, TX 75501 5054
Tel: 903 794 2149
Fax: 903 794 2139
http://www.txar-publib.org/home.htm

CALIFORNIA

Office of Vital Records
304 'S' Street
Sacramento, CA 95814
Tel: 916 445 1719
Fax: 800 858 5553
http://www.dhs.cahwnet.gov/hisp/chs/
OVR/Ordercert.htm

California State Archives
1020 'O' Street
Sacramento, CA 95814
Tel: 916 653 7715
Fax: 916 653 7636
http://www.ss.ca.gov/archives/
archives_contacts.htm

National Archives and Records
Administration Pacific Region
Southwest
24000 Avila Road
Laguna Niguel, CA 92677 3497
Tel: 949 360 2641
Fax: 949 360 2424
E-mail: center@laguna.nara.gov
http://www.nara.gov/regional/
laguna.html

National Archives and Records
Administration Pacific Region
1000 Commodore Drive
San Bruno, CA 94006
Tel: 415 876 9009
Fax: 415 876 9233
E-mail: archives@sanbruno.nara.gov
http://www.nara.gov/nara/sanfranc.html

California State Library
914 Capitol Mall
P.O. Box 942837
Sacramento, CA 94237 0001
Tel: 916 654 0261
Fax: 916 654 0241
E-mail: cslsirc@library.ca.gov
http://www.library.ca.gov/html/
cslgen3.html

California State Library
Sutro Branch
480 Winston Drive
San Francisco, CA 94132
Tel: 415 564 4010
Fax: 415 564 3606
http://www.library.sfsu.edu/special/
larc.html

San Diego Historical Society
P.O. Box 81825
San Diego, CA 92138
Tel: 619 232 6203
Fax: 619 232 6297
http://www.sandiegohistory.org/links/
writeus.htm

California Genealogical Society
1611 Telegraph Avenue, Suite 200
Oakland, CA 94612 2152
Tel: 510 663 1358
http://www.calgensoc.com

San Diego Genealogical Society
1050 Pioneer Way, Suite E
El Cajon, CA 92020-1943
Tel: 619 588 0065
http://www.rootsweb.com/~casdgs

COLORADO

Vital Records Office
4300 Cherry Creek Drive South
Denver, CO 80246 1530
Tel: 303 692 2224
Fax: 800 423 1108
http://www.cdphe.state.co.us/hs/certs.asp

Colorado State Archives
1313 Sherman Street, I-B20
Denver, CO 80203
Tel: 303 866 2358
Fax: 303 866 2257
E-mail: archives@state.co.us
http://www.archives.state.co.us/
geneal.html

National Archives and Records
Administration Rocky Mountain
Region
Building 48, Denver Federal Center
P.O. Box 25307
Denver, CO 80225 0307
Tel: 303 236 0817
Fax: 303 236 9297
E-mail: archives@denver.nara.gov
http://www.nara.gov/regional/
denver.html

Colorado Genealogical Society
P.O. Box 9218
Denver, CO 80209 0218
Tel: 303 571 1535
http://www.cogensoc.org/cgs/
cgs-home.htm

Denver Public Library
10 W. Fourteenth Avenue Parkway
Denver, CO 80204
Tel: 720 865 1111
http://www.denver.lib.co.us/dpl/
aboutdpl.html

CONNECTICUT

Connecticut State Vital Records
410 Capitol Avenue, 1st Floor
Hartford, CT 06134
Tel: 860 509 7897
Fax: 860 509 7964
E-mail: angela.kasek@po.state.ct.us
http://www.state.ct.us/dph/OPPE/
hpvital.htm

Connecticut State Library
231 Capitol Avenue
Hartford, CT 06106
Tel: 860 566 5650
Fax: 860 566 1421
http://www.cslnet.ctstateu.edu/
archives.htm

Connecticut Historical Society
1 Elizabeth Street
Hartford, CT 06105
Tel: 860 236 5621
Fax: 860 236 2664
http://www.chs.org

Connecticut Society of Genealogists
175 Maple Street
East Hartford, CT 06118
Mailing address: P.O. Box 435
Glastonbury, CT 06033 0435
Tel: 860 569 0002

DELAWARE

Vital Records Office
Division of Public Health
P.O. Box 637
Dover, DE 19903
Tel: 302 739 4721
Fax: 302 736 1862

Delaware Public Archives
Hall of Records
121 Duke of York Street
Dover, DE 19901
Tel: 302 739 5318
Fax: 302 739 2578
http://www.archives.lib.de.us

Historical Society of Delaware
505 North Market Street
Wilmington, DE 19801
Tel: 302 655 7161
Fax: 302 655 7844
http://www.hsd.org

Delaware Genealogical Society
505 North Market Street
Wilmington, DE 19801 3091
http://delgensoc.org

Hugh M. Morris Library
University of Delaware Library
181 South College Avenue
Newark, DE 19717 5267
Tel: 302 831 2965

DISTRICT OF COLUMBIA

Vital Records Department
825 North Capitol Street NE
1st Floor, Room 1312
Washington, D.C. 20002
Tel: 202 442 9009
Fax: 202 783 0136

Library of Congress
Humanities and Social Sciences
Division
Thomas Jefferson Building
Room LJ G42
Washington, D.C. 20540 4660
Tel: 202 707 5522
Fax: 202 707 1389
http://www.lcweb.loc.gov/rr/main

National Archives and Records Administration
Seventh and Pennsylvania Avenues N.W.
Washington, D.C. 20408
Tel: 301 713 6800
Fax: 301 713 6905
E-mail: inquire@arch2.nara.gov
http://www.nara.gov/nara/dc/
Archives_info.html

Daughters of the American Revolution Library
1776 D. Street, NW
Washington, D.C. 20006 5392
Tel: 202 879 3229
Fax: 202 879 3227
http://www.dar.org/library/default.html

FLORIDA

Vital Records Office
Department of Health
P.O. Box 210, 1217 Pearl Street
Jacksonville, FL 32202
Tel: 904 359 6900
Fax: 904 359 6993
http://www.doh.state.fl.us

Florida State Archives
500 South Bronough Street
Tallahassee, FL 32611
Tel: 850 487 2073
Fax: 850 488 4890
http://www.dos.state.fl.us/dlis/barm/
fsa.html

Florida Historical Society
435 Brevard Ave
Cocoa, FL 32922
Tel: 321 690 1971
Fax: 321 690 4388
E-mail: information@florida-historical-soc.org
http://www.florida-historical-soc.org

Florida State Genealogical Society
P.O. Box 10249
Tallahassee, FL 32302 2249
http://www.rootsweb.com/~flsgs

GEORGIA

Vital Records Service
State Dept of Human Resources
47 Trinity Avenue SW, Room 217-H
Atlanta, GA 30334
Tel: 877 572 6343
Fax: 404 524 4278
E-mail: GDPHINFO@dhr.state.ga.us

Georgia Department of Archives
330 Capitol Avenue, SE
Atlanta, GA 30334
Tel: 404 656 2393
Fax: 404 657 8427
http://www.sos.state.ga.us/archives

National Archives and Records Administration Southeast Region
1557 St. Joseph Avenue
East Point, GA 30344 2593
Tel: 404 763 7474
Fax: 404 763 7033
E-mail: center@atlanta.nara.gov
http://www.nara.gov/regional/
atlanta.html

Georgia Historical Society
501 Whittaker Street
Savannah, GA 31401
Tel: 912 651 2128
Fax: 912 651 2831
E-mail: ghslib@georgiahistory.com
(library and archives)
http://www.georgiahistory.com

Georgia Genealogical Society
P.O. Box 54575
Dept. W
Atlanta, GA 30308 0575
http://www.gagensociety.org

HAWAII

Vital Records Office
Department of Health
P.O. Box 3378
1250 Punch Bowl Avenue, Room 103
Honolulu, HI 96801
Tel: 808 586 4533
E-mail: vr-info@mail.health.state.hi.us
http://kumu.icsd.hawaii.gov/health/
records/vr_howto.html

Hawaii State Archives
Iolani Palace Grounds
Honolulu, HI 96813
Tel: 808 586 0329
http://www.hawaii.gov/dags/archives

Hawaii Historical Society
560 Kawaiahoa Street
Honolulu, HI 96813
Tel: 808 537 6271
Fax: 808 537 6271
http://www.hawaiianhistory.org/
index.html

IDAHO

Vital Records Office
450 W. State Street, 1st Floor
P.O. Box 83720
Boise, ID 83720
Tel: 208 334 5988
Fax: 208 389 9096
http://www2.state.id.us/dhw/hwgd_www/
health/vs/appmenu.html

Idaho State Library
325 West State Street
Boise, ID 83702
Tel: 208 334 2150
Fax: 208 334 4016
E-mail: cbolles@isl.state.id.us
http://www.state.id.us/ishs/index/htm

Idaho State Historical Society
450 North 4th Street
Boise, ID 83702
Tel: 208 334 5335
Fax: 208 334 3198
http://www2.state.id.us/ishs/Index.html

Idaho Genealogical Society
4620 Overland Road #204
Boise, ID 83705 2867
Tel: 208 384 0542

ILLINOIS

Vital Records Office
605 W. Jefferson Street
Springfield, IL 62702 5097
Tel: 217 782 6553
Fax: 217 523 2648
http://www.idph.state.il.us/vital/
vitalhome.htm

Illinois State Archives
Margaret Cross Norton Building
Capitol Complex
Springfield, IL 62756
Tel: 217 782 4682
Fax: 217 524 3930
http://www.sos.state.il.us/depts/archives/
arc_home.html

**National Archives and Resource
Administration Great Lakes Region**
7358 South Pulaski Road
Chicago, IL 60629 5898
Tel: 773 581 7816
Fax: 312 353 1294
E-mail: archives@chicago.nara.gov
http://www.nara.gov/regional/
chicago.html

Illinois State Library
300 South Second Street
Springfield, IL 62701 1796
Tel: 217 785 5600
Fax: 217 524 0041
http://www.sos.state.il.us/depts/library/
isl_home.html

Illinois State Historical Library
Old State Capitol
Springfield, IL 62701
Tel: 217 524 7216
Fax: 217 785 6250
http://www.state.il.us/hpa/lib

Illinois State Genealogy Society
P.O. Box 10195
Springfield, IL 62791 0195
Tel: 217 789 1968
http://www.tbox.com/isgs

Newberry Library
60 West Walton Street
Chicago, IL 60610 3305
Tel: 312 943 9090
http://www.newberry.org/nl/
newberryhome.html

INDIANA

Indiana State Vital Records Office
2 North Meridian Street
Indianapolis, IN 46204
Tel: 317 233 2700
Fax: 317 233 2710
http://www.state.in.us/isdh/bdcertifs/
bdcert.html

Indiana State Archives
117 State Library Building
140 North Senate Avenue
Indianapolis, IN 46204
Tel: 317 232 3660
Fax: 317 233 1085
http://www.state.in.us/icpr/webfile/
archives/homepage.html

Indiana State Library
Genealogy Division
140 North Senate Avenue, Room 250
Indianapolis, IN 46204
Tel: 317 232 3689
http://www.statelib.lib.in.us/WWW/
INDIANA/GENEALOGY/
genmenu.HTML

Indiana Historical Society
315 West Ohio Street
Indianapolis, IN 46202 3269
Tel: 317 232 1882
Fax: 317 233 6615
http://www.indianahistory.org

Allen County Public Library
900 Webster Street
P.O. Box 2270
Fort Wayne, IN 46801
Tel: 219 421 1225
Fax: 219 422 9688
http://www.acpl.lib.in.us

IOWA

State Vital Records Office
321 E. 12th, 4th Floor
Des Moines, IA 50319 0075
Tel: 515 281 4944
http://www.idph.state.ia.us/pa/vr.htm

Iowa State Historical Society
Capitol Complex
600 East Locust
Des Moines, IA 50319 0290
Tel: 515 281 5111
Fax: 515 242 6498
E-mail: staylor@max.state.ia.us
http://www.culturalaffairs.org

Iowa Genealogical Society
P.O. Box 7735
Des Moines, IA 50322 7735
Tel: 515 276 0287
Fax: 515 727 1824
E-mail: igs@iowagenealogy.org
http://www.iowagenealogy.org

KANSAS

Office of Vital Statistics
900 SW Jackson
Topeka, KS 66612
Tel: 785 296 3253
Fax: 785 357 4332
E-mail: info@kdhe.state.ks.us
http://www.kdhe.state.ks.us/vital/
index.html

Kansas State Historical Society
6425 SW Sixth Avenue
Topeka, KS 66615
Tel: 785 272 8681
Fax: 785 272 8683
http://www.kshs.org

Midwest Historical and Genealogical Society
P.O. Box 1121
Wichita, KS 67201
Tel: 316 264 3611
http://skyways.lib.ks.us/genweb/mhgs/
index.html

Kansas Council of Genealogical Societies
P.O. Box 3858
Topeka, KS 66604 6858
http://skyways.lib.ks.us/genweb/kcgs

KENTUCKY

State Vital Records Office
275 East Main Street
Frankfort, KY 40621
Tel: 502 564 4212
Fax: 502 227 0032
http://publichealth.state.ky.us/vital.htm

Kentucky Department for Libraries and Archives
300 Coffee Tree Road
P.O. Box 537
Frankfort, KY 40602 0537
Tel: 502 564 8300
Fax: 502 564 5773
http://www.kdla.state.ky.us

Kentucky Historical Society
300 West Broadway
P.O. Box 1792
Frankfort, KY 40602
Tel: 502 564 1792
http://www.state.ky.us/agencies/khs

The Filson Club Historical Society
1310 S. Third Street
Louisville, KY 40205
Tel: 502 636 0471
Fax: 502 635 5086
http://www.filsonclub.org

National Society Sons of the American Revolution
1000 South Fourth Street
Louisville, KY 40203
Tel: 502 589 1776
Fax: 502 589 1671
http://www.sar.org

LOUISIANA

State Vital Records Office
P.O. Box 60630
New Orleans, LA 70160
Tel: 504 568 5152
http://www.dhh.state.la.us/oph/vital/
Index.htm

Louisiana State Archives
P.O. Box 94125
3851 Essen Lane
Baton Rouge, LA 70809 2137
Tel: 225 922 1208
E-mail: archives@sec.state.la.us
http://www.sec.state.la.us/archives/
archives/archives-index.htm

Louisiana State Library
701 North 4th Street
Baton Rouge, LA 70802
Tel: 225 342 4923
Fax: 225 219 4804
http://www.state.lib.la.us

Louisiana Historical Association
P.O. Box 42808, UL Lafayette
Lafayette, LA 70504 2808
http://www.louisiana.edu/Academic/
LiberalArts/CLS/lahist.html

Louisiana Genealogical and Historical Society
P.O. Box 82060
Baton Rouge, LA 70884 2060
E-mail: LGHS@aol.com
http://usersA.usunwired.net/mmoore/
lghs/lghs.htm

MAINE

State Vital Records Office
Department of Human Services
State House Station 11
Augusta, ME 04333 0011
Tel: 207 287 3181

Maine State Archives
State House Station #84
Augusta, ME 04333 0084
Tel: 207 287 5790
Fax: 207 287 5739
http://www.state.me.us/sos/arc/general/
admin/mawww001.htm

Maine State Library
State House Station 64
Augusta, ME 04333
Tel: 207 287 5615
Fax: 207 287 5622
http://www.state.me.us/msl

The Center for Maine History
485 Congress Street
Portland, ME 04101
Tel: 207 774 1822
Fax: 207 775 4301
E-mail: info@mainehistory.org
http://www.mainehistory.org/home.html

Maine Genealogical Society
P.O. Box 221
Farmington, ME 04938 0221
http://www.rootsweb.com/~megs/
MaineGS.htm

MARYLAND

State Vital Records Office
P.O. Box 68760
4201 Patterson Avenue
Baltimore, MD 21215 0020
Tel: 410 764 3068
Fax: 410 358 0738
http://www.dhmh.state.md.us/html/
vitalrec.htm

Maryland State Archives
350 Rowe Boulevard
Annapolis, MD 21401
Tel: 410 974 3914
Fax: 410 974 3895
E-mail: archives@mdarchives.state.
md.us
http://www.mdarchives.state.md.us

**National Archives and Records
Administration**
8601 Adelphi Road
College Park, MD 20740 6001
Tel: 301 713 7200
Fax: 301 713 7205
http://www.nara.gov/nara/dc/
archives2_directions.html

**National Archives and Records
Administration**
Washington National Records Center
4205 Suitland Road
Suitland, MD 20746 8001
Tel: 301 457 7000
Fax: 301 457 7117
E-mail: center@suitland.nara.gov
http://www.nara.gov/records/wnrc.html

Maryland Historical Society
201 West Monument Street
Baltimore, MD 21201 4674
Tel: 410 685 3750
Fax: 410 385 2105
E-mail: web-comments@mdhs.org
http://www.mdhs.org

The Maryland Genealogical Society
201 West Monument Street
Baltimore, MD 21201 4674
http://www.rootsweb.com/~mdsgs

MASSACHUSETTS

Registry of Vital Records
150 Mount Vernon Street, 1st floor
Dorchester, MA 02125 3105
Tel: 617 740 2600
Fax: 617 825 7755
http://www.state.ma.us/dph/rvr.htm

Massachusetts State Archives
220 Morrissey Boulevard
Boston, MA 02125
Tel: 617 727 2816
Fax: 617 258 8429
E-mail: archives@sec.state.ma.us
http://www.magnet.state.ma.us/sec/arc

**National Archives and Records
Administration Northeast Region**
380 Trapelo Road
Waltham, MA 02452 6399
Tel: 781 647 8104
Fax: 781 647 8088
E-mail: archives@waltham.nara.gov
http://www.nara.gov/regional/
boston.html

**National Archives and Records
Administration Northeast Region
(Pittsfield)**
10 Conte Drive
Pittsfield, MA 01201 8230
Tel: 413 445 6885
Fax: 413 445 7305
E-mail: archives@pittsfield.nara.gov
http://www.nara.gov/regional/
pittsfie.html

American Antiquarian Society
185 Salisbury Street
Worcester, MA 01609
Tel: 508 755 5221
Fax: 508 753 3311
E-mail: library@mwa.org
http://www.americanantiquarian.org/
index.htm

**New England Historic Genealogical
Society**
101 Newbury Street
Boston, MA 02116 3007
Tel: 617 536 5740
Fax: 617 536 7307
http://www.nehgs.org

Boston Public Library
700 Boylston Street
Copley Square
Boston, MA 02117
Tel: 617 536 5400
http://www.bpl.org

MICHIGAN

State Vital Records Office
Michigan Dept of Community Health
3423 N. Martin Luther King Boulevard
P.O. Box 30721
Lansing, MI 48909
Tel: 517 335 8666
http://www.mdch.state.mi.us

State Archives of Michigan
Michigan Library and Historical Center
717 West Allegan Street
Lansing, MI 48918 1800
Tel: 517 373 3559
http://www.sos.state.mi.us/history/
archive/archtour.html

Library of Michigan
717 West Allegan Street
P.O. Box 30007
Lansing, MI 48909 7507
http://www.libraryofmichigan.org

**Marquette County Historical Society
and Museum**
213 N. Front Street
Marquette, MI 49855
Tel: 906 226 3571
http://www.haja.com/dest_up/upcd_ads/
Np010001.htm

Detroit Public Library
Burton Historical Collection
5201 Woodward Avenue
Detroit, MI 48202
Tel: 313 833 1480
http://www.detroit.lib.mi.us/burton

MINNESOTA

State Vital Records Office
Minnesota Department of Health
717 Delaware Street, SE
P.O. Box 9441
Minneapolis, MN 55440
Tel: 612 676 5121
Fax: 612 331 5776
http://www.health.state.mn.us

Minnesota Historical Society
345 Kellogg Boulevard West
St. Paul, MN 55102 1906
Tel: 651 296 2143
Fax: 651 296 6126
http://www.mnhs.org

Immigration History Research Center
University of Minnesota
222 21st Avenue South
Minneapolis, MN 55455 0439
Tel: 612 625 4800
Fax: 612 626 0018
E-mail: ihrc@tc.umn.edu
http://www1.umn.edu/ihrc

Minnesota Genealogical Society
5768 Olsen Memorial Highway
Golden Valley, MN 55422
Tel: 612 595 934 (library)
http://www.mtn.org/mgs

Duluth Public Library
520 West Superior Street
Duluth, MN 55802
Tel: 218 723 3800
Fax: 218 723 3822
http://www.duluth.lib.mn.us

MISSISSIPPI

State Vital Records Office
2423 North State Street
P.O. Box 1700
Jackson, MS 39215 1700
Tel: 601 576 7960
Fax: 601 576 7505
http://www.msdh.state.ms.us/phs

Mississippi Department of Archives and History
Capers Building
100 South State Street
P.O. Box 571
Jackson, MS 39205 0571
Tel: 601 359 6850
Fax: 601 359 6964
http://www.mdah.state.ms.us

Family Research Association of Mississippi
P.O. Box 13334
Jackson, MS 39236 3334
E-mail: FRA99JF@aol.com

MISSOURI

Bureau of Vital Records
P.O. Box 570
920–930 Wildwood Drive
Jefferson City, MO 65102 0570
Tel: 573 751 6387
http://www.health.state.mo.us

Missouri State Archives
P.O. Box 1747
Jefferson City, MO 65102
Tel: 573 751 3280
Fax: 573 526 7333
http://mosl.sos.state.mo.us/rec-man/arch.html

National Archives and Records Administration Central Plains Region
2312 East Bannister Road
Kansas City, MO 64131 3011
Tel: 816 926 6272
Fax: 816 926 6982
E-mail: archives@kansascity.nara.gov
http://www.nara.gov/regional/kansas.html

National Archives and Records Administration Central Plains Region
200 Space Center Drive
Lee's Summit, MO 64064 1182
Tel: 816 478 7079
Fax: 816 478 7625
E-mail: center@kccave.nara.gov
http://www.nara.gov/regional/leesumit.html

State Historical Society of Missouri
1020 Lowry Street
Columbia, MO 65201 7298
Tel: 573 882 7083
Fax: 573 884 4950
E-mail: shsofmo@umsystem.edu
http://www.system.missouri.edu/shs/welcome.html

Missouri State Genealogical Association
Dept. W, P.O. Box 833
Columbia, MO 65205 0833
http://www.umr.edu/~mstauter/mosga

Mid-Continent Public Library
Genealogy and Local History
317 W. 24 Highway
Independence, MO 64050
Tel: 816 252 7228
http://www.mcpl.lib.mo.us/branch/ge

MONTANA

State Vital Records Office
DPHHS/Vital Records
P.O. Box 4210
111 North Sanders
Helena, MT 59604 4210
Tel: 406 444 4228
http://www.imt.net/~corkykn/vital.html

Montana Historical Society
P.O. Box 201201
225 North Roberts Street
Helena, MT 59620
Tel: 406 444 2694
http://www.his.state.mt.us

Montana State University
Bozeman Libraries
P.O. Box 173320
Bozeman, MT 59717 3320
Tel: 406 994 3119
Fax: 406 994 2851
http://www.lib.montana.edu

NEBRASKA

Office of Vital Statistics
P.O. Box 95065
301 Centennial Mall South
Lincoln, NE 68509
Tel: 402 471 2871
E-mail: doh7151@vmhost.cdp.state.ne.us
http://www.hhs.state.ne.us/ced/cedindex.htm

Nebraska State Historical Society
P.O. Box 82554
1500 'R' Street
Lincoln, NE 68501 2554
Tel: 402 471 3270
Fax: 402 471 3100
http://www.nebraskahistory.org/

Nebraska State Genealogical Society
P.O. Box 5608
Lincoln, NE 68505 0608
http://www.rootsweb.com/~nesgs

NEVADA

Division of Health/Vital Statistics
505 East King Street, Rm #102
Carson City, NV 89710
Tel: 775 684 4242
Fax: 775 687 6151
http://www.state.nv.us/health

Nevada State Archives and Records
100 North Stewart Street
Carson City, NV 89710
Tel: 775 784 3310
Fax: 775 887 2273
http://lahontan.clan.lib.nv.us/polpac/
html_client/default.asp

Nevada Historical Society
1650 N. Virginia Street
Reno, NV 89503
Tel: 775 688 1190

Nevada State Genealogical Society
P.O. Box 20666
Reno, NV 89515 0666
http://www.rootsweb.com/~nvsgs

NEW HAMPSHIRE

Bureau of Vital Records
6 Hazen Drive
Concord, NH 03301
Tel: 603 271 4650
Fax: 603 223 6614
E-mail: vitalrecords@dhhs.state.nh.us
http://www.dhhs.state.nh.us/
CommPublicHealth/VitalRec.nsf

State of New Hampshire Division of Records Management and Archives
71 South Fruit Street
Concord, NH 03301
Tel: 603 271 2236
http://www.state.nh.us/state/index.html

New Hampshire State Library
20 Park Street
Concord, NH 03301
Tel: 603 271 2392
Fax: 603 271 6826
http://www.state.nh.us/nhsl/index.html

New Hampshire Historical Society
The Tuck Library
30 Park Street
Concord, NH 03301 6394
Tel: 603 225 3381
Fax: 603 224 0463
http://www.nhhistory.org

New Hampshire Society of Genealogists
P.O. Box 2316
Concord, NH 03302 2316
Tel: 603 225 3381
http://nhsog.org/genealogy.htm

NEW JERSEY

Department of Health and Senior Services
State Registrar Search Unit
P.O. Box 370
Trenton, NJ 08625 0370
Tel: 609 292 4087
Fax: 609 392 4292
http://www.state.nj.us/health/vital/
vs11.htm

New Jersey Division of Archives
185 West State Street, Level 2
New Jersey State Library Building
Trenton, NJ 08625 0307
Tel: 609 292 6260
Fax: 609 396 2454
E-mail: info@archive.sos.state.nj.us
http://www.state.nj.us/state/darm/
archives.html

New Jersey State Library
State Library Building
185 West State Street
Trenton, NJ 08625 0520
Tel: 609 292 6220
Fax: 800 364 9783
http://www.njstatelib.org

NEW MEXICO

Vital Records Office
P.O. Box 26110
1105 St. Francis Drive
Santa Fe, NM 87502
Tel: 505 827 0121/2338 (24 hours)
Fax: 505 984 1048

New Mexico State Records Center and Archives
404 Montezuma Street
Santa Fe, NM 87503
Tel: 505 827 7332
Fax: 505 476 7901
http://www.state.nm.us/cpr

New Mexico Genealogical Society
P.O. Box 8283
Albuquerque, NM 87198 8283
Tel: 505 848 1376
http://www.nmgs.org

NEW YORK

Vital Records Section
Genealogy Unit
P.O. Box 2602
Albany, NY 12220 2602
Tel: 518 474 3077
Fax: 518 432 6286
http://www.health.state.ny.us/nysdoh/
consumer/vr.htm

New York State Archives and Records Administration
Room 11D40
Cultural Education Center
New York State Education Department
Albany, NY 12230
Tel: 518 474 8955
E-mail: sarainfo@mail.nysed.gov
http://www.archives.nysed.gov

National Archives and Records Administration Northeast Region (New York City)
201 Varick Street
New York, NY 10014 4811
Tel: 212 337 1300
Fax: 212 337 1306
E-mail: archives@newyork.nara.gov
http://www.nara.gov/regional/
newyork.html

New York State Library
Cultural Education Center
Empire State Plaza
Albany, NY 12230
Tel: 518 474 5355
http://www.nysl.nysed.gov/contact.htm

The New York Public Library
Room 121
5th Avenue and 42nd Street
New York, NY 10018
Tel: 212 592 7200.
http://www.nypl.org

Brooklyn Historical Society
128 Pierrepont Street
Brooklyn, NY 11201
Tel: 718 254 9830
Fax: 718 254 9869
http://www.brooklynhistory.org

**New York Genealogical and
Biographical Society**
122 East 58th Street
New York, NY 10022 1939
Tel: 212 755 8532
Fax: 212 754 4218
http://www.nygbs.org

NORTH CAROLINA

North Carolina Vital Records
1903 Mail Service Center
Raleigh, NC 27699 1903
Tel: 919 733 3526
http://www.schs.state.nc.us/SCHS/
certificates

**North Carolina Division of Archives
and History**
109 East Jones Street
Raleigh, NC 27601 2807
Tel: 919 733 7305
Fax: 919 733 8807
http://www.ah.dcr.state.nc.us

State Library of North Carolina
109 East Jones Street
Raleigh, NC 27601 2807
Tel: 919 733 3270
Fax: 919 733 5679
http://statelibrary.dcr.state.nc.us

North Carolina Genealogical Society
P.O. Box 22
Greenville, NC 27835 0022
http://www.rootsweb.com/~ncgs/
index.html

North Carolina Museum of History
4650 Mail Service Center
Raleigh, NC 27699 4650
Tel: 919 715 0200
Fax: 919 733 8655
http://nchistory.dcr.state.nc.us/museums

NORTH DAKOTA

Division of Vital Records
State Capitol
600 East Boulevard Avenue
Bismarck, ND 58505
Tel: 701 328 2360
http://www.health.state.nd.us/ndhd/
default.asp

North Dakota State Library
604 East Boulevard Avenue,
Dept. 250
Bismarck, ND 58505 0800
Tel: 701 328 4622
http://ndsl.lib.state.nd.us

**State Historical Society of North
Dakota**
North Dakota Heritage Center
612 East Boulevard Avenue
Bismark, ND 58505 0830
Tel: 701 328 2668
http://www.state.nd.us/hist/sal.htm

**North Dakota State University
Libraries**
1301 North University Drive
P.O. Box 5599
Fargo, ND 58105 5599
Tel: 701 231 8876
Fax: 701 231 6128
http://www.lib.ndsu.nodak.edu/newsite/
Sitemap/index.html

OHIO

Vital Statistics Unit
35 East Chestnut Street
P.O. Box 15098
Columbus, OH 43215 0098
Tel: 614 466 2531
http://www.odh.state.oh.us

State Library of Ohio
Jeffrey Mining Corporate Center
274 E. 1st Avenue
Columbus, OH 43201
Tel: 614 644 7061
Fax: 614 466 3584
http://winslo.state.oh.us

**National Archives and Records
Administration Great Lakes Region
(Dayton)**
3150 Springboro Road
Dayton, OH 45439 1883
Tel: 937 225 2852
Fax: 937 225 7236
E-mail: center@dayton.nara.gov
http: www.nara.gov/regional/
dayton.html

Ohio Historical Society
Archives/Library Reference Questions
1982 Velma Avenue
Columbus, OH 43211 2497
Tel: 614 297 2300
http://www.ohiohistory.org

Western Reserve Historical Society
10825 East Boulevard
University Circle
Cleveland, OH 44106
Tel: 216 721 5722
Fax: 216 721 0645
http://www.wrhs.org/index.htm

OKLAHOMA

Vital Records Service
1000 Northeast Tenth, Room 117
Oklahoma City, OK 73117
Tel: 405 271 4040
http://www.health.state.ok.us/index.html

**Oklahoma State Archives and
Records**
200 Northeast 18th Street
Oklahoma City, OK 73105 3298
Tel: 405 521 2502
Fax: 405 525 7804
http://www.odl.state.ok.us/oar

Oklahoma Historical Society
2100 N. Lincoln Boulevard
Oklahoma City, OK 73105 4997
Tel: 405 521 2491
http://www.ok-history.mus.ok.us

Oklahoma Genealogical Society
P.O. Box 12986
Oklahoma City, OK 73157
http://www.rootsweb.com/~okgs/
index.htm

OREGON

State Vital Records
P.O. Box 14050
Portland, OR 97293
Tel: 503 731 4108/4095
Fax: 503 234 8417
http://www.ohd.hr.state.or.us/chs/certif/
certfaqs.htm

Oregon State Archives
800 Summer Street NE
Salem, OR 97310
Tel: 503 373 0701
http://www.arcweb.sos.state.or.us

Oregon State Library
250 Winter Street NE
Salem, OR 97310
Tel: 503 378 4277
http://www.osl.state.or.us/oslhome.html

Oregon Historical Society
1200 SW Park Avenue
Portland, OR 97205 2483
Tel: 503 222 1741
Fax: 503 221 2035
http://www.ohs.org/homepage.html

Genealogical Forum of Oregon
P.O. Box 42567
Portland, OR 97242 0567
Tel: 503 963 1932
Fax: 561 325 7676
E-mail: info@gfo.org
http://www.gfo.org

PENNSYLVANIA

Vital Records, State Dept. of Health
P.O. Box 1528
101 South Mercer Street
New Castle, PA 16103
Tel: 724 656 3100
Fax: 724 652 8951
http://www.health.state.pa.us/HPA/
apply_bd.htm

Pennsylvania State Archives
P.O. Box 1026
Harrisburg, PA 17108 1026
Tel: 717 783 3281
http://sites.state.pa.us/PA_Exec/
Historical_Museum/DAM/overview.htm

**National Archives and Records
Administration Mid Atlantic Region
(Center City, Philadelphia)**
900 Market Street
Philadelphia, PA 19107 4292
Tel: 215 597 3000
Fax: 215 597 2303
E-mail:archives@philarch.nara.gov
http: www.nara.gov/regional/
philacc.html

**National Archives and Records
Administration Mid Atlantic Region
(Northeast Philadelphia)**
14700 Townsend Road
Philadelphia, PA 19154 1096
Tel: 215 671 9027
Fax: 215 671 8001
E-mail: center@philfrc.nara.gov
Web: www.nara.gov/regional/
philane.html

State Library of Pennsylvania
Commonwealth Avenue & Walnut Street
P.O. Box 1601
Harrisburg, PA 17105 1601
Tel: 717 783 5950
http://www.statelibrary.state.pa.us

**The Historical Society of
Pennsylvania**
1300 Locust Street
Philadelphia, PA 19107 5699
Tel: 215 732 6200
Fax: 215 732 2680
http://www.hsp.org

Genealogical Society of Pennsylvania
1305 Locust Street 3rd Floor
Philadelphia, PA 19107 5405
Tel: 215 545 0391
Fax 215 545 0936
E-mail: gsppa@aol.com
http://www.libertynet.org/gspa

RHODE ISLAND

Vital Records Office
Department of Health
3 Capitol Hill, Room 101
Providence, RI 02908 5097
Tel: 401 222 2811
http://www.health.state.ri.us

**Rhode Island State Archives and
Public Records Administration**
337 Westminster Street
Providence, RI 02903 3302
Tel: 401 277 2353
Fax: 401 222 3199
E-mail: reference@archives.state.ri.us
http://www.state.ri.us/archives

Rhode Island State Library
State House Room 208
Providence, RI 02903
Tel: 401 222 2473
Fax: 401 331 6430
http://www.state.ri.us/library/web.htm

Rhode Island Historical Society
121 Hope Street
Providence, RI 02903
Tel: 401 331 8575
Fax: 401 351 0127
http://www.rihs.org

Rhode Island Genealogical Society
P.O. Box 433
Greenville, RI 02828
E-mail: RIGenSociety@myfamily.com
http://users.ids.net/~ricon/rigs.html

SOUTH CAROLINA

Office of Vital Records
2600 Bull Street
Columbia, SC 29201 1708
Tel: 803 898 3630

**South Carolina Department of
Archives and History**
8301 Parklane Road
Columbia, SC 29223
Tel: 803 896 6100
Fax: 803 896 6198
E-mail: sox@scdah.state.sc.us
http://www.state.sc.us/scdah/
homepage.htm

South Carolina State Library
1500 Senate Street
P.O. Box 11469
Columbia, SC 29211
Tel: 803 734 8666
Fax: 803 734 8676
http://www.state.sc.us/scsl

South Carolina Historical Society
100 Meeting Street
Charleston, SC 29401
Tel: 843 723 3225
Fax: 843 723 8584
http://www.schistory.org

SOUTH DAKOTA

Vital Records Office
600 East Capitol
Pierre, SD 57501 2536
Tel: 605 773 4961
E-mail: kathimu@doh.state.sd.us
http://www.state.sd.us/doh/VitalRec/
Vital.htm

South Dakota State Archives
900 Governors Drive
Pierre, SD 57501 2217
Tel: 605 773 3804
Fax: 605 773 6041
E-mail: Archref@state.sd.us
http://www.state.sd.us/deca/cultural/
archives.htm

South Dakota State Historical Sciety
Mercedes MacKay Building
800 Governors Drive
Pierre, SD 57501 2294
Tel: 605 773 3131
Fax: 800 423 6665
http://www.state.sd.us/deca/cultural/
index.htm

South Dakota Genealogical Society
P.O. Box 1101
Pierre, SD 57501 1101
http://www.rootsweb.com/~sdgenweb/
gensoc/sdgensoc.html

TENNESSEE

Tennessee Vital Records
Central Services Building, 1st Floor
421 5th Avenue North
Nashville, TN 37247 0450
Tel: 615 741 1763
Fax: 615 726 2559
http://www.state.tn.us/health/vr/
index.html

Tennessee State Library And Archives
403 Seventh Avenue North
Nashville, TN 37243 0312
Tel: 615 741 2764
http://www.state.tn.us/sos/statelib/
tslahome.htm

Tennessee Genealogical Society
9114 Davies Plantation Road
Brunswick, TN 38014
Tel: 901 381 1447
http://www.rootsweb.com/~tngs

TEXAS

Bureau of Vital Statistics
P.O. Box 12040
Austin, TX 78711 2040
Tel: 512 458 7111
E-mail: register@tdh.state.tx.us
http://www.tdh.state.tx.us/bvs/
default.htm

Texas State Library and Archives
P.O. Box 12927
1201 Brazos Street
Austin, TX 78711 2927
Tel: 512 463 5460 (archives)
Tel: 512 463 5463 (genealogy)
E-mail (archives):
archinfo@tsl.state.tx.us
E-mail (genealogy):
geninfo@tsl.state.tx.us
http://www.tsl.state.tx.us/lobby

National Archives and Records Administration Southwest Region
501 West Felix Street, Building 1
Fort Worth, TX 76115 3405
Tel: 817 334 5525
Fax: 817 334 5621
E-mail: archives@ftworth.nara.gov
http://www.nara.gov/regional/
ftworth.html

Texas State Genealogical Society
P.O. Box 110842
Carrollton, TX 75011 0842.
http://www.rootsweb.com/~txsgs

Dallas Public Library
1515 Young Street
Dallas, TX 75201 5415
Tel: 214 670 7803
Fax: 214 670 7839
http://www.ci.dallas.tx.us/html/library.html

Clayton Library
5300 Caroline
Houston, TX 77004 6896
Tel: 713 284 1999
http://www.hpl.lib.tx.us/clayton

UTAH

Bureau of Vital Records
P.O. Box 141012
Salt Lake City, UT 84114 1012
Tel: 801 538 6380
Fax: 801 538 9467
http://hlunix.hl.state.ut.us/bvr

Utah State Archives
P.O. Box 141021
State Capitol Archive Building
Salt Lake City, UT 84114 1021
Tel: 801 538 3031
Fax: 801 538 3354
E-mail: research@das.state.ut.us
http://www.archives.state.ut.us

Utah State Library
250 N. 1950 W., Suite A
Salt Lake City, UT 84116 7901
Tel: 801 524 8200
http://www.state.lib.ut.us

Utah State Historical Society Library
300 South Rio Grande
Salt Lake City, UT 84101
Tel: 801 533 3545
http://www.history.utah.org/#top

Family History Library
The Church of Jesus Christ of
Latter-Day Saints
35 North West Temple
Salt Lake City, UT 84150
Tel: 801 240 2331/1054
Fax: 801 240 5551
E-mail: fhl@ldschurch.orgUnofficial
http://www.familysearch.org/eng/
Library/FHL/frameset_library.asp

VERMONT

Vital Records Section
P.O. Box 70
108 Cherry Street
Burlington, VT 05402
Tel: 802 863 7275
http://www.state.vt.us/gsd/pubrec.htm

Vermont State Archives
26 Terrace Street
Drawer 09
Montpelier, VT 05609 1101
Tel: 802 828 2363
Fax: 802 828 2467
E-mail: gsanford@sec.state.vt.us
http://www.sec.state.vt.us/archives/
archdex.htm

Vermont Agency of Administration
Public Records Division
6 Baldwin Street
Montpelier, VT 05602

Historical Society Library
First floor, Pavilion Building
109 State Street
Montpelier, VT 05609 1101
Tel: 802 828 2308
Fax: 802 828 3638
E-mail: vhs@vhs.state.vt.us
http://www.state.vt.us/vhs

Genealogical Society of Vermont
P.O. Box 1553
St. Albans, VT 05478 1006
http://www.rootsweb.com/~vtgsv

VIRGINIA

Office of Vital Records
P.O. Box 1000
Richmond, VA 23208 1000
Tel: 804 225 5000
E-mail: jtyler@sover.net
http://www.vdh.state.va.us

The Library Of Virginia
800 East Broad Street
Richmond, VA 23219
Tel: 804 692 3500
http://www.lva.lib.va.us

Virginia Historical Society
428 North Boulevard
Richmond, VA 23220
Tel: 804 358 4901
http://www.vahistorical.org

Virginia Genealogical Society
5001 West Broad Street, Suite 115
Richmond, VA 23230 3023
Tel: 804 285 8954
E-mail: mail@vgs.org
http://www.vgs.org

WASHINGTON

Vital Records Office (Center for Health Statistics)
P.O. Box 9709
Olympia, WA 98507 9709
Tel: 360 236 4313
Fax: 360 352 2586
http://www.doh.wa.gov/EHSPHL/CHS/
divorce.htm

Washington State Archives
1120 Washington Street SE
P.O. Box 40238
Olympia, WN 98504 0238
Tel: 360 753 5485
http://www.secstate.wa.gov/archives

Washington State Archives Center
415 15th Avenue SW
Olympia, WA 98504 2460
Tel: 360 753 3087
Fax: 360 586 7575
E-mail: archives@secstate.wa.gov
http://www.secstate.wa.gov/archives/
main.htm

National Archives and Records Administration Pacific Alaska Region
6125 Sand Point Way NE
Seattle, WA 98115 7999
Tel: 206 526 6501
Fax: 206 526 6575
E-mail: archives@seattle.nara.gov
http://www.nara.gov/regional/
seattle.html

Washington State Genealogical Society
P.O. Box 1422
Olympia, WA 98507 1422
http://www.rootsweb.com/~wasgs

Fiske Genealogical Library
1644 43rd Avenue E
Seattle, WA 98112
Tel: 206 328 2716
http://www.fiske.lib.wa.us

WEST VIRGINIA

Vital Registration, Division of Health
State Capitol Complex
Building 3, Room 513
Charleston, WV 25305
Tel: 304 558 2931
Fax: 304 558 1051
http://www.wvdhhr.org/bph/oehp/hsc/vr/
birtcert.htm

West Virginia State Archives
The Cultural Center
1900 Kanawha Boulevard, East
Charleston, WV 25305 0300
Tel: 304 558 0230
http://www.wvculture.org/history/
index.html

West Virginia University Libraries
Colson Hall, West Virginia University
P.O. Box 6464
Morgantown, WV 26506 6464
Tel: 304 293 3536
Fax: 304 293 3981
http://www.libraries.wvu.edu/
wvcollection

West Virginia Historical Society
The Cultural Center, Capitol Complex
1900 Kanawha Boulevard
East Charleston, WV 25305 0300
Tel: 304 348 2277

West Virginia Genealogical Society
P.O. Box 249
Elkview, WV 25071

WISCONSIN

Vital Records Office
P.O. Box 309
1 West Wilson Street, Rm 158
Madison, WI 53701
Tel: 608 266 1371
E-mail: VitalRecords@dhfs.state.wi.us
http://www.dhfs.state.wi.us/VitalRecords

State Historical Society of Wisconsin
816 State Street
Madison, WI 53706
Tel: 608 264 6460
Fax: 608 264 6472
http://www.shsw.wisc.edu

Milwaukee Public Library
814 W. Wisconsin Avenue
Milwaukee, WI 53233
Tel: 414 286 3000
Fax: 414 286 2798
http://www.mpl.org

Wisconsin State Genealogical Society
2109 Twentieth Avenue
Monroe, WI 53566
Email: wsgs@chorus.net
http://www.rootsweb.com/~wsgs/index.htm

WYOMING

Vital Records Services
Hathaway Building
Cheyenne, WY 82002
Tel: 307 777 7591
Fax: 307 635 4103
http://wdhfs.state.wy.us/vital_records

Wyoming State Archives
Barrett Building
Cheyenne, WY 82002
Tel: 307 777 7013
Fax: 307 777 7044
http://spacr.state.wy.us/CR/Archives

Wyoming State Library
2301 Capitol Avenue
Cheyenne, WY 82002 0060
Tel: 307 777 7283
Fax: 307 777 6289
http://www.wsl.state.wy.us

Wyoming Pioneer Historical Society
P.O. Drawer 10
Douglas, WY 82633

RELIGIOUS ARCHIVES

BAPTIST

North American Baptist Seminary Library
11525–23 Avenue
Edmonton, AL 57105
Tel: 780 437 1960
http://www.nabcebs.ab.ca/library/

Partee Center for Baptist Historical Studies
William Jewell College
500 College Hill
Liberty, MO 64068 1896
Tel: 816 781 7700
http://www.jewell.edu/academia/currylibrary/partee/partee.html

CATHOLIC

United States Catholic Historical Society
1011 First Avenue
New York, NY 10022
http://www.catholic.org/uschs

EPISCOPAL

Archives of the Episcopal Church
P.O. Box 2247
606 Rathervue Place
Austin, TX 78768

Episcopal Church Center
Records Administration Office
815 Second Avenue
New York, NY 10017 4594
http://episcopalarchives.org

EVANGELICAL

Evangelical and Reformed Historical Society
Philip Schaff Library
Lancaster Theological Seminary
555 West James Street
Lancaster, PA 17603

Evangelical Lutheran Church in America
8765 W. Higgins Road
Chicago, IL 60631
Tel: 800 638 3522
Fax: 773 380 1465
http://www.elca.org

HUGUENOT

Huguenot Historical Society
18 Broadhead Avenue
New Paltz, NY 12561 0339
Tel: 845 255 1660
http://www.hhs-newpaltz.org

Library and Archives
88 Huguenot Street
New Paltz, NY 12561
Tel: 914 255 6738
Fax: 914 255 0376

The National Huguenot Society
9033 Lyndale Avenue S. #108
Bloomington, MN 55420 3535
Tel: 612 885 9776
http://www.huguenot.netnation.com

JEWISH

American Jewish Historical Society
2 Thornton Road
Waltham, MA 02453 7711
Tel: 781 891 8110
Fax: 781 899 9208
E-mail: ajhs@ajhs.org
http://www.ajhs.org

International Association of Jewish Genealogical Societies
Howard Margol, President
4430 Mt. Paran Parkway NW
Atlanta, GA 30327 3747
E-mail: HoMargol@aol.com
http://www.jewishgen.org/ajgs

Center for Jewish History
15 West 16th Street
New York, NY 10011
Tel: 212 294 8301
Fax: 212 294 8302
Email: CGI@cjh.org
http://www.centerforjewishhistory.com

LATTER-DAY SAINTS

Family History Library
35 North West Temple Street
Salt Lake City, UT 84150 3400
Tel: 801 240 2331
Fax: 801 240 5551
http://www.familysearch.org/Eng/Library/FHL/frameset_library.asp

MENNONITE

Historical Committee and Archives of the Mennonite Church
1700 South Main Street
Goshen, IN 46526 4794
Tel: 219 535 7477
Fax: 219 535 7756
http://www.goshen.edu/mcarchives

Mennonite Family History Library
10 W. Main Street
Elverson, PA 19520 0171
Tel: 610 286 0258
Fax: 610 286 6860
http://feefhs.org/men/frg-mfh.html

Mennonite Historians of Eastern Pennsylvania
P.O. Box 82
565 Yoder Road
Harleysville, PA 19438
Tel: 215 256 3020
Fax: 215 256 3023
http://www.mhep.org/welcome.html

Early Russian Mennonite History
http://members.aol.com/jktsn/
mennohis.htm

METHODIST

United Methodist Church
General Commission on Archives and History
P.O. Box 127
36 Madison Avenue
Madison, NJ 07940
Tel: 973 408 3189
Fax: 973 408 3909
http://www.gcah.org

PRESBYTERIAN

The Presbyterian Historical Society
425 Lombard Street
Philadelphia, PA 19147 1516
Tel: 215 627 1852
Fax: 215 627 0509
http://history.pcusa.org

Presbyterian College Library
503 South Broad Street
Clinton, SC 29325
Tel: 864 833 8299
http://www.presby.edu/library

Historical Foundation of the Cumberland Presbyterian Church
1978 Union Avenue
Memphis, TN 38104
Tel: 901 276 8602
Fax: 901 272 3913
http://www.cumberland.org/hfcpc

QUAKER

Friends General Conference of the Religious Society of Friends
1216 Arch Street #2B
Philadelphia, PA 19107
Tel: 215 561 1700
Fax: 215 561 0759
http://www.fgcquaker.org

Friends Collection
Earlham College Libraries
Richmond, IN 47374
Tel: 765 983 1511 (college archivist)
http://www.earlham.edu/~libr/quaker

SHAKER

Shaker Heritage Society
1848 Shaker Meeting House
Albany-Shaker Road
Albany, NY 12211
Tel: 518 456 7890
Fax: 518 452 7348
E-mail: shakerwv@crisny.org
http://www.crisny.org/not-for-profit/
shakerwv

WESLEYAN

Wesley Theological Seminary Library
4500 Massachussetts Avenue NW
Washington, D.C. 20016
Tel: 202 885 8695
Fax: 202 855 8691
http://www.wesleysem.org

NATIONAL ORGANIZATIONS

American Local History Network
http://members.xoom.com/abame/
lib-arch.html

Federation of Genealogical Societies
P.O. Box 200940
Austin, TX 78720 0940
Tel: 888 FGS 1500
Fax: 888 380 0500
E-mail: fgs-office@fgs.org
http://www.fgs.org

The Balch Institute of Ethnic Studies
18 South Seventh Street
Philadelphia, PA 19106
Tel: 215 925 8090
E-mail: info@balchinstitute.com
http://www.libertynet.org/balch

Local County Library and Historical Society Directory
http://www.state.in.us/icpr/webfile/
archives/loclsocs.html

National Archives and Records Administration Personnel Records Center
Civilian Personnel Records
111 Winnebago Street
St. Louis, MO 63118 4199
Tel: 314 538 5761
E-mail: center@cpr.nara.gov
http://www.nara.gov/regional/cpr.html

National Archives and Records Administration Military Personnel Records Center
9700 Page Avenue
St. Louis, MO 63132 5100
Tel: 314 538 4243 (Air Force)
Tel: 314 538 4261 (Army)
Tel: 314 538 4141 (Navy, Marine Corps, Coast Guard)
E-mail: center@stlouis.nara.gov
http://www.nara.gov/regional/mpr.html

National Genealogical Society Library
4527 17th Street North
Arlington, VA 22202
Tel: 703 525 0050
Fax: 800 473 0060
http://www.ngsgenealogy.org

Canada

ALBERTA

Government Services, Alberta Registries
Vital Statistics, Box 2023
Edmonton, AL T5J 4W7
Tel: 780 427 7013
http://www.gov.ab.ca/ma/REG/vs/
overv.htm

Provincial Archives of Alberta
12845, 102 Avenue
Edmonton, AB T5N 0M6
Tel: 780 427 1750
Fax: 780 427 4646
E-mail: paa@mcd.gov.ab.ca
http://www.gov.ab.ca/mcd/mhs/paa/
paa.htm

Alberta Genealogical Society
Prince of Wales Armouries Heritage
Centre
#116, 10440, 108 Avenue
Edmonton, AB T5H 3Z9
Tel: 780 424 4429
Fax: 780 423 8980
E-mail: agsoffice@compusmart.ab.ca
http://www.compusmart.ab.ca/abgensoc

Alberta Family Histories Society
P.O. Box 30270, Station B
Calgary, AB T2M 4P1
Tel: 403 214 1447
http://www.calcna.ab.ca/afhs/library.html

**Mennonite Historical Society of
Alberta**
c/o George Paetkau, P.O. Box 100
Gem, AB T0J 1M0
http://www.rootsweb.com/~abmhsa/
index.html

BRITISH COLUMBIA

Division of Vital Statistics
818 Fort Street
Victoria, BC V8W 1H8
Tel: 250 952 2681
Fax: 250 952 1829
http://www.hlth.gov.bc.ca/vs

British Columbia Archives
P.O. Box 9419, Station Prov Govt
Victoria, BC V8W 9V1
Tel: 250 387 1952
Fax: 250 387 2072
http://www.bcarchives.gov.bc.ca/
index.htm

City of Victoria Archives
1 Centennial Square
Victoria, BC V8W 1P6
Tel: 250 361 0375
Fax: 250 361 0394
E-mail: careyp@ch.city.victoria.bc.ca
http://www.city.victoria.bc.ca/depts/
archives/index.htm

Surrey Public Library
41 Cloverdale
5642, 176A Street
Surrey, BC V3S 4G9
Tel: 604 576 1384
Fax: 604 576 0120
http://www.bcpl.gov.bc.ca/interlink/
systems/surrey.htm

MANITOBA

Division of Vital Statistics
254 Portage Avenue
Winnipeg, MB R3C 0B6
Tel: 204 945 8177/3701 (recording)
Fax: 204 948 3128
E-mail: vitalstats@cca.gov.mb.ca
http://www.gov.mb.ca/cca/vital.html

Provincial Archives of Manitoba
Hudson's Bay Company Archives
200 Vaughan Street
Winnipeg, MB R3C 1T5
Tel: 204 945 3971
Fax: 204 948 2672
E-mail: pam@gov.mb.ca
http://www.gov.mb.ca/chc/archives/
index.html

Legislative Library of Manitoba
200 Vaughan Street
Winnipeg, MB R3C 1T5
Tel: 204 945 4330
Fax: 204 948 2008
E-mail: legislative_library@gov.mb.ca
http://www.gov.mb.ca/chc/
leglib_index.html

Manitoba Genealogical Society
Unit E, 1045 St. James Street
Winnipeg, MB R3H 1B1
Tel: 204 783 9139
http://www.mbnet.mb.ca/~mgs

NEW BRUNSWICK

Registrar General
Division of Vital Statistics
Centennial Building, Box 6000
Fredericton, NB E3B 5H1
Tel: 506 453 2385/444 5525 (recording)
http://www.gov.nb.ca/0379/en/index.htm

**Provincial Archives of New
Brunswick**
P.O. Box 6000
Bonar Law-Bennett Building
23 Dineen Drive
U.N.B. Campus, Fredericton
NB E3B 5H1
Tel: 506 453 2122
Fax: 506 453 3288
E-mail: provincial.archives@gnb.ca
http://www.gov.nb.ca/archives/e

New Brunswick Legislative Library
P.O. Box 6000
706 Queen Street
Fredericton, NB E3B 5H1
Tel: 506 453 2506
Fax: 506 453 7154
http://www.gov.nb.ca/legis/library.htm

University of New Brunswick Library
Archives and Special Collections
P.O. Box 7500
Fifth Floor, Harriet Irving Library
Fredericton, NB E3B 5H5
Tel: 506 453 4748
Fax: 506 453 4595
http://www.unbsj.ca/library

**The New Brunswick Genealogical
Society**
P.O. Box 3235, Station B
Fredericton, NB E3A 5G9
http://www.bitheads.ca/nbgs

NEWFOUNDLAND AND
LABRADOR

Vital Statistics
Department of Government Services
and Lands
P.O. Box 8700, 5 Mews Place
St. John's, NF A1B 4J6
Tel: 709 729 3308
Fax: 709 729 0946
http://www.gov.nf.ca/gsl/gslvfaq.htm

**Provincial Archives of Newfoundland
and Labrador**
Colonial Building
Military Road
St. John's, NF A1C 2C9
Tel: 709 729 3065
Fax: 709 729 0578
http://www.gov.nf.ca/panl/client3.htm

Newfoundland and Labrador Genealogical Society
Colonial Building
Military Road
St. John's, NF A1C 2C9
Tel: 709 754 9525
Fax: 709 754 9525
http://www.wordplay.com/newfoundland/
nonprofitorgs/genealogicalsociety.html

St. John's Provincial Public Library
1st. Floor, Arts and Culture Centre
St. John's, NF A1B 3A3
Tel: 709 737 3953
Fax: 709 737 2660
http://www.publib.nf.ca/libraries/stjohns/
index.html

NORTHWEST TERRITORIES

Registrar General, Vital Statistics
Department of Health and Social
Services
Government of NWT, Bag 9
Inuvik, NT X0E 0T0
Tel: 867 777 7420
Fax: 867 777 3197

Northwest Territories Archives
P.O. Box 1320
Yellowknife, NT X1A 2L9
Tel: 867 873 7240
Fax: 867 873 0279
http://www.urova.fi/home/arktinen/
polarweb/polar/lbcdnwar.htm

The NWT Genealogical Society
P.O. Box 1715
Yellowknife, NT X1A 2P3
Fax: 867 873 9304
E-mail: xdennis@ssimicro.com
http://www.ssimicro.com/nonprofit/
nwtgs/

NOVA SCOTIA

Deputy Registrar General
1723 Hollis Street
P.O. Box 157
Halifax, NS B3J 2M9
Tel: 902 424 4381/4380 (recording)
http://www.gov.ns.ca/snsmr

Public Archives of Nova Scotia
6016 University Avenue
Halifax, NS B3H 1W4
Tel: 902 424 6060
Fax: 902 424 0628
http://museum.gov.ns.ca/mikmaq/
pans.htm

Genealogical Association of Nova Scotia
P.O. Box 641
Station 'Central'
Halifax, NS B3J 2T3
Tel: 902 454 0322
http://www.chebucto.ns.ca/Recreation/
GANS/

Acadia University Library
Acadia Street, Box D
Wolfeville, NS B0P1XO
Tel: 902 585 1241
Fax: 902 585 1748
http://www.acadiau.ca/vaughan/

Yarmouth County Museum and Archives
22 Collins Street
Yarmouth, NS B5A 3C8
Tel: 902 742 5539
Fax: 902 749 1120
http://www.ycn.library.ns.ca/museum/
yarcomus.htm

NUNAVUT (est. April 1999)

Registrar General
Vital Statistics, Government of Nunavut
Bag #3, Rankin Inlet, NT X0C 0G0
Tel: 867 645 5002
Fax: 867 645 5001

ONTARIO

Office of the Registrar General
Box 4600, 189 Red River Road
Thunder Bay, ON P7B 6L8
Tel: 416 325 8305
www.ccr.gov.on.ca/mccr/orgindex.htm

National Archives of Canada
395 Wellington Street
Ottawa, ON K1A 0N3
Tel: 613 995 5138
Tel: 613 996 7458 (genealogy)
Fax: 613 995 6274
http://www.archives.ca

Oshawa Historical Society Archives
1450 Simcoe Street
South Oshawa, ON L1H 8S8
Tel: 905 436 7624
Fax: 905 436 7625
http://www.oshawamuseum.org/
index.html

Ontario Genealogical Society
40 Orchard View Blvd., Suite 102
Toronto, ON M4R 1B9
Tel: 519 824 6220
http://www.ist.uwaterloo.ca/~marj/
genealogy/ww.html

Mennonite Archives of Ontario
Conrad Grebel College
Waterloo, ON N2L 3G6
Tel: 519 885 0220

Kingston Public Library
130 Johnson Street
Kingston, ON K7L 1X8
Tel: 613 549 8888
http://www.kfpl.library.on.ca

York University Library Archives and Special Collections
Room 305 Scott Library
4700 Keele Street
Toronto, ON, M3J 1P3
Tel: 416 736 5442
Fax: 416 650 8039
http://www.info.library.yorku.ca/depts/
asc/archives.htm

PRINCE EDWARD ISLAND

Division of Vital Statistics
35 Douses Road, Box 3000
Montague, PE C0A 1R0
Tel: 902 838 0880/0881
Fax: 902 838 0883
http://www.gov.pe.ca/vitalstatistics/
index.php3

Public Archives of Prince Edward Island
P.O. Box 1000
Charlottetown, PEI C1A 7M4
Tel: 902 368 4290
Fax: 902 668 6327
E-mail: archives@gov.pe.ca
http://www2.gov.pe.ca/educ/archives/
archives_index.asp

The Prince Edward Island Genealogical Society
P.O. Box 2744
Charlottetown, PEI C1A 8C4
E-mail: peigs_queries@hotmail.com>
http://www.islandregister.com/
peigs.html

The Prince Edward Island Museum and Heritage Foundation
2 Kent Street
Charlottetown, PEI C1A 1M6
Tel: 902 368 6600
Fax: 902 368 6608
http://www.metamedia.pe.ca/
peimuseum/

QUÉBEC

Direction de l'état civil
Le Directeur de l'état civil
205, rue Montmagny
Quebec, QC G1N 2Z9
Tel: 418 643 3900
http://www.etatcivil.gouv.qc.ca/
ENGLISH/Default.htm

Montreal Centre of Archives
535 Avenue Viger Est
Montreal, QC
http://www.anq.gouv.qc.ca/
ANQ-B-02.html

Société de généalogie de Québec
Salle 4266, Pavillon Louis-Jacques-
Casault, Cité Universaire
Case Postale 9066
Sainte-Foy, QC G1V 4A8
Tel: 418 651 9127
Fax: 418 651 2643
http://www.genealogie.org/club/sgq/
sgq.htm

Québec Family History Society
P.O. Box 1026
Pointe Claire, QC, H9S 4M5
Tel: 514 695 1502
http://www.cam.org/~qfhs/index.html

SASKATCHEWAN

Division of Vital Statistics
Department of Health
1942 Hamilton Street
Regina, SK S4P 3V7
Tel: 306 787 3092

Saskatchewan Archives Board
University of Regina
Regina, SK S4S 0A2
Tel: 306 787 4068
Fax: 306 787 1975
http://www.gov.sk.ca/govt/archives/
offices.htm

Saskatchewan Genealogical Society
2nd Floor, 1870 Lorne Street
P.O. Box 1894
Regina, SK S4P 3E1
Tel: 306 780 9207
Fax: 306 781 6021
http://www.saskgenealogy.com

YUKON TERRITORIES

Registrar of Vital Statistics
P.O. Box 2703
Whitehorse, YT Y1A 2C6
Tel: 403 667 5207

Yukon Archives
P.O. Box 2703
Whitehorse, YT Y1A 2C6
Tel: 867 667 5321
Fax: 867 393 6253
http://www.yukoncollege.yk.ca/archives/
yukarch.html

RELIGIOUS ARCHIVES

BAPTIST

Canadian Baptist Archives
McMaster Divinity College
1280 Main St. W.
Hamilton, ON L8S 4K1
Tel: 905 525 9140 ext. 23511 (archives)
Fax: 905 577 4782
http://www.mcmaster.ca/divinity/
archives.html

CATHOLIC

The Canadian Catholic Historical Association
1155 Yonge Street
Toronto, ON M4T 1W2
Tel: 416 934 0606
Fax: 416 934 3444
http://www.umanitoba.ca/colleges/
st_pauls/ccha/index2.html

JEWISH

Jewish Historical Society of Western Canada
C116–123 Doncaster Street
Winnipeg, MB R3N 2B2
Tel: 204 477 7460
Fax: 204 477 7365
http://www.jhcwc.mb.ca

MENNONITE

Centre for Mennonite Brethren Studies
1-169 Riverton Avenue
Winnipeg, MB R2L 2E5
Tel: 204 669 6575
Fax: 204 654 1865
http://www.mbconf.ca/mbstudies

PRESBYTERIAN

Presbyterian Church Archives
50 Wynford Drive
Toronto, ON M3C 1J7
Tel: 416 441 1111/800 619 7301
Fax: 416 441 2825
http://www.presbyterian.ca/archives

UNITED CHURCH OF CANADA

The United Church of Canada
Victoria University Archives
73 Queen's Park Crescent
East Toronto, ON M5S 1K7
Tel: 416 585 4563
Fax: 416 585 4584
http://vicu.utoronto.ca/archives/
archives.htm

NATIONAL ORGANIZATIONS

American-Canadian Genealogical Society
P.O. Box 6478
Manchester, NH 03108 6478
http://www.acgs.org

National History Society
478-167 Lombard Avenue
Winnipeg, MB R3B 0T6
Tel: 204 988 9300
Fax: 204 988 9309

East European Genealogical Society
P.O. Box 2536
Winnipeg, MB R3C 4A7
Tel: 204 989 3292
http://www.eegsociety.org/index.html

WEBSITES

Canada GenWeb Project
http://www.rootsweb.com/~canwgw

National Library of Canada
http://www.nlc-bnc.ca/about/eabout.htm

The United Church of Canada Archives Network
http://www.uccan.org/archives/home.htm

Society Hill: A Directory of Genealogy and History Societies
http://www.daddezio.com/
societyindex.html

Countries A–Z

Argentina

Archivo General de la Nación (National Archives)
Avenida Leandro N. Alem 246
1003 Buenos Aires
Tel: 4331 5531/2/3/6642
Fax: 4334 0065
http://www.archivo.gov.ar

Archivo del Registro Nacional del Estado Civil y Capacidad de Las Personas (Vital Records)
Jean Jaures 970
1215 Buenos Aires

Biblioteca Nacional de la República Argentina (National Library)
Agüero 2502
Ciudad Autónoma de Buenos Aires 1425
Tel: 11 4806 4721/1929/2081
http://www.bibnal.edu.ar

WEBSITES

Argentina GenWeb
http://www.rootsweb.com/~argwgw

Armenia

Outside Armenia
Armenian Genealogical Society
P.O. Box 1383
Provo, UT 84603 1383, U.S.A.
http://www.feefhs.org/am/frg-amgs.html

Armenian Research Center and Society for Armenian Studies
University of Michigan-Dearborn
4901 Evergreen Road
Dearborn, MI 48128 1491, U.S.A.
http://www.umd.umich.edu/dept/
armenian/sas

Armenian Historical Association of Rhode Island
P.O. Box 28142
Providence, RI 02908, U.S.A.
http://members.aol.com/Gaghjayan/
riaha.html

WEBSITES

Armenia Genealogy (WorldGenWeb)
http://www.rootsweb.com/~armwgw

Armenian Church Directory
http://www.cilicia.com/armo_church_
directory.html

Armenian Diasporan Archives
http://users.erols.com/guerig

Armenian Genealogical Home Page
http://members.aol.com/Gaghjayan/
homepage.htm

Distant Cousins: Armenian Genealogy Resources
http://www.distantcousin.com/Links/
Ethnic/Armenia.html

Genealogy for Armenians
http://www.itsnet.com/home/gfa

Australia

For each Australian state or territory, directory entries start with the contact addresses for vital records. This is followed by contact details for state archives, national archives (where appropriate), state and provincial libraries, genealogical and historical societies, and specialist libraries.

AUSTRALIAN CAPITAL TERRITORY

Registrar-General's Office
(G.P.O. Box 788)
Allara House, Allara Street
Canberra ACT 2601
Tel: (0) 2 6207 0460
http://www.act.gov.au/NewServices/law/
registrar.html

Probate Office
Supreme Court of the Australian
Capital Territory
Knowles Place
Canberra ACT 2601
Tel: (0) 2 6267 2707
Fax: (0) 2 6257 3668

Australian Capital Territory Public Trustee
4 Mort Street
Canberra ACT 2601
Tel: (0) 2 6207 9800
Fax: (0) 2 6207 9811

National Archives of Australia
Queen Victoria Terrace
Parkes ACT 2600
Tel: (0) 2 6212 3600
Fax: (0) 2 6212 3699
http://www.aa.gov.au

The Canberra and District Historical Society
25 Blaxland Crescent
Griffith ACT 2604
Tel: (0) 2 6232 6212
Fax: (0 2 6207 6498
http://www.history.org.au/act

The Heraldry and Genealogy Society of Canberra
G.P.O. Box 585
Canberra ACT 2601
Tel: (0) 2 6282 9356
E-mail: hagsoc @ hagsoc.org.au
http://www.hagsoc.org.au

NEW SOUTH WALES

Registry of Births, Deaths, and Marriages
(G.P.O. Box 30, Sydney 2001)
191 Thomas Street
Haymarket NSW 2000
Tel: (0) 2 9243 8585
E-mail: bdm-mail@agd.nsw.gov.au
http://www.bdm.nsw.gov.au

The Registrar of Probate
Supreme Court of New South Wales
King Street
Sydney NSW 2000
Tel: (0) 2 9228 7377
Fax: (0) 2 9228 7388

Public Trustee
19 O'Connell Street
Sydney NSW 2000
Tel: (0) 2 9252 0523
Fax: (0) 2 9231 4527

State Records New South Wales
2 Globe Street
The Rocks
Sydney NSW 2000
Tel: (0) 2 8276 5600
Fax: (0) 2 8276 5604
http://www.records.nsw.gov.au/services/
visit.htm

Society of Australian Genealogists
Richmond Villa
120 Kent Street,
Sydney NSW 2000
Tel: (0) 2 9247 3953
Fax: (0) 2 9241 4872
http://www.sag.org.au/contact.htm

Little Forest Family History Research Group
P.O. Box 87
Milton NSW 2538
E-mail: cathyd@shoalhaven.net.au
http://www.shoalhaven.net.au/~cathyd/
groups.html

Royal Australian Historical Society
History House
133 Macquarie Street
Sydney NSW 2000
Tel: (0) 2 9247 8001
Fax: (0) 2 9247 7854
http://www.rahs.org.au/
RAHS%20Home.html

Brisbane Water Historical Society
218 Gertrude Street
Gosford NSW 2250
Tel: (0) 2 4325 2270
E-mail: brisbanewater@hotmail.com
http://www.terrigal.net.au/~bwhs

Wentworth Historical Society
Wentworth Shire Library
Corner Short and Murray Streets
Wentworth NSW 2648
Tel: (0) 3 5027 3287
Fax: (0) 3 5027 2137
http://www.wentworth.nsw.gov.au/
library/libhist.html

NORTHERN TERRITORY

Registrar-General's Office
(G.P.O. Box 3021, Darwin 0801)
Nichols Place
Corner of Bennett and Cavenagh Street
Darwin NT 0800
Tel: (0) 8 8999 6119
Fax: (0) 8 8999 6324
http://www.ke.com.au/bdmaus/bdmnt/
index.html

The Registrar of Probate
Supreme Court of the Northern
Territory
51 Mitchell Street
Darwin NT 0800
Tel: (0) 8 8999 6562
Fax: (0) 8 8999 5446

Public Trustee
45 Mitchell Street
Darwin NT 0800
Tel: (0) 8 8999 7271
Fax: (0) 8 8999 7882

Genealogical Society of the Northern Territory
P.O. Box 37212
Winnellie NT 0821
Tel: (0) 8 8981 7363
E-mail: gsnt@austarnet.com.au
http://sites.archivenet.gov.au/gsnt

Northern Territory Library
Parliament House
Darwin NT 0800
Tel: (0) 8 8999 5558
Fax: (0) 8 8999 6390
http://www.ntlis.nt.gov.au

QUEENSLAND

Registrar-General's Office
Registry of Births, Deaths. and
Marriages
(P.O. Box 188, Albert Street,
Brisbane 4002)
501 Ann Street
Brisbane Qld 4000
(visitors to 501 Ann Street, Brisbane)
Tel: (0) 7 3247 9203
Fax: (0) 7 3247 5803
http://kestrel.ke.com.au/bdmaus/bdmqld/
index.html

The Registrar of Probate
Supreme Court of Queensland
George Street
Brisbane Qld 4000
Tel: (0) 7 3247 4313

Public Trust Office
Trustee House
444 Queen Street
Brisbane Qld 4000
Tel: (0) 7 3213 9288
Fax: (0) 7 3213 9485

Queensland State Archives
(P.O. Box 1397)
435 Compton Road
Runcorn Qld 4113
Tel: (0) 7 3875 8755
Fax: (0) 7 3875 8764
http://www.archives.qld.gov.au/services/
public/BDM.html

**Central Queensland Family Historical
Association**
P.O. Box 6000
Central Queensland Mail Centre
Qld 4701
http://sites.archivenet.gov.au/cqfha

Genealogical Society of Queensland
Resource Centre, First Floor
Woolloongabba Post Office
Corner of Hubert and Stanley Streets
Woolloongabba Qld 4102
Tel: (0) 7 3891 5085
http://www.home.st.net.au/~dunn/
gsq.htm

**Maryborough Family Heritage
Institute**
Ground Floor
Maryborough Heritage Centre
(P.O. Box 913)
164 Richmond Street
Maryborough Qld 4650
Tel: (0) 7 4123 1620
Fax: (0) 7 4123 1884
http://www.satcom.net.au/mfhi

Queensland Family History Society
P.O. Box 171
Indooroopilly Qld 4068
Tel: (0) 7 3857 5744
http://www.qfhs.org.au

SOUTH AUSTRALIA

**Births, Deaths, and Marriages
Registration Office of South Australia**
(G.P.O. Box 1351, Adelaide 5001)
Level 2, Chesser House
91–97 Grenfell Street
Adelaide SA 5000
Tel: (0) 8 8204 9599
Fax: (0) 8 8204 9605
http://www.ocba.sa.gov.au/
bdm_contact.htm

Probate Registry
301 King William Street
Adelaide SA 5000
Tel: (0) 8 8204 0505

Public Trustee Office
25 Franklin Street
Adelaide SA 5000
Tel: (0) 8 8226 9200
Fax: (0) 8 8231 9518

State Records Office
(P.O. Box 1056, Blair Athol West,
SA 5084)
222 Marion Road
Netley SA 5037
Tel: (0) 8 8343 6800
E-mail: staterecords@saugov.sa.gov.au
www.archives.sa.gov.au/about/contact.htm

**South Australian Genealogy and
Heraldry Society**
G.P.O. Box 592
Adelaide SA 5001
Tel: (0) 8 8272 4222
Fax: (0) 8 8272 4910
http://www.sags.mtx.net

**Yorke Peninsula Family History
Group**
Northern Yorke Peninsula Public
Library
Graves Street
Kadina SA 5554
Tel: (0) 8 8821 2704
http://www.asap.unimelb.edu.au/asa/
directory/data/319.htm

TASMANIA

**Registry of Births, Deaths, and
Marriages**
(G.P.O. Box 198, Hobart Tas 7001)
Lands Building
134 Macquarie Street
Hobart Tas 7000
Tel: (0) 3 6233 3793
Fax: (0) 3 6233 6444
http://www.justice.tas.gov.au/bdm/
contact_bdm.htm

Probate Registry
Supreme Court of Tasmania
Salamanca Place
Hobart Tas 7000
Tel: (0) 3 6233 3716
Fax: (0) 3 6223 7816

Public Trustee
116 Murray Street
Hobart Tas 7000
Tel: (0) 3 6233 7598
Fax: (0) 3 6231 0621

Archives Office of Tasmania
77 Murray Street
Hobart Tas 7000
Tel: (0) 3 6233 7488
Fax: (0) 3 6233 7471
E-mail: Archives.Tasmania@
Central.tased.edu.au
http://www.archives.tas.gov.au/
contact-hours.asp

Genealogical Society of Tasmania
Hobart Branch
G.P.O. Box 640
Hobart Tas 7001
Tel: (0) 3 6243 6200
http://www.southcom.com.au/~gsthobt/
contacts.htm

Ulverstone Local History Museum
P.O. Box 340
Ulverstone Tas 7315
E-mail: info@leven.tassie.net.au
http://www.leven.tassie.net.au/ULHM

VICTORIA

Registy of Births, Deaths, and Marriages
(G.P.O. Box 4332, Melbourne 3001)
589 Collins Street
Melbourne Vic 3000
Tel: (0) 3 9603 5888
Fax: (0) 3 9603 5880
http://www.justice.vic.gov.au/
DOJsite.nsf/all+by+key/
BirthsDeathsAndMarriagesHome?open
document

Probate Office
436 Lonsdale Street
Melbourne Vic 3000
Tel: (0) 3 9603 9296
Fax: (0) 3 9628 0656

State Trustees Ltd
168 Exhibition Street
Melbourne Vic 3000
Tel: (0) 3 9667 6444
Fax: (0) 3 9663 4260

Public Record Office
P.O. Box 2100
North Melbourne Vic 3051
Tel: (0) 3 9348 5600
Fax: (0) 3 9285 7953
E-mail: ask.prov@dpc.vic.gov.au
http://www.prov.vic.gov.au/about/
operations.htm

Australian Institute of Genealogical Studies
P.O. Box 339
Blackburn Vic 3130
Tel: (0) 9 877 3789
Fax: (0) 9 877 9066
http://www.alphalink.com.au/~aigs

Dromana and District Historical Society
(P.O. Box 30)
Old Shire Offices
359A Point Nepean Road
Dromana Vic 3936
Tel: (0) 3 5982 2735
E-mail: dromana@r150.aone.net.au
http://home.vicnet.net.au/~dromana

First Fleet Fellowship Victoria
C/- Polly Woodside Maritime Park
Lorimer Street East
Southbank Vic 3006
Tel: (0) 3 9370 9590
http://home.vicnet.net.au/~firstff

The Geelong Family History Group
P.O. Box 1187
Geelong Vic 3220
http://www.home.vicnet.net.au/
~gfamhist/index.htm

The Genealogical Society of Victoria
Level 6, 179 Queen Street
Melbourne Vic 3000
Tel: (0) 3 9670 7033
Fax: (0) 3 9670 4490
http://www.alphalink.com.au/~gsv

Mildura and District Genealogical Society
P.O. Box 1187
Mildura Vic 3502
Tel: (0) 3 5024 5330
http://users.mildura.net.au/users/
genealogy

West Gippsland Genealogical Society
P.O. Box 225
Warragul Vic 3820
Tel: (0) 3 5625 2743
http://home.vicnet.net.au/~wggs

Australian Association of Genealogists and Records Agents
P.O. Box 268
Oakleigh Vic 3166
Tel: (0) 3 9699 9548
Fax: (0) 3 9699 2382
http://www.aagra.asn.au

WESTERN AUSTRALIA

Registry of Births, Deaths, and Marriages
Level 10
141 St Georges Terrace
Perth WA 6000
Tel: (0) 8 9264 1555
Fax: (0) 8 9264 1599
E-mail: rgoperth@justice.wa.gov.au
http://www.moj.wa.gov.au/birth/min2.htm

Probate Office
Supreme Court of Western Australia
14th Floor, 111 St George's Terrace
Perth WA 6000
Tel: (0) 8 9261 7699

Public Trust Office
565 Hay Street
Perth WA 6000
Tel: (0) 8 9222 6777
Fax: (0) 8 9221 1102

Library and Information Service of Western Australia
Alexander Library Building
Perth Cultural Centre
Francis Street
Perth WA 6000
Tel: (0) 8 9427 3111
Fax: (0) 8 9427 3256
E-mail: info@liswa.wa.gov.au
http://www.liswa.wa.gov.au/contacts.htm

Western Australian Genealogical Society
6/48 May Street
Bayswater WA 6053
Tel: (0) 8 9271 4311
Fax: (0) 8 9271 4311
http://cleo.murdoch.edu.au/~wags

Geraldton Family History Society
P.O. Box 2502
Geraldton WA 6531
http://www.wn.com.au/gfhs/aboutus.htm

Austria

Austrian National Library
Josefsplatz 1
Postfach 308
A-1015 Vienna
Tel: 1 53410 201
Fax: 1 53410 280
http://www.onb.ac.at/english.htm
(English)
http://www.onb.ac.at (German)

Austrian State Archives
Nottendorfergasse 2
A-1030 Vienna
Tel: 1 79540 504
http://www.oesta.gv.at/engdiv/
geneal.htm

Heraldisch-Genealogische Gesellschaft "ADLER"
Universitaetsstrasse 6, Tuer 10
A-1096 Vienna

Institute for Historical Family Research
Pantzergasse 30/8
A-1190 Vienna
Tel: 1 369 9729
Fax: 1 369 9730
http://ihff.nwy.at/index.htm

OUTSIDE AUSTRIA

Federation of East European Family History Societies
P.O. Box 510898
Salt Lake City, UT 94151 0898
U.S.A.
http://feefhs.org

Gottscheer Heritage and Genealogy Association
P.O. Box 725
174 South Hoover Avenue
Louisville, CO 80027 0725
U.S.A.
http://www.gottschee.org/~ghga/
ghga.htm

WEBSITES

Archives in Austria by Andreas Hanacek
http://my.bawue.de/~hanacek/info/
aarchive.htm

Burgenland Bunch
http://www.spacestar.com/users/
hapander/burgen.html

German Genealogy: Austria
http://www.genealogy.net/gene/reg/
AUT/austria-en.html

Belgium

Association Généalogique du Hainaut Belge
Monsieur Jean-Claude Pirson
Avenue Mascaux 457
B-6001 Marcinelle
Tel: (0) 7 143 05 58

Etudes Généalogiques et Demographiques de Belgique
S.C.G.D.
Chausée de Haecht 147
1030 Bruxelles
Tel: (0) 2 374 14 92

Les Archives générales du Royaume
Rue de Ruysbroeck 2
1000 Bruxelles
Tel: (0) 2 513 76 80
Fax: (0) 2 513 76 81
http://arch.arch.be/AGR_F.HTML

Vlaamse Vereniging voor Familiekunde
Van Heybeekstraat 3
B-2170 Merksem, Antwerpen
Tel: (0) 3 646 99 88
Fax: (0) 3 644 46 20
http://www.vvfmerksem.yucom.be

OUTSIDE BELGIUM

Genealogical Society of Flemish Americans (GSFA)
18740 13 Mile Road
Roseville, MI 48066
U.S.A.
http://www.rootsweb.com/~gsfa

WEBSITES

Archives in Belgium (in English)
http://members.xoom.com/janssen_BE/
genealogy/BEL-archives/arch.html

How to find your Roots in Belgium!
http://www.ping.be/picavet

The Belgium Roots Project (English)
http://belgium.rootsweb.com/
index.html

Digital Resources: Netherlands and Belgium
http://geneaknowhow.net/digi/
resources.html

Genealogy Benelux Home Page
http://www.ufsia.ac.be/genealogy/
genealog.htm

Genealogical and Historical Society
http://www.geocities.com/Heartland/
Hollow/6442/home

Bulgaria

Bulgarian Genealogy Society
Obshtobalgarski komitet Vasil Levski
Batemberg Str. 4
1000 Sofia

Charakchiev & Son Representation
7 May Street
4000 Plovdiv
Tel: 32 227373 (Bulgaria)
Tel: 773 622 2337 (U.S.A.)
Fax: 32 632331
E-mail: ncharak@plov.omega.bg
E-mail: charakchiev@hotmail.com
http://www.geocities.com/Broadway/
Balcony/7632

Chile

Archivo Nacional
Miraflores # 50
Santiago
Tel: 562 681 7979
http://www.dibam.renib.cl/ISC145

China

Universities Service Centre (USC)
The Chinese University of Hong Kong
Shatin, N.T., Hong Kong
Tel: 2609 8765
Fax: 2603 5030
E-mail: usc@cuhk.edu.hk
http://www.usc.cuhk.edu.hk

OUTSIDE CHINA

Chinese Culture Center
750 Kearny Street, 3rd Floor
San Francisco, CA 94108
U.S.A.
Tel: 415 986 1822
Fax: 415 986 2825
http://www.c-c-c.org

Chinese Historical Society of America
644 Broadway Street, Suite 402
San Francisco, CA 94133
U.S.A.
Tel: 415 391 1188
Fax: 415 391 1150
http://www.chsa.org

WEBSITES

Chinese Genealogical Resources
http://fuzzo.com/genealogy/Asia/
chinagen.htm

ChineseRoots.com
http://www.chineseroots.com

ChinaGenWeb
http://www.rootsweb.com/~chnwgw

Croatia

Croatia Genealogy Home Page
P.O. Box 510898
Salt Lake City, UT 84151 0898
U.S.A.
http://feefhs.org/cro/frg-hr.html

Croatian Genealogical and Heraldic Society
2527 San Carlos Avenue
San Carlos, CA 94070 1747
U.S.A.
http://feefhs.org/cro/frg-cghs.html

WEBSITES

A Guide to Croatian Genealogy, by Adam S. Eterovich
http://feefhs.org/cro/cghs-gcg.html

Croatian Research at the Family History Library, by Thomas K. Edlund
http://www.feefhs.org/frl/cro/
edlund1.html

Cross Index of Croatian Surnames (and Locations) in Roman Catholic Parishes of Croatia
http://feefhs.org/cro/parish/
hrparish.html

Genealogy in Croatia
http://www.appleby.net/genealogy.html

Cuba

OUTSIDE CUBA

Cuban Genealogical Society
P.O. Box 2650
Salt Lake City, UT 84110
U.S.A.

WEBSITES

CubaGenWeb
http://www.cubagenweb.org

Czech Republic

Archivni Sprava
Ministerstva vnitra CR
Milady Horakove 133
166 21 Praha 6
Tel: (0) 2 3332 0274

Státní ústrední archiv v Praze
Karmelitská 2
118 01 Praha 1
Malá Strana
Tel: (0) 2 5732 0338 41
Tel: (0) 2 5731 2535 37
Fax: (0) 2 5732 0275
http://www.mvcr.cz/archivy/index.htm

OUTSIDE THE CZECH REPUBLIC

California Czech and Slovak Club
P.O. Box 20542
Castro Valley, CA 94546 8542
U.S.A.
http://feefhs.org/czs/frg-ccsc.html

The Czech and Slovak American Genealogy Society of Illinois
P.O. Box 313
Sugar Grove, IL 60554
U.S.A.
http://www.csagsi.org

Czechoslovak Genealogical Society International
P.O. Box 16225
St. Paul, MN 55116 0225
U.S.A.
http://feefhs.org/czs/cgsi/frg-cgsi.html

WEBSITES

Czech Republic, Bohemia, and Moravia Genealogical Research
http://www.iarelative.com/czech

Find a Czech Ancestor
http://www.muselik.com/cac

Genealogical Research in the Czech Republic
http://www.czech.cz/washington/cons/
genealogy.htm

Czech Genealogy
http://freepages.genealogy.rootsweb.com
/~elainetmaddox/czgenealogy.htm

Czech Republic WorldGenWeb Page
http://www.rootsweb.com/~czewgw

Czech Genealogy
http://www.geocities.com/Heartland/
Plains/2064/czechgen.htm

Denmark

Danish Emigration Archives
Arkivstræde 1
P.O. Box 1731
DK 9100 Aalborg
Tel: 99 31 42 20
Fax: 98 10 22 48
http://emiarch.homepage.dk

Frederiksberg Kommunes Biblioteker
Solbergvej 21-25
DK-2000 Frederiksberg
Tel: 38 21 18 00
Fax: 38 21 17 99
http://www.fkb.dk

Rigsarkivet (State Archives)
Rigsdagsgården 9
DK-1218 København K
Tel: 33 92 33 10
Fax: 33 15 32 39
http://www.sa.dk

Samfundet for dansk genealogi og Personalhistorie
(The Society for Danish Genealogy and
Biography)
Elsebeth Paikin
Kildevænget 37
2100 København Ø
http://www.genealogi.dk/index.htm

110 års indholdsfortegnelse til Personalhistorisk Tidsskrift
(A 110 Year Index of the Periodical of
Biography)
http://www.genealogi.dk/110.htm

OUTSIDE DENMARK

The Anglo-Danish Society
Mrs A.M. Eastwood
"Danewood"
4 Daleside
Gerrards Cross
Bucks SL9 7JF
United Kingdom
Tel: (0) 1753 884846

Danish Genealogy Group
c/o Minnesota Genealogical Society
5768 Olson Memorial Highway
Golden Valley, MN 55422
U.S.A.
http://www.mtn.org/mgs/branches

The Danish Immigrant Museum
2212 Washington Street
P.O. Box 470
Elk Horn, IA 51531 0470
U.S.A.
Tel: 712 764 7001
Fax: 712 764 7002
http://dkmuseum.org

The Scandinavian Society of Nova Scotia
Lisbeth Truelstrup Hansen
31 Ilsley Avenue
Darthmouth
NS B3B 1L5
Canada
Tel: 902 468 6844 (Lissi Jeppesen)
Fax: 902 468 2642
http://www.spodnet.uk.com/~pasht/
scandinavian/Society.html

WEBSITES

Computers in Genealogy Society of Denmark
http://dis-danmark.dk/indexuk.htm

Genealogy Resource Index for Denmark
http://fp.image.dk/fpemartin

Hvem Forsker Hvad
http://www.hvemforskerhvad.dk

Estonia

Population Register (in Estonian)
Suur-Ameerika 1
10122 Tallinn
Tel: (0) 611 3183/3176; (0) 611 3181
Fax: (0) 631 1275
E-mail: teenus@andmevara.ee
http://www.andmevara.ee/Andmek/
RRAB.htm

Statistical Office of Estonia
Endla 15, 15174 Tallinn
Tel: (0) 625 9300/9202
Fax: (0) 625 9370
E-mail: stat@stat.ee
http://www.stat.ee/wwwstat/eng_stat/
contacts_fr.html

Rahvusarhiiv (National Archive)
J. Liivi 4, Tartu 50409
Tel: (0) 742 1337
Fax: (0) 742 1482
E-mail ra@ra.ee
http://www.ra.ee

Ajaloo Instituut (Institute of History)
Rüütli-6
10130 Tallinn
Tel: (0) 644 6594
Fax: (0) 644 3714
E-mail: ai@teleport.ee
http://ai.ai.ee

Estonian Genealogical Society
Pk 4419
10511 Tallinn
Tel: (0) 677 5011 (Ants Roomets, vice
chairperson)
E-mail: kalle.keskula@energia.ee
(chairperson)
http://www.genealoogia.ee

WEBSITES

Estonian GenWeb
http://www.fortunecity.com/meltingpot/
estonia/200/genweb.html

Finland

Genealogical Society of Finland
Liisankatu 16 A
FIN-00170 Helsinki
Tel: (0) 9 278 1188
Fax: (0) 9 278 1199
http://sss.genealogia.fi
http://sss.genealogia.fi/historia/
indexe.htm

Institute of Migration
Piispankatu 3
20500 Turku
Tel: (0) 2 2317 536
Fax: (0) 2 2333 460
http://www.utu.fi/erill/instmigr

Finnish Canadian Society
P.O. Box 282
00121 Helsinki
http://www.sci.fi/~suomikan/home.html

League of Finnish-Australian Societies
Mariankatu 8
00170 Helsinki
Tel: (0) 9 631 546
Fax. (0) 9 622 2594
http://www.pp.clinet.fi/~ozleague/
english.html

OUTSIDE FINLAND

Finnish American Heritage Society of Connecticut
P.O. Box 252
Canterbury, CT 06331
U.S.A.
Tel: 860 546 6671
http://www.fahs-ct.org

Finnish-American Historical Society of the West
P.O. Box 5522
Portland, OR 97228
U.S.A.
http://www.teleport.com/~finamhsw

Immigration History Research Center
University of Minnesota
311 Andersen Library
222 21st Avenue S.
Minneapolis, MN 55455 0439
U.S.A
Tel: 612 625 4800
Fax: 612 626 0018
http://www1.umn.edu/ihrc

Finnish Historical Society of Canada
P.O. Box 911
Sudbury, ON P3E 4S4
Canada

Swedish Finn Historical Society
P.O. Box 17264
Seattle, WA 98107 0964
U.S.A.
Tel: 206 706 0738
Fax: 206 782 5813
http://home1.gte.net/SFHS/index.htm

WEBSITES

Family History Finland
http://www.open.org/~rumcd/genweb/
finn.html

Finnish Genealogy: Where do I Begin? by Timothy Laitila Vincent
http://www.utu.fi/erill/instmigr/art/
finngeneal.htm

List of Finnish societies
http://sss.genealogia.fi/stutkyh

Web History of Finland
http://kyyppari.hkkk.fi/~k21206/
finhist.html

France

Bibliothèque Nationale de France
Site François-Mitterrand/Tolbiac
Collections audiovisuelles et imprimées
11, quai François Mauriac
75706 Paris cedex 13
Tel: (0) 1 53 79 53 79
http://www.bnf.fr

Site Richelieu
Collections spécialisées
58, rue de Richelieu/2, rue de Louvois
75002 Paris
Tel: (0) 1 47 03 81 26

Fédération Francaise de Généalogie
3, rue Turbigo
75001 Paris
Tel: (0) 1 40 13 00 88
Fax: (0) 1 40 13 00 89
http://www.genefede.org

La recherche des origines familiales des pionniers du Québec
Search of the family origins of the
pioneers of Québec
http://www.genefede.org/7_coopinter/
frqc.html

Karolus (Genealogical Directory)
13, Street of the Brothers Dreyfus
02600 Villers-Cotterêts
http://www.karolus.org

Librairie Généalogique de la Voûte
24, rue de la voûte
75012 Paris
Tel/Fax: (0) 1 43 07 81 63
http://perso.cybercable.fr/voute

OUTSIDE FRANCE

American-French Genealogical Society
78 Earle Street
Woonsocket, RI 02895
U.S.A.
Tel/Fax: 401 765 6141
Mailing Address:
P.O. Box 2113
Pawtucket, RI 02861 0113
U.S.A.
http://www.afgs.org

Anglo-French Family History Society
31 Collingwood Walk
Andover, Hampshire SP10 1PU
United Kingdom
http://www.karolus.org/membres/affhs/
AS-AFFHS.HTM

La Société généalogique canadienne-française
3440, rue Davidson
Montrèal, QC H1W 2Z5
Canada
Tel: 514 527 1010
Fax: 514 527 0265

WEBSITES

Acadian and French-Canadian Genealogy
http://ourworld.compuserve.com/
homepages/lwjones

Acadian Genealogy Home Page
http://www.acadian.org

France GenWeb
http://francegenweb.org

FrancoGene.com
http://www.francogene.com

Geneactes: Search for civil-status records in France
http://www.geneactes.org

Genealogy and History in France
http://www.gefrance.com

Germany

Arbeitskreis donauschwäbischer Familienforscher e.V.
(Working Group of Danube-Swabian Genealogists)
AKdFF-Bibliothek
Goldmühlestr 30
71065 Sindelfingen
http://www2.genealogy.net/gene/vereine/AKdFF/akdff-en.html

Bundesarchiv (Federal Archives)
Potsdamer Strasse 1
56075 Koblenz
Tel: (0) 2615 050
Fax: (0) 2615 0522 6
http://www.bundesarchiv.de

Branches:
Aachen
Abteigarten 6
52076 Aachen
Tel: (0) 2408 1470
Fax: (0) 2408 1473 7

Bayreuth
Postfach 5025
95424 Bayreuth
Tel: (0) 9214 6010
Fax: (0) 9214 6011 11

Berlin
Postfach 450 569
12175 Berlin
Tel: (0) 1888 7770 0
Fax: (0) 1888 7770 111

Dahlwitz-Hoppegarten
Lindenallee 55–57
15366 Dahlwitz-Hoppegarten
Tel: (0) 3342 2368 0
Fax: (0) 3342 3006 28

Freiburg
Postfach, 79024 Freiburg
Wiesentalstasse 10
79115 Freiburg
Tel: (0) 7614 7817 0
Fax: (0) 7614 7817 900

Ludwigsburg
Schorndorfer Strasse 58
71638 Ludwigsburg
Mailing address:
Postfach 1144
71611 Ludwigsburg
Tel: (0) 7141 8992 14
Fax: (0) 7141 8992 12

Rastatt
Schloß, Herrenstrasse 18
76437 Rastatt
Mailing Address:
Postfach 1235
76402 Rastatt
Tel: (0) 7222 7713 90
Fax: (0) 7222 7713 97

St. Augustin-Hangelar
Bundesgrenzschutzstr. 100
53757 St. Augustin-Hangelar
Tel: (0) 1888 7400 00
Fax: (0) 2241 9283 33

Deutsche Zentralstelle für Genealogie
(German Central Office for Genealogy)
Sächsisches Staatsarchiv Leipzig
Abt. Deutsche Zentralstelle für Genealogie
Schongauer Strasse 1
D-04329 Leipzig
Tel: (0) 3412 5555 51
Fax: (0) 3412 5555 55
http://www.genealogy.net/gene/reg/DEU/dzfg-en.html (unofficial page)

Zentralstelle für Personen und Familiengeschichte
(Institut für Genealogie)
Birkenweg 13
D-61381 Friedrichsdorf

East European Genealogical Society
P.O. Box 2536
Winnipeg, MB R3C 4A7
Canada
Tel: 204 989 3292 (voicemail)
http://www.eegsociety.org

Society for German Genealogy in Eastern Europe
P.O. Box 905, Stn 'M'
Calgary, AB T2P 2J3
Canada
http://www.sggee.org

Anglo-German Family History Society
14 River Reach
Teddington, TW11 9QL
United Kingdom
http://www.art-science.com/agfhs/index.html

American Historical Society of Germans from Russia
631 D Street
Lincoln, NE 68502 1199
U.S.A.
Tel: 402 474 3363
Fax: 402 474 7229
http://www.ahsgr.org

Bukovina Society of the Americas
P.O. Box 81
Ellis, KS 67637 0081
U.S.A.
Tel: 913 625 9492
Fax: 913 726 4568
http://members.aol.com/LJensen/bukovina.html

Federation of East European Family History Societies
P.O. Box 510898
Salt Lake City, UT 94151 0898
U.S.A.
http://feefhs.org

Galizien German Descendants
653 Douglas Avenue
Elgin, IL 60120 3633
U.S.A.
http://feefhs.org/gal/ggd/frg-ggd.html

German Genealogical Society of America

2125 Wright Avenue, Suite C-9
La Verne, CA 91750
U.S.A.
Tel: 909 593 0509
http://feefhs.org/ggsa/frg-ggsa.html

German-Bohemian Heritage Society

P.O. Box 822
New Ulm, MN 56073 0822
U.S.A.
http://www.rootsweb.com/~gbhs

Gluckstal Colonies Research Association

611 Esplanade
Redondo Beach, CA 90277 4130
U.S.A.
Tel: 310 540 1872
http://www.feefhs.org/FRGGCRA/gcra.html

Palatines to America

611 East Weber Road
Columbus, OH 43211 1097
U.S.A.
Tel: 614 267 4700
http://genealogy.org/~palam/ia_index.htm

WEBSITES

Genealogy: German Migration to South Africa

http://www.genealogy.net/gene/reg/WELT/rsa.html

Genealogy Page of Andreas Hanacek

http://my.bawue.de/~hanacek/egene/egenepag.htm

German Genealogy: Resources for Genealogists in German-speaking Areas

http://www.genealogy.net/gene/genealogy.html

German Migration Resource Center

http://www.germanmigration.com

German Records in the Russian State Historic Archive

http://feefhs.org/blitz/blitzgr.html

German South African Resource Page

http://www.geocities.com/Heartland/Meadows/7589/index.html

Odessa—German-Russian Genealogical Library

http://pixel.cs.vt.edu/library/odessa.html

Greece

Historical and Ethnological Society of Greece

National Historical Museum
The Old Parliament Building
Stadiou Strasse
105 61 Athens
Tel: 132 37 617/132 22 266/132 26 370
Fax: 132 13 786
http://www.culture.gr/4/42/421/42103/42103e/e42103e1.html

OUTSIDE GREECE

Greek Association of Family History and Tradition

P.O. Box 711027
Salt Lake City, UT 84171
U.S.A.
E-mail: 801 569 9201
http://www.sipeo.org

WEBSITES

GreeceGenWeb

http://mediterraneangenweb.org/greece

Greek Legacy

http://www.greeklegacy.com

Hungary

National Archives of Hungary

1014 Budapest
Bécsi kapu tér 2–4
Mailing address:
P.O. Box 3
1250 Budapest
Tel: 1 356 5811
Fax: 1 212 1619
http://www.natarch.hu/english/mol.htm

Stadtarchiv Budapest

(Budapest City Archives)
H-1052 Budapest
Városház u. 9–11
Tel: 1 317 2033
Fax: 1 318 3319
http://www.bparchiv.hu

OUTSIDE HUNGARY

Arbeitskreis donauschwäbischer Familienforscher e.V.

(Danube-Swabian Genealogists)
AKdFF-Bibliothek
Goldmühlestr. 30
71065 Sindelfingen
Germany
http://www2.genealogy.net/gene/vereine/AKdFF/akdff-en.html

Federation of East European Family History Societies

P.O. Box 510898
Salt Lake City, UT 94151 0898
U.S.A.
http://feefhs.org/

Hungarian/American Friendship Society: Hungarian & Slovak Genealogy

2701 Corabel Lane #34
Sacramento, CA 95821 5233
U.S.A.
Tel: 916 489 9599
http://www.dholmes.com/hafs.html

Hungarian Genealogical Society of Greater Cleveland

c/o Gustav Enyedy
7830 Sugar Bush Lane
Gates Mills, OH 44040
U.S.A.
Tel: 440 423 3469
http://community.cleveland.com/cc/hungariangenealogy

Society for German Genealogy in Eastern Europe
P.O. Box 905, Stn 'M'
Calgary, AB T2P 2J3
Canada
http://www.sggee.org

WEBSITES

Alex Glendinning's Hungarian Genealogy Pages
http://user.super.net.uk/~glen/Hungarianintro.html

Danube-Swabians—Donauschwaben
http://www2.genealogy.net/gene/reg/ESE/dschwaben.html

Hungarian Genealogy
http://hallai.cjb.net

Hungarotips
http://www.hungarotips.com

HungaryGenWeb
http://www.rootsweb.com/~wghungar

Radix: Genealogy Research in Hungary
http://www.bogardi.com/gen

Slovak and Carpatho-Rusyn Genealogy
http://www.iarelative.com/slovakia.htm

India

National Archives of India
Janpath
New Delhi 110001
Tel: (0) 755 540017
http://nationalarchives.nic.in

OUTSIDE INDIA

The British Library
Oriental and India Office Collections
96 Euston Road
London NW1 2DB
United Kingdom
Tel: (0) 207 412 7873
Fax: (0) 207 412 7641
http://www.bl.uk/collections/oriental/records/overview.html

East India Group, NZ Society of Genealogists
Jacquie Fisher
34 Sarah Todd Lane
Waimauku 1250
New Zealand
http://www.ozemail.com.au/~clday/nzsg.htm

Families in British India Society
Tony Fuller, Secretary FIBIS
81 Rosewood Avenue
Elm Park, Hornchurch
Essex RM12 5LD
United Kingdom
http://www.links.org/FIBIS

Indische Genealogische Vereniging (Dutch Indies Genealogical Association)
c/o Volendamlaan 1030
2547 CS The Hague
The Netherlands
http://www.ozemail.com.au/~clday/igsh.htm

WEBSITES

Cochin Churchbook, India, 1751–1804
http://members.home.nl/dessa/cochin.htm

Family History in India
http://www.ozemail.com.au/~clday

Passages to India: Genealogy Resources In British India
http://users.synflux.com.au/~sylcec/index.htm

European Cemeteries in India
http://www.ozemail.com.au/~clday/cem.htm

Iceland

Ministry of Health and Social Security
Laugavegi 116
IS-150 Reykjavík
Tel: 560 9700
Fax: 551 9165

OUTSIDE ICELAND

The Icelandic National League of North America
Sigrid Johnson
330 Brock Street, Winnipeg
MB R3N 0Y9, Canada
Tel: 204 474 6345
E-mail: sjonso1@videon.wave.ca

Embassy of Iceland
1156 15th Street, NW, Suite 1200
Washington, D.C. 20005 1704
U.S.A.
Tel: 202 265 6653
Fax: 202 265 6656
E-mail: icemb.wash@utn.stjr.is
Home page: http://www.iceland.org

Ireland

Also refer to United Kingdom entry for Northern Ireland

The Genealogical Office
2 Kildare Street
Dublin 2
Tel: (0) 1 661 8811
http://www.scripts.ireland.com/ancestor/browse/emigration/australia/genealogical.html

General Register Office
Joyce House
8–11 Lombard Street
Dublin 2
Tel: (0) 1 635 4000
http://www.groireland.ie

The National Archives of Ireland
Bishop Street
Dublin 8
Tel: (0) 1 407 2300
Fax: (0) 1 407 2333
E-mail: mail@nationalarchives.ie
http://www.nationalarchives.ie/general.html

The National Library of Ireland
Kildare Street
Dublin 2
Tel: (0) 1 603 0200
Fax: (0) 1 676 6690
http://www.heanet.ie/natlib/contact.html

Registry of Deeds
King's Inn
Henrietta Street
Dublin 1
Tel: (0) 1 670 7500
Fax: (0) 1 804 8406
http://www.irlgov.ie/landreg/
rd_order.htm

Land Registry (Louth, Monaghan, Cavan, Donegal, Longford, Leitrim, Meath, Westmeath)
Chancey Lane
Dublin 7
http://www.irlgov.ie/landreg/
about_us.htm

Land Registry (Dublin, Sligo, Mayo, Galway, Clare, Roscommon)
Setanta Centre
Nassau Street
Dublin 2
http://www.irlgov.ie/landreg/
about_us.htm

Land Registry (Kildare, Wicklow)
Irish Life Centre
Block 1
Lower Abbey Street
Dublin 1
http://www.irlgov.ie/landreg/
about_us.htm

Land Registry (Carlow, Kerry, Waterford, Wexford, Limerick, Laois, Offaly, Tipperary)
Cork Road
Waterford
Tel: (0) 51 303 000
http://www.irlgov.ie/landreg/
about_us.htm

Society of Friends Library
Swanbrook House
Morehampton Road
Donnybrook
Dublin 4
http://www.local.ie/content/25654.shtml

Royal Irish Academy
19 Dawson Street
Dublin 2
Tel: (0) 1 676 2570
Fax: (0) 1 676 4222
http://www.ria.ie/index.html

Trinity College Library
College Street
Dublin 2
Tel: (0) 1 677 2941
Fax: (0) 1 671 9003
http://www.tcd.ie/Library

WEBSITES

Repositories of Irish Records
http://www.ihaonline.com/ref_reposit.
htm

Ireland Now
www.irelandnow.com/genealogy/
intro.html

Italy

Archivio Centrale Dello Stato
(Central Archives of the State)
Piazzale degli Archivi
27 00144 Roma
Tel: 06 545 481
Fax: 06 541 3620
E-mail: acs@archivi.beniculturali.it
http://www.archivi.beniculturali.it

OUTSIDE ITALY

Italian Genealogical Group
P.O. Box 626
Bethpage, NY 11714 0626
U.S.A.
E-mail: info@italiangen.org
http://www.italiangen.org/default.stm

Italian Genealogy Society of America
P.O. Box 8571
Cranston, RI 02920 8571
U.S.A.
http://users.loa.com/~del2jdcd/
igsa.html

Italian Historical Society of America
111 Columbia Heights
Brooklyn, NY 11201
U.S.A.
Tel: 718 852 2929
http://www.italianhistorical.org/

WEBSITES

Introduction to Italian Genealogy
http://www.regalis.com/introgen.htm

Italian Genealogy, Heritage, Culture, and Databases on the WWW
http://www.cimorelli.com/pie

Italian Genealogy Homepage
http://www.italgen.com

Italian History Index
http://www.iue.it/LIB/SISSCO/VL/
hist-italy/archives.html

Lou Alfano's Italian Genealogy
http://www.geocities.com/Athens/Acropol
is/1709/index.html

Jamaica

National Library of Jamaica and Jamaica Historical Society
12 East Street, Kingston
Jamaica, West Indies

Registrar General's Office
Twickenham Park, Spanish Town
Jamaica, West Indies

Jamaica Archives
Spanish Town
Jamaica, West Indies

LDS Family History Center,
48 Gore Terrace, Kingston
Jamaica, West Indies
Tel: 876 925 8492

Japan

National Archive Japan
Kitanomaru Koen 3–2
Chiyoda-ku, Tokyo 102
Tel: (0) 3 3214 0621
Fax: (0) 3 3212 8806
http://www.sorifu.go.jp/koubunsho

Department of Social Welfare and War Victims' Relief Bureau
2–2, Kasumigaseki 1 Chome
Chiyoda-ku, Tokyo
Tel: (0) 3 3503 1711

OUTSIDE JAPAN

Japanese American National Museum
369 East First Street
Los Angeles, CA 90012
U.S.A.
Tel: 213 625 0414
Fax: 213 625 1770
http://www.lausd.k12.ca.us/janm/
index.htm

WEBSITES

Japan GenWeb
http://www.rootsweb.com/~jpnwgw

Latvia

Central State History Archives
Centralais Valsts vestures arhivs
Slokas iela 16
Riga, LV 226007
Tel: 613118

Central State Archives
Centralais Valsts vestures arhivs
Bezdeligu iela 1
Riga, LV 226007

Centralais Valsts Kino-Foto-Fono-Dokumentu arhivs
(Central State Cine-Phono-Photo
Document Archives)
Skuna iela 11
Riga, LV 226007

OUTSIDE LATVIA

Herder Institute Marburg
Gisonenweg 5-7
D-35037 Marburg
Germany
Tel: (0) 6421 1840
Fax: (0) 6421 1841 39
http://www.uni-marburg.de/herder-institut/english/welcome.html

WEBSITES

Dag's Latvian Genealogy Page
http://feefhs.org/baltic/lv/frg-dag.html

East Prussian Genealogy Homepage
http://www.halleluja.de/genealogy

The Latvian Genealogy Homepage
http://www.world4you.com/genealogy/
latvia

Latvian History
http://www.latnet.lv/info_Latvia/
history.html

Lithuania

Central Vital Records
(vital records after 1915)
Lietuvos Centrinis Metriku Archyvas
K. Kalinausko g. 21. 2000 Vilnius
Tel: 2 637846

State Historical Archives
(vital records up to 1915)
Gerosios Vilties 10
Vilnius 2015
Tel: 2 765290
Fax: 2 765318

Central State Archives
(property records)
Oskaro Milasiaus 21
2051 Vilnius

Archives of Public Organizations
(World War II records)
Gedimino 12
2039 Vilnius

OUTSIDE LITHUANIA

The Balzekas Museum of Lithuanian Culture
6500 South Pulaski Road
Chicago, IL 60629 5136
U.S.A.
Tel: 773 582 6500

Mexico

El Archivo General de la Nación
Eduardo Molina y Albañiles s/n
Col. Penitenciaría Ampliación
Deleg. Venustiano Carranza
15350, México, D.F.
Tel: 5133 9900 ext. 19371 and 19402
Fax: 5789 5296
http://www.agn.gob.mx

Academia Mexicana de Genealogía y Heráldica
Jorge V. Barbabosa y Torres, Presidente
Calle Misión #11, Fraccionamiento
Lomas de Santa Fé
D.F. CP 01210M

OUTSIDE MEXICO

Hispanic Genealogical Society
P.O. Box 231271
Houston, TX 77223 1271
U.S.A.
http://www.brokersys.com/~joguerra/
jose.html

Institute of Genealogy and History for Latin America
316 West 500 North
St. George, UT 84770
U.S.A.
Tel: 801 652 1710
Fax: 801 674 5787
E-mail: lplatt@infowest.com

WEBSITES

MexicoGenWeb
http://www.rootsweb.com/~mexwgw

Netherlands

Centraal Bureau voor Genealogie
Prins Willem Alexanderhof 22
Postbus 11755
2502 AT The Hague
Tel: (0) 70 315 0500
http://www.cbg.nl

Nederlandse Genealogische Vereniging
Dutch Genealogical Society
P.O. Box 976
1000 AZ Amsterdam
http://www.ngv.nl

Rijksarchiefdienst (State Archives)
Prins Willem-Alexanderhof 20
The Hague
Mailing address:
Postbus 90520
2509 LMís-Gravenhage
Tel: (0) 70 331 5400
Fax: (0) 70 331 5499
http://www.archief.nl/rad
http://www-lias.rad.archief.nl/genlias

Royal Netherlands Society for Genealogy and Heraldry
Prins Willem-Alexanderhof 24
The Hague
Mailing address:
Postbus 85630
NL-2508 CH The Hague
Tel: (0) 70 385 5965
http://www.knggw.nl/indexuk.html

OUTSIDE THE NETHERLANDS

Dutch Australian Centre
222 Waldron Road
Chester Hill NSW 2162
Australia
Tel: (0) 2 9644 7327
http://www.zip.com.au/%7Ejoopmul/dac.html

WEBSITES

A Dutch-Australian Connection
http://users.bigpond.net.au/dutch_aussie

Dutch-Canadian Online
http://www.magma.ca/~louievb/index.html

Dutch GenWeb
http://members.tripod.com/~westland/index.htm

Dutch Immigrants to New Zealand
http://www.geocities.com/SoHo/Veranda/2663/klompen.html

Digital Resources: Netherlands and Belgium
http://geneaknowhow.net/digi/resources.html

NedGen Genealogy
http://genealogie.thewebconnection.nl

Yvette's Dutch Genealogy Web Page
http://www.twente.nl/~genealogy

New Zealand

Births, Deaths and Marriages Office
Central Registry
(PO Box 31 115)
191 High Street
Lower Hutt
Tel: (0) 4 570 6300
Fax: (0) 4 566 5311
E-mail: bdm.nz@dia.govt.nz
http://www.bdm.govt.nz/DIAwebsite.nsf/

Archives New Zealand
Auckland Regional Office
525 Mt Wellington Highway
Auckland
Tel: (0) 9 270 1100
Fax: (0) 9 276 4472
E-mail: auckland@archives.govt.nz
http://www.archives.govt.nz/archivesnz/offices/offices.html

Archives New Zealand
Head Office
10 Mulgrave Street
Thorndon, Wellington
Tel: (0) 4 499 5595
Fax: (0) 4 495 6210
E-mail: wellington@archives.govt.nz
http://www.archives.govt.nz/archivesnz/offices/offices.html

Archives New Zealand
Christchurch Regional Office
90 Peterborough Street
Christchurch
Tel: (0) 3 377 0760
Fax: (0) 3 365 2662
E-mail: christchurch@archives.govt.nz
http://www.archives.govt.nz/archivesnz/offices/offices.html

Archives New Zealand
Dunedin Regional Office
556 George Street
Dunedin
Tel: (0) 3 477 0404
Fax: (0) 3 477 0422
E-mail: dunedin@archives.govt.nz
http://www.archives.govt.nz/archivesnz/offices/offices.html

Central City Library
44–46 Lorne Street
Auckland
Tel: (0) 9 377 0209
Fax: (0) 9 307 7741
http://www.akcity.govt.nz/library/family/family.html

Central City Library
Corner of Gloucester Street and Oxford Terrace
Christchurch
Tel: (0) 3 379 6914
Fax: (0) 3 365 1751
http://www.ccc.govt.nz/library/Central

WEBSITES

New Zealand Genealogy Search Engine
http://www.downtown.co.nz/genealogy/search.shtml

New Zealand Record Categories
http://www.spicercowan.co.nz/~pycroftb/AGWebNZL/nzlcat.htm

Norway

Norwegian Emigrant Museum and Genealogical Society
Åkershagan
2312 Ottestad
Tel: 62 57 48 50
Fax: 62 57 48 51
http://www.hamarnett.no/emigrantmuseum

Norwegian Emigration and Genealogy Center
Strandkaien 31
N-4005 Stavanger
Tel: 51 53 88 60
Fax: 51 53 88 63
http://www.utvandrersenteret.no

Norwegian Historical Data Center
The Faculty of Social Sciences
University of Tromsø
N-9037 Tromsø
Tel: 77 64 41 77
http://draug.rhd.isv.uit.no/rhd/
indexeng.htm

Riksarkivaren (National Archives)
Folke Bernadottes vei 21
Postboks 4013 Ullevl stadion
N-0806 Oslo
Tel: 22 02 26 00
Fax: 22 23 74 89
http://digitalarkivet.uib.no/
index-eng.htm

**Statsarkivet i Oslo (Østfold,
Akershus, Oslo)**
(Regional Records)
Folke Bernadottes vei 21
Postboks 4015 Ullevl stadion
N-0806 Oslo
Tel: 22 02 26 00
Fax: 22 23 74 89

**Statsarkivet i Hamar (Hedmark,
Oppland)**
(Regional Records)
Lille Strandgate 3
Postboks 533
N-2304 Hamar
Tel: 62 52 36 42
Fax: 62 52 94 48

**Statsarkivet i Kongsberg (Buskerud,
Vestfold, Telemark)**
(Regional Records)
Frogsvei 44
N-3611 Kongsberg
Tel: 32 86 99 00
Fax: 32 86 99 10

**Statsarkivet i Kristiansand (Aust-
Agder, Vest-Agder)**
(Regional Records)
Märthas vei 1
Serviceboks 402, 4604 Kristiansand
N-4613 Kristiansand
Tel: 38 14 55 00
Fax: 38 14 55 01

Statsarkivet i Stavanger (Rogaland)
(Regional Records)
Bergjelandsgt. 30
N-4012 Stavanger
Tel: 51 50 12 60
Fax: 51 50 12 90

**Statsarkivet i Bergen (Hordaland,
Sogn og Fjordane)**
(Regional Records)
Årstadveien 22
N-5009 Bergen
Tel: 55 31 50 70
Fax: 55 32 12 65

**Statsarkivet i Trondheim (Møre og
Romsdal, Sør-Trøndelag, Nord-
Trøndelag, Nordland)**
(Regional Records)
Høgskoleveien 12
Postboks 2825 ElgesEter
N-7432 Trondheim
Tel: 73 88 45 00
Fax: 73 88 45 40

**Statsarkivet i Tromsø (Records from
Troms, Finnmark, Spitsbergen)**
(Regional Records)
N-9293 Tromsø
Tel: 77 67 66 11
Fax: 77 67 65 20

University of Oslo
(Regional Records)
The Documentation Project
4. floor, N.H. Abels house
Blindern
Mailing address:
P.O. Box 1123, Blindern
0317 Oslo
Tel: 22 85 49 82
Fax: 22 85 49 83
http://www.dokpro.uio.no/engelsk
/index.html

OUTSIDE NORWAY

Carl B. Ylvisaker Library
Concordia College
Moorhead, MN 56562
U.S.A.
Tel: 218 299 3237/3241
http://home.cord.edu/dept/library/
Library_Departments/genealogy_
services.html

**Norwegian-American Genealogical
Association**
c/o Minnesota Genealogical Society
5768 Olson Memorial Highway
Golden Valley, MN 55422 5014
U.S.A.
http://www.mtn.org/mgs/branches/naga/
nagaindx.htm

WEBSITES

The Bygdelag Page
http://www.hfaa.org/bygdelag/index.
shtml

**Norwegian Surname database from
Statistics Norway**
http://www.ssb.no/english/subjects/00/
navn_en

Peru

Archivo General de la Nacion
Jr. Manuel Cuadros
s/n Palacio de Justicia
Lima
Tel: 427 5930/5939
Fax: 428 2829
http://agn.perucultural.org.pe

Philippine Republic

National Statistics Office
Vital Statistics Section
3rd floor, Vibal Building
Times Street cor EDSA
West Triangle, Quezon City
Tel: 926 73 04
http://www.census.gov.ph/data/aboutnso/
centralofcs.html

WEBSITES

Philippines GenWeb
http://www.geocities.com/Heartland/
Ranch/9121

Tanikalang Ginto
http://www.filipinolinks.com/home/
genealogy.html

Poland

Archives in Poland
00-950 Warszawa
P.O. Box 1005
ul.Dluga 6
Tel: 22 31 32 06
Fax: 22 31 75 63
http://ciuw.warman.net.pl/alf/archiwa/
index.eng.html

Archiwum Glówne Akt Dawnych
(Central archives of Historical Records
in Warsaw)
ul. Dluga 7, Pl 00-263 Warszawa
Tel: 22 831 54 91
Fax: 22 831 16 08
http://members.nbci.com/agadadm

Polskie Towarzystwo Heraldyczne
Rynek Starego Miasta 29/31
00-272 Warszawa
http://www.dig.com.pl/PTHer/
index.html

OUTSIDE POLAND

Federation of East European Family History Societies
P.O. Box 510898
Salt Lake City, UT 94151 0898
U.S.A.
http://feefhs.org

Polish American Cultural Center
308 Walnut Street
Philadelphia, PA 19106
U.S.A.
Tel: 215 922 1700
Fax: 215 922 1518
http://www.polishamericancenter.org

The Polish American Museum
16 Belleview Avenue
Port Washington, New York 11050
U.S.A.
Tel: 516 883 6542/767 1936
http://www.liglobal.com/t_i/attractions/
museums/polish

Polish Genealogical Society of America
Polish Museum of America
984 North Milwaukee Avenue
Chicago, IL 60622 4199
U.S.A.
Tel: 773 384 3352
http://www.pgsa.org

WEBSITES

Poland GenWeb
http://www.rootsweb.com/~polwgw

Genealogia Polska
http://republika.pl/slucki

Genealogia Dynastyczna (Dynastic Genealogy)
http://www.befado.com.pl/JuRy/
RJ_Genealogia.html

Historia Polski
http://intercafe.zamosc.tpsa.pl/linki/
Histpol.htm

PolishRoots.org
http://polishroots.org

Polish Genealogy Research In The Russian State Historic Archives
http://feefhs.org/blitz/blitzprr.html

Portugal

Arquivo National da Torre do Tombo (National Archive)
Largo de S. Bento, 1200
Lisboa

Biblioteca Nacional de Lisboa (National Library)
Campo Grande 83
1749-081 Lisboa
Tel: (0) 21 798 2000
Fax: (0) 21 798 2140
http://www.bn.pt

OUTSIDE PORTUGAL

American-Portuguese Genealogical and Historical Society
P.O. Box 644
Taunton, MA 02780 0644
U.S.A.
http://www.tauntonma.com/apghs

Portuguese Ancestry
Rosemarie Capodicci
1155 Santa Ana
Seaside, CA 93955
U.S.A.
http://www.dholmes.com/ancestry.html

WEBSITES

António Carlos Godinho Janes Monteiro
http://planeta.clix.pt/janesmonteiro

AOL Hispanic Genealogy Group
http://members.aol.com/mrosado007/
index.htm

Genealogía
http://www.genealogia.com

Portuguese Genealogy Home Page, by Doug da Rocha Holmes
http://www.dholmes.com/rocha1.html

Puerto Rico

Sociedad Puertorriqueña de Genealogía
OSS # 239, Apartado Postal 70292
San Juan de Puerto Rico 00936-8292
E-mail: spg@genealogiapr.com
http://www.GenealogiaPR.com

OUTSIDE PUERTO RICO

The Hispanic Genealogical Society of New York
Murray Hill Station, P.O. Box 818
New York, NY 10156 0602
http://www.hispanicgenealogy.com

The Genealogy of Puerto Rico
http://www.rootsweb.com/~prwgw/
index.html

Romania

Center for Romanian Studies
Oficiul Postal I
Casuta Postala 108
6600 Iasi
Tel: (0) 32 219 000
Fax (0) 32 219 010
http://www.romanianstudies.ro

GenealogyRO Group
O.P. 2—C.P. 416
Timisoara—Cod 1900
Judetul Timis
Tel: (0) 92 378 390
http://www.feefhs.org/ro/genro/
frggenro.html

Romanian State Archives
Str. Andrei Mocioni nr 8
1900 Timisoara
Tel: (0) 56 193 463

OUTSIDE ROMANIA

Bukovina Society of the Americas
P.O. Box 81
Ellis, KS 67637 0081
http://members.aol.com/LJensen/
bukovina.html

United Romanian Society
18405 West Nine Mile Road
Southfield, MI 48075
Mailing address:
P.O. Box 03189
Detroit, MI 48203
U.S.A.
http://www.feefhs.org/ro/urs/
hurs-toc.html

WEBSITES

Donauschwaben in the Banat, Including the Arader Land
http://www.genealogy.net/gene/reg/ESE/
dsbanat.html

Jewish Genealogical Records in Romania at the Timisoara, Arad, and Caransebes State Archives
http://www.feefhs.org/ro/genro/rosa1jew.
html

Romania WorldGenWeb
http://www.rootsweb.com/~romwgw

Russia

Russian-American Genealogical Archival Service
1929 18th Street N.W., Suite 1112
Washington, D.C. 20009 1710
U.S.A
http://feefhs.org/ragas/frgragas.html

Russian-Baltic Information Center
Dumskaya ulitsa, dom 3, 5 etazh, PEN-club
St. Petersburg, 191011
Tel: 312 14 40
Fax: 314 87 85
http://feefhs.org/blitz/frgblitz.html

Russian Germans of St.Petersburg
22–24 Nevsky Avenue
Petrikirche
St. Petersburg
Tel: 219 40 96
Fax: 219 40 95
http://www.d-inter.ru/rg-acad/
default.htm

OUTSIDE RUSSIA

American Historical Society of Germans from Russia
631 D Street
Lincoln, NE 68502 1199
U.S.A.
Tel: 402 474 3363
Fax: 402 474 7229
http://www.ahsgr.org

Bukovina Society of the Americas
P.O. Box 81
Ellis, KS 67637 0081
U.S.A.
http://members.aol.com/LJensen/
bukovina.html

Germans from Russia Heritage Society
1008 East Central Avenue
Bismarck, ND 58501
U.S.A.
Tel: 701 223 6167
http://www.grhs.com

Glückstal Colonies Research Association
611 Esplanade
Redondo Beach, CA 90277 4130
U.S.A.
Tel: 310 540 1872
http://www.feefhs.org/FRGGCRA/
gcra.html

Russian-American Genealogical Archival Service
1929 18th Street N.W., Suite 1112
Washington, D.C. 20009 1710
U.S.A.
http://feefhs.org/ragas/frgragas.html

Russian-Baltic Information Center
907 Mission Avenue
San Rafael, CA 94901
U.S.A.
Fax:415 453 0343
http://feefhs.org/blitz/frgblitz.html

WEBSITES

Jewish Genealogy Research In Russia
http://feefhs.org/blitz/blitzjgr.html

Odessa: A German Russian Genealogical Library
http://pixel.cs.vt.edu/library/
odessa.html

Russian Archives Online
http://www.abamedia.com/rao/
index.html

Slovak Republic

Archival Research in Slovakia
Archives Department, Ministry of Interior
Krikzova 7
81104 Bratislava
Tel: 7 5249 6051
http://www.civil.gov.sk/arch.htm

Matica Slovenska
Ustav pre zahranicnych Slovakov
(Foreign Slovaks Institute)
Frantiskanska 2, Bratislava
Tel. 7 335 374
http://www.matica.sk

Slovak Genealogical-Heraldic Society at the Matica slovenská
Nám. J.C. Hronského 1
036 52 Martin
Tel: 1 842 31371
Fax: 1 842 33188
http://www.genealogy-heraldry.sk
http://www.genealogy-heraldry.sk/eng/eng.htm (English)

OUTSIDE THE SLOVAK REPUBLIC

Carpatho-Rusyn Knowledge Base and Society
125 Westland Drive
Pittsburgh, PA 15217
U.S.A.
http://www.carpatho-rusyn.org

WEBSITES

Slovak Republic GenWeb
http://www.rootsweb.com/~svkwgw

Carpatho-Rusyn Genealogy Web Page
http://www.rusyn.com

Eastern Slovakia: Slovak and Carpatho-Rusyn Genealogy Research Pages
http://www.iarelative.com/slovakia.htm

Slovenia

Archives of the Republic of Slovenia
Zvezdarska 1
SLO-1000 Ljubljana
Tel: 61 125 1122
Fax: 61 216 5511

Slovenian Genealogical Society
(Skofja Loka, Slovenia)
Lipica 7
4220 Skofja Loka
http://www.feefhs.org/slovenia/si/frg-sigs.html

OUTSIDE SLOVENIA

Slovenian Genealogical Society, International
34 Camp Street
Dayleford Vic 3460
Australia
http://www.sloveniangenealogy.org/Australia.htm

Slovenian Genealogical Society, International
631 Dobson Road
Duncan, BC V9L 2L8
Canada
http://www.sloveniangenealogy.org/BritColumbia.htm

Slovenian Genealogical Society
Frank Pinter, Jr.
145 Athenia Drive
Stoney Creek, ON L8J 1T5
Canada
http://www.sloveniangenealogy.org/Ontario.htm

Slovenian Genealogical Society, International
52 Old Farm Road
Camp Hill, PA 17011 2604
U.S.A.
http://www.sloveniangenealogy.org

WEBSITES

Slovenia Genealogy Research
http://www.angelfire.com/ca/LucyFlick/SloveniaGenealogy.html

South Africa
(Republic of South Africa)

National Archives Depot
Private Bag X236
Pretoria, 0001

South African Data Archive
National Research Foundation
P.O. Box 2600
Pretoria 0001
Tel: (0) 12 481 4192/4158
Fax: (0) 12 481 4020
http://www.nrf.ac.za/sada/index.stm

Durban Archives Repository
Private Bag X22
Nashua House
14 De Mazenod Road
Greyville, Durban 4023
Tel: (0) 31 309 5681/4
Fax: (0) 31 309 5685

Pietermaritzburg Archives Repository
Private Bag X9012
231 Pietermaritz Street
Pietermaritzburg 3200
Tel: (0) 331 42 4712
Fax: (0) 331 94 4353

Transvaal Archives Department
Private Bag X236
24 Hamilton Street
Pretoria 0001
Tel: (0) 12 323 5300
Fax: (0) 12 323 5287

Cape Archives Department
Private Bag X9025
Cape Town 8000
Tel: (0) 21 462 4050
Fax: (0) 21 452 960
http://www.3.fast.co.za/~alittle/rsa.htm#address

Free State Archives Department
Private Bag X20504
37 Elizabeth Street
Bloemfontein 9300

Port Elizabeth Archives Repository
Private Bag X3932
1 De Villiers Street
North End
Port Elizabeth 6056
Tel: (0) 41 54 6451
Fax: (0) 41 54 6451

The State Library
P.O. Box 397
Pretoria

The South African Library
5 Queen Victoria St
Cape Town 8001
Tel: (0) 21 424 6320

Albany Museum Genealogy Department and 1820 Settler Museum
Somerset Street
Grahamstown 6140

Genealogical Institute of South Africa
P.O. Box 3033
Matieland 7602
Tel : (0) 21 887 5070
Fax : (0) 21 887 5031
E-mail: gisa@renet.sun.ac.za
http://www.sun.ac.za/gisa/index1.htm

The Genealogical Society of South Africa
Suite 143
Postnet X2600
Houghton 2041
http://www.rootsweb.com/~zafgssa/Eng

The Cory Library for Historical Research
Rhodes University Library
P.O. Box 184
Grahamstown 6140
Tel: (0) 46 603 8438 (voicemail)
Fax: (0) 46 622 3487
E-mail: S.Rowoldt@ru.ac.za
http://www.rhodes.ac.za/library/cory

Family History Library
Church of the Latter Day Saints
P.O. Box 33642
Johannesburg
Tel: (0) 11 618 1890

WEBSITES

Genealogy Help list
http://www.helplist.org/zaf/index.shtml

Genealogy Home Page
http://home.global.co.za/~mercon

South Korea

WEBSITES

Korean History Project
E-mail: director@koreanhistoryproject.org
http://www.rootsweb.com/~korwgw-s

Spain

Archivo Histurico Nacional
Serrano, 115
28006 Madrid
Tel: 915 618 001/005
Fax: 915 631 199
http://www.mcu.es/lab/archivos/AHN.html

Biblioteca Nacional
Paseo Recoletos 20
28071 Madrid
Tel: 915 807 891/7 757
Fax: 915 775 634
http://www.bne.es

Secciun Nobleza del Archivo Histurico Nacional
Hospital Tavera
C/. Duque de Lerma, 2
45071 Toledo
Tel: 925 210 354
Fax: 925 210 668
http://www.mcu.es/lab/archivos/SN.html

OUTSIDE SPAIN

Hispanic Genealogical Society
P.O. Box 231271
Houston, TX 77223
U.S.A.
http://www.brokersys.com/~joguerra

Spanish American Genealogical Association
P.O. Box 794
Corpus Christi, TX 78403 0794
U.S.A.
Tel: 512 855 1183
http://members.aol.com/sagacorpus/saga.htm

WEBSITES

AOL Hispanic Genealogy Group
http://members.aol.com/mrosado007/index.htm

Archiespa: Spanish Archives Web Page Index
http://rayuela.uc3m.es/~pirio/archiespa

Basque Genealogy Homepage
http://www.primenet.com/~fybarra

Buber's Basque Page
http://students.washington.edu/buber/Basque

Genealogía
http://www.genealogia.com

Genealogía espanola
http://www.geocities.com/CapitolHill/Senate/4593/geneal.html

Our Spanish Heritage: History and Genealogy of South Texas and Northeast Mexico
http://www.geocities.com/Heartland/Ranch/5442

Sweden

Föreningen Släktdata
c/o Gösta Dryselius
Nedergrdsgatan 18
416 54 Göteborg
Tel: (0) 31 84 34 08
http://sd.datatorget.educ.goteborg.se
(includes parish registers on-line)

Krigsarchivet (Military Archives)
Banérgatan 64
SE-115 88 Stockholm
Tel: (0) 87 82 41 00
Fax: (0) 87 82 69 76
http://www.ra.se/KRA/index.html

Riksarchivet (National Archives)
Fyrverkarbacken 13–17
Mailing Address:
P.O. Box 12541
102 29 Stockholm
Tel: (0) 87 37 63 50
Fax: (0) 87 37 64 74
http://www.ra.se
http://www.ra.se/en/index.html (English)

Regional Archives
Landsarkivet i Östersund (Jämtland)
Arkivvägen 1 831 31
S–Östersund
Tel: (0) 63 10 84 85
Fax: (0) 63 12 18 24

Landsarkivet i Uppsala
P.O. Box 135
S–751 04 Uppsala
Tel: (0) 18 65 21 00
Fax: (0) 18 65 21 03

Landsarkivet i Härnösand
P.O. Box 161
S 871 24 Härnösand
Tel: (0) 61 18 35 00
Fax: (0) 61 18 35 28

Landsarkivet i Vadstena
P.O. Box 126
S–592 23 Vadstena
Tel: (0) 6 14 31 30 30
Fax: (0) 6 14 31 02 54

Stockholms stadsarkiv
P.O. Box 22063
S–104 22 Stockholm
Tel: (0) 87 85 83 00
Fax: (0) 86 50 23 30

Landsarkivet i Göteborg
P.O. Box 3009
S–400 10 Göteborg
Tel: (0) 3 17 78 68 00
Fax: (0) 3 17 78 68 25

Landsarkivet i Visby
Visborgsgatan 1
S–621 57 Visby
Tel: (0) 4 98 21 05 14
Fax: (0) 4 98 21 29 55

Landsarkivet i Lund
P.O. Box 2016
S–220 02 Lund
Tel: (0) 46 19 70 00
Fax: (0) 46 19 70 70

Svenska Emigrantinstitutet
Utvandrarnas Hus
P.O. Box 201
351 04 Växjä
Tel: (0) 47 02 01 20
Fax: (0) 47 03 94 16
http://www.svenskaemigrantinstitutet.
g.se

OUTSIDE SWEDEN

**Sveriges Släktforskarfärbund
(Federation of Swedish Genealogical
Societies)**
Tordmulegränd 6
FIN-22100 Mariehamn
Finland
Tel: (0) 18 21204
http://www.genealogi.se/index.htm

American Swedish Institute
2600 Park Ave
Minneapolis, MN 55407
U.S.A.
Tel: 612 871 4907
Fax: 612 871 8682

**Swedish Ancestry Research
Association**
P.O. Box 70603
Worcester, MA 01607 0603
U.S.A.
http://www.members.tripod.com/
~SARAssociation/sara/SARA_Home_
Page.htm

Swedish Finn Historical Society
P.O. Box 17264
Seattle, WA 98107 0964
U.S.A.
Tel: 206 706 0738
Fax: 206 782 5813
http://home1.gte.net/SFHS/index.htm

Swedish Genealogy Society
c/o Minnesota Genealogical Society
5768 Olson Memorial Highway
Golden Valley, MN 55422
U.S.A.
http://www.mtn.org/mgs/sweden/
index.htm

**Swenson Swedish Immigration
Research Center**
Augustana College
639 38th Street
Rock Island, IL 61201 2296
U.S.A.
Tel: 309 794 7204
Fax: 309 794 7443
http://www.augustana.edu/
administration/swenson/index.htm

WEBSITES

**Guidelines for Swedish-American
Genealogical Research**
http://www.augustana.edu/administration/
swenson/fhguide.htm

**Lindesberg, Orebro, Sweden, Vital
Statistics**
http://userdb.rootsweb.com/vitals

**Skånsk Släktforskning (Scanian
Genealogy)**
http://www.algonet.se/~anderzb/genea/
skane.htm

Swedish Genealogy Page
http://www.acc.umu.se/~petersj/
swegen.html

Switzerland

**Schweizerisches Bundesarchiv
(Swiss Federal Archives)**
Archivstrasse 24
CH-3003 Bern
Tel: (0) 31 322 89 89
Fax: (0) 31 322 78 23
http://www.admin.ch/bar

**Schweizerische Landesbibliothek
(Swiss National Library)**
Hallwylstrasse 15
CH-3003 Berne
Switzerland
Tel: (0) 31 322 89 11
Fax: (0) 31 322 84 63
http://www.snl.ch

Schweizerische Gesellschaft für Familienforschung (Swiss Genealogical Society)
Postfach 54
3608 Thun
Switzerland

OUTSIDE SWITZERLAND

Orangeburgh German-Swiss Genealogical Society (OG-SGS)
P.O. Box 974
Orangeburg, SC 29116 0974
U.S.A.
http://www.netside.com/~genealogy/orangeburgh.htm

WEBSITES

Genealogy in French-speaking Switzerland
http://www.unige.ch/biblio/ses/jla/gen/swiss-e.html

Index of Archival Collections held in Swiss Libraries and Archives
http://www.snl.ch/repertoi/alsrep.htm

Neuchael Genealogy Society
http://www.junod.ch/SNG/index_eng.html

Swiss-American Genealogy
http://www.usaswiss.org/swissweb/genealog.html

Swiss Genealogy on the Internet
http://www.eye.ch/swissgen/home-m.htm

Taiwan
(China, Republic of Taiwan)

TaiwanGenWeb
http://www.rootsweb.com/~twnwgw

Turkey

Directorate of Ottoman Archives
Basbakanlik Devlet Arsivleri Genel Müdürlügü Osmanli Arsivi Daire Baskanligi Ticarethane Sokak
Nu: 12.
34410 Sultanahmet Istanbul
Tel.: 212 513 88 70/71/72
Fax: 212 511 75 86

Directorate of Republican Archives
Basbakanlik Devlet Arsivleri Genel Müdürlügü Dokümantasyon Daire Baskanligi Ivedik Caddesi
Nu: 59.
06180 Yenimahalle Ankara
Tel: 312 344 59 09
Fax: 312 315 10 00

WEBSITES

General Directorate of State Archives
http://www.archimac.marun.edu.tr/Organizations/DAGM.spml

TurkeyGenWeb
http://www.rootsweb.com/~turwgw

Ukraine

Tsentral'nyi gosudarstvennyi istoricheskii arkhiv Ukrainy, Kiev (Central State Historical Archive of Ukraine)
252601, Kyïv, vul. Solomians'ka, 24
Tel: (0) 277 30 02/82 22

Tsentral'nyi gosudarstvennyi istoricheskii arkhiv Ukrainy, L'vov (Central State Historical Archive of Ukraine in Lviv)
290008, L'viv, pl. Soborna, 3-a
Tel: (0) 322 72 30 63
Fax: (0) 322 72 35 08

OUTSIDE UKRAINE

Carpatho-Rusyn Knowledge Base and Society
125 Westland Drive
Pittsburgh, PA 15217
U.S.A.
http://www.carpatho-rusyn.org

WEBSITES

Archives in Ukraine
http://www.sabre.org/huri/abbukr

Carpathian Connection
http://www.tccweb.org

Slovak and Carpatho-Rusyn Genealogy
http://www.iarelative.com/slovakia.htm

Theresientaler Heimatbund/ Bernreuther Karpatho-Ukraine (Austrian Immigration)
http://feefhs.org/cru/heimatb1.html

Ukraine WorldGenWeb
http://www.rootsweb.com/~ukrwgw/index.html

United Kingdom

ENGLAND

Public Record Office
Ruskin Avenue
Richmond
Surrey TW9 4DU
Tel: (0) 20 8392 5200
Fax: (0) 20 8392 5286
http://www.pro.gov.uk/readers/enquiry.htm

Family Records Centre
1 Myddelton Street
London EC1R 1UW
Tel: (0) 20 8392 5300
Tel: (0) 151 471 4816 (certificate enquiries)
Fax: (0) 20 8392 5307
E-mail: certificate.services@ons.gov.uk

London Metropolitan Archives
40 Northampton Road
London EC1R 0HB
Tel: (0) 20 7332 3820
Fax: (0) 20 7833 9136.
http://www.corpoflondon.gov.uk/
organisation/services/records.htm

The Corporation of London Records Office
Guildhall
London EC2P 2EJ
Tel: (0) 20 7332 1251
http://www.corpoflondon.gov.uk/
organisation/services/records.htm

The British Library
Great Russell Street
London WC1B 3DG
Tel: (0) 20 7412 7332
http://www.bl.uk/index.html

The British Library
Newspaper Library
Colindale Avenue
London NW9 5HE
Tel: (0) 20 7412 7353
Fax: (0) 20 7412 7379
http://www.bl.uk/collections/newspaper

Lambeth Palace Library
London SE1 7JU
Tel: (0) 20 7928 6222
http://www.ihr.sas.ac.uk/lambeth/
welcome.html

Society of Genealogists
14 Charterhouse Buildings
Goswell Road
London EC1M 7BA
Tel: (0) 20 7253 5235
Fax: (0) 20 7250 1800
http://www.sog.org.uk/acatalog

Central Library
St Peter's Square
Manchester M2 5PD
Tel: (0) 161 234 1980
http://www.gmcro.u-
net.com/purple1.htm

Methodist Archives and Research Centre
John Rylands Library University of
Manchester
150 Deansgate
Manchester M3 3EH
Tel: (0) 161 834 5343/6765
Fax: (0) 161 834 5574
http://www.rylibweb.man.ac.uk/data1/
dg/text/method.html

Federation of Family History Societies
The Benson Room
Birmingham and Midland Institute
Margaret Street
Birmingham B3 3BS
http://www.ffhs.org.uk

Hyde Park Family History Centre
64–68 Exhibition Road
London SW7 2PA
Tel: (0) 20 7589 8561

British Society of Sports History (worldwide links to sports archives)
http://www.umist.ac.uk/sport/
index2.html

Catholic Family History Society
45 Gates Green Road
West Wickham, Kent BR4 9DE
http://feefhs.org/uk/frg-cfhs.html

SCOTLAND

General Register Office for Scotland
New Register House
3 West Register Street
Edinburgh EH1 3YT
Tel: (0) 131 334 0380
http://www.open.gov.uk/gros/
groshome.htm

Scottish Record Office
HM General Register House
Princes Street
Edinburgh EH13YY
Tel: (0) 131 535 1314

General Register Office for Scotland
New Register House
Edinburgh EH1 3YY
Tel: (0) 131 314 4444
http://www.wood.ccta.gov.uk/grosweb/
grosweb.nsf

Edinburgh City Archives
Corporate Services
City Chambers
High Street
Edinburgh EH1 1YJ
Tel: (0) 131 529 4616
http://www.edinburgh.gov.uk/CEC/
Corporate_Services

Glasgow City Archives
The Mitchell Library
North Street
Glasgow G3 7DN
Tel : (0) 141 287 2910
Fax : (0) 141 226 8452
http://www.mitchelllibrary.org/
archives.htm

National Library of Scotland
George IV Bridge
Edinburgh EH1 1EW
Tel: (0) 131 226 4531
Fax: (0) 131 622 4803
http://www.nls.ac.uk

Aberdeen Central Library
Rosemount Viaduct
Aberdeen AB25 1GW
Tel: (0) 1224 652511
Fax: (0) 1224 624118
http://www.urie.demon.co.uk/genuki/
ABD/archives.html#citylibrary

Scots Ancestry Research Society
8 York Road
Edinburgh EH5 3EH
Tel: (0) 131 552 2028
http://www.2.vpl.vancouver.bc.ca/DBs/
cod/orgPgs/1/1500.html

The Scottish Genealogy Society
Library and Family History Centre,
15 Victoria Terrace
Edinburgh EH1 2JL
Tel: (0) 131 220 3677
Fax: (0) 131 220 3677
http://www.sol.co.uk/s/scotgensoc

Library and Archive Sources in Scotland
http://www.ifb.co.uk/~kinman/
archlib.html

WALES

Welsh Archives Council
National Library of Wales
Aberystwyth
Ceredigion SY23 3BU
Tel: (0) 1970 632857
Fax: (0) 1970 632883
http://www.llgc.org.uk/cac/cac0051.htm

National Library of Wales
Aberystwyth
Ceredigion
Wales SY23 3BU
Tel: (0) 1970 632800
Fax: (0) 1970 615709
http://www.llgc.org.uk

WEBSITES

Local History Directory for Wales
http://www.local-history.co.uk/Groups/
wales.html

Digging up Your Roots in Wales
http://www.everton.com/GENEALOG/
GENEALOG.WALES1

Links to Genealogical services
http://www.afhs.ab.ca/wales.html

GenealogyPro
Professional Genealogical Services
http://www.genealogypro.com

NORTHERN IRELAND

General Register Office
Oxford House
49–55 Chichester Street
Belfast BT1 4HL
Tel: (0) 28 9025 2021/2/3/4/5
http://www.nisra.gov.uk/gro

Public Record Office for Northern Ireland
66 Balmoral Avenue
Belfast BT9 6NY
Northern Ireland
Tel: (0) 28 9025 1318
Fax: (0) 28 90 255999
E-mail: proni@doeni.gov.uk
http://proni.nics.gov.uk

General Register Office Northern Ireland (GRO)
Oxford House, 49–55 Chichester Street
Belfast BT1 4HC
Tel: (0) 1232 251318

Ulster Historical Foundation
12 College Square East
Belfast BT1 6DD
Tel: (0) 28 90 332288
Fax: (0) 28 90 239885
http://www.ancestryireland.com

Society of Friends Library
Meeting House
Railway Street
Lisburn, County Antrim
http://www.local.ie/content/25654.shtml

WEBSITES

British Isles GenWeb project
http://www.britishislesgenweb.org

GenUK
http://www.genuki.org.uk

Familia (directory of family history resources)
http://www.earl.org.uk/familia

Venezuela

WEBSITES

Genealogía de Venezuela
http://www.geocities.com/Heartland/
Ranch/2443

Web-only Resources

MAJOR GENEALOGY SITES

Ancestry.com
http://www.ancestry.com

Family Search
http://www.familysearch.org

Genealogy Toolbox
http://www.genealogy.tbox.com

Roots Surname List
http://www.rootsweb.com

Online Genealogy Records
http://msnhomepages.talkcity.com/
PicnicPl/bertaut/online.html

Seniors Search Genealogy
http://www.seniorssearch.com/cgi-
bin/page.asp?cn=11107

Family Genealogy Online
http://www.familygenealogyonline.com

Family Search
http://www.familysearch.org

Snap: Genealogy
http://www.snap.com/directory/category/
0,16,-17303,00.html?st.sn.fd.0.
dir-17303

Genealogy at a Search Engine Galore
http://www.searchenginesgalore.com/
gen.html

LINKS SITES

Cyndi's List
http://www.CyndisList.com

Interactive Genealogy Searches
http://www.hometown.aol.com/Sftrail/
inter-gen2.html

About.com
http://genealogy.about.com/hobbies/
genealogy/index.htm

Genealogy Gateway
http://www.gengateway.com

Ancestor Roots Information
http://www.dcn.davis.ca.us/~vctinney/
database.htm

I Found It
http://www.gensource.com/ifoundit

Ancestral Links
http://aklein.webhostme.com

What's New in Genealogy Today
http://www.genealogytoday.com

Genealogy Site Finder
http://www.genealogysitefinder.com

Genealogy Home Page
http://www.genhomepage.com

Lineages' Web Site
http://www.lineages.com

Vital Records Information (U.S. and International)
http://vitalrec.com

SURNAME SITES

Guild of One-name Studies
http://www.one-name.org

Surname Web
http://www.surnameweb.org

Genealogy Roots Corner
http://ourworld.compuserve.com/
homepages/Strawn/roots.htm

Surname Search Engines
http://freepages.genealogy.rootsweb.com/
~darci/search.htm

Genealogy Exchange and Surname Registry
http://www.genexchange.com/index.cfm

Genealogy Directory of Surname Sites
http://members.1stnetusa.com/a/
genealogy

Surname Springboard
http://www.geocities.com/~alacy/
spring.htm

Genealogy's Most Wanted
http://www.citynet.net/mostwanted

Genealogy and Acadian Connections
http://www.geocities.com/Heartland/
Acres/9466/geneaintro.html

In Memory of Them.com
http://www.inmemoryofthem.com

Connect with Surnames Genealogy Registry
http://www.geocities.com/Heartland/
Bluffs/7708

ADOPTION AND REUNION

Adoption Genealogy Forum
http://genforum.genealogy.com/
adoption

William Spoon's First Nations (Native American Adoption)
http://members.tripod.com/
~SkyatDawn/index-4.html

Reunions Magazine
http://www.reunionsmag.com

REGIONAL AND ETHNIC WEBSITES

Hispanic Genealogy Resources
http://www.elanillo.com/recursos.html

South American GenWeb
http://www.southamericangenweb.org

Asian GenWeb
http://www.rootsweb.com/~asiagw

Pacific Genealogy Message Board
www.InsideTheWeb.com/mbs.cgi/
mb120345

NativeWeb (native peoples around the world)
http://www.nativeweb.org

Afrigeneas (African ancestry)
http://www.msstate.edu/Archives/History/
afrigen

Christine's Genealogy Website (African-American Research)
http://www.ccharity.com

JewishGen: The Home of Jewish Genealogy
http://www.jewishgen.org

Getting Started With Czech-Jewish Genealogy
http://www.jewishgen.org/bohmor/
czechguide.html

Sephardim.com
http://www.sephardim.com

CHARTS AND FORMS

Correspondence Records
http://www.ancestry.com/save/charts/
correcord.htm

Family Group Sheets
http://www.ancestry.com/save/charts/
familysheet.htm

Pedigree (or Ancestral) Charts
http://www.ancestry.com/save/charts/
ancchart.htm

Research Calendars
http://www.ancestry.com/save/charts/
researchcal.htm

Research Extracts
http://www.ancestry.com/save/charts/
researchext.htm

Source Summaries
http://www.ancestry.com/save/charts/
sourcesum.htm

MAPS

Lycos RoadMaps
http://maps.lycos.com

MapQuest
http://www.mapquest.com

Odden's Bookmarks: The Fascinating World of Maps and Mapping
http://oddens.geog.uu.nl/index.html

Pam Rietsch's 1895 U.S. Atlas
http://www.livgenmi.com/1895.htm

U.S.G.S. Location Finder
http://www-nmd.usgs.gov

Ordinance Survey (United Kingdom)
http://www.ordnancesurvey.co.uk

Ordinance Survey Historic Maps
http://www.old-maps.co.uk

DIRECTORIES

555-1212.com (area code lookups, reverse look-ups, international directories, etc.)
http://555-1212.com

AOL International Directories
http://www.aol.com/netfind/
international.html

Death (cemeteries worldwide)
http://www.totentanz.de

U.S. Post Office Zip Code Lookup
http://www.framed.usps.com/ncsc

TRANSLATION SERVICES

AltaVista Babel Fish Translation
http://babel.altavista.com/translate.dyn

Travlang's Translating Dictionaries
http://dictionaries.travlang.com

Tour Companies

Heritage Tours (African American)
280 Hernando
Memphis, TN 38126
U.S.A.
Tel: 901 527 3427
E-mail: heritage@mobbs.com
http://www.mobbs.com/heritage

The Educated Traveler
P.O. Box 220822
Chantilly, VA 20153
U.S.A.
Tel: 800 648 5168
http://www.educated-traveler.com

Ashton Drye Associates
95 Squire Place
Orchard Park, NY 14127
U.S.A.
Tel: 800 785 7785/716 667 3359
E-mail: ashdrye@aol.com
http://www.educated-traveler.com

Mir Corp (Russia, Central Asia, Eastern Europe)
Suite 210, 85 South Washington Street
Seattle, WA, 98104
U.S.A.
Tel: 800 424 7289
http://www.mircorp.com

Extraordinary Places
2325 NW Market Street
Seattle, WA 98107
U.S.A.
Tel: 800 891 4706
http://www.eplaces.com

Elderhostel
75 Federal Street
Boston, MA 02110 1941
U.S.A.
Tel: 877 426 8059
http://www.elderhostel.org

History America Tours
P.O. Box 797687
Dallas, TX 75379
U.S.A.
Tel: 800 628 8542
http://www.historyamerica.com

Jewish Heritage Tours
630 Third Avenue
New York, NY 10017
U.S.A.
Tel: 800 223 7460/212 661 1193
Fax: 212 370 1477
E-mail: info@jhtours.com
http://www.jhtours.com/default.asp

EUROPEAN TOURS

Routes to Roots
136 Sandpiper Key
Secaucus, NJ 07094
U.S.A.
http://www.routestoroots.com

European Focus
P.O. Box 550
Bountiful, UT 84011 0550
U.S.A.
Tel: 800 401 7802
http://www.eurofocus.com

Czech Slovak Travel Tours
6805 West Cermak Road
Berwyn, IL 60402
U.S.A.
Tel: 708 749 1333
Fax: 708 749 1350
http://www.webertravel.com

Old Country Tours
P.O. Box 340
Flourtown, PA 19031 0340
U.S.A.
Tel: 800 953 5812
http://www.oldcountrytours.com

Old Country Tours
P.O. Box 324
Esher, Surrey KT10 0XD
United Kingdom
Tel: (0) 20 8398 5368
Fax: (0) 20 8398 5594
www.oldcountrytours.com/
maintour.html

Tours of Acadian-Cajun Locations
P.O. Box 99
Clements, CA 95227 0099
Tel: 209 759 3788
Fax: 209 759 3513
http://genweb.net/acadian-cajun/
tours.htm

Custom Designed Holidays
4931 Timberline Drive
Middletown, OH 45042
U.S.A.
Tel: 513 422 9445
Fax: 513 422 4414

Custom Designed Holidays
7 Victor Court
Abbs Cross Gardens
Hornchurch, Essex, RM12 4XF
United Kingdom
Tel: (0) 1708 456 281
Fax: (0) 1708 620 999
www.combstravel.com/cdh

Genealogy Germany
Heritage Travel, Uwe Porten
Im Mittelpfad 11A
D-55411 Bingen
Germany
Tel: (0) 6721 990022
Fax: (0) 6721 990044
www.genealogy-germany.de

Heritage Tours (Czeck and Slovak)
4219 Thornhill Lane
St. Paul, MN 55127 7822
U.S.A.

Joyce Ireland Tours
34 Carragh Hill, Knocknacarragh
Galway, Ireland
Tel/Fax: (0) 91 521699
Email: joytour@iol.ie
http://www.failte.com/heritage

Spanish Heritage Tours
116–47 Queens Boulevard Forest Hills
NY 11375
U.S.A.
Tel: 800 456 5050
Fax: 718 793 4278
http://www.shtours.com

TourMagination
1011 Cathill Road
Sellersville, PA 18960
U.S.A.
Tel: 800 565 0451/215 723 8413

TourMagination
9 Willow Street, Waterloo
ON N2J 1V6
Canada
Tel: 519 885 2522
www.tourmagination.com

TOUR COMPANY WEBSITES

Czech & Slovak Heritage Tours
www.czechheritage.net

Czech, Slovak Travel Information and Tours
http://members.aol.com/jzel/travel.htm

Budget Travel Online
www.frommers.com/vacations/
mainstream/roots

INDEX

Page numbers in italics refer to captions.

photograph albums 25, 79,
  82
  restoring 85, *85*
photographs:
  copying 79
  dating 50
  digital 7
  digital tinting *80*
  family portraits *38*
  on family trees 122–3
  of houses *56*
  as interview aids 20, 21,
    21
  laminating 80
  learning from 48–9
  negatives, storing 81
  on-line information on
    107
  rescue and repair 81
  storing 78–9, *78–9*
  storing negatives 81
  technology 50
  tinted black-and-white *50*
  tinting 80
  of trips 144
  wedding *135*
platinum prints 50
Poland, border changes 63
poor, tracing records 8
poorhouses 8
population surveys,
  local 53
Portuguese colonies 67
postcards, storing *76*
preservation of materials
  75–93
printers:
  dye-sublimation *92*, *93*
  inkjet *93*
printing, deciphering 132,
  133
probate records 42–3
professional associations 71
professions, clues to 45
property:
  deeds *29*, 56
  storage 82
  ownership 52
  taxes 56–7, 109
Provincetown, Massachusetts
  60
public records offices 29, 30,
  31

Q
Quakers 111
questionnaires 20, 24–5

R
real estate *see* property
record offices *see* public
  record offices
recording equipment 18–19
recording information 14–15
relationships 134
relatives, interviewing 17
religious communities:
  memorial customs 39
  records on-line 111
research plan 30
research skills 14–15
residential care, interviews in
  21
Roman Catholics:
  maintaining records 63
  memorial masses 39
  records on-line 111
Roman numerals 137
Romania:
  birth certificate *33*
  burials *41*
Roots Surname List 98
Rosicrucians *111*
Russians, naming traditions
  130

S
safe, fireproof 83, *83*
scanners 80, 92, *92*
  film 92, *93*
Schneider, Dale 106
school records 70
Scotland:
  adoption 34
  baptismal records 33
  naming traditions 130
  probate documents 42
scrapbooks 25, 82, 83, *84*
  restoring 85
ships, passenger lists 58, 60,
  108
Siena, Italy *139*
signatures 132–3, *133*
slaves:
  on census returns 52, 64
  freed 10, 65
  records on-line 110
Social Security Death Index
  (SSDI) 101
social welfare 8
societies 72
Society of Genealogists,
  London 72
sound cards 93
Soundex system 54–5

South Africa:
  census records 53
  probate documents 42
Spanish colonies 67
storage 75–93
  methods 82–3
  organizing 83
storage boxes 82, *82*
street plans 57
surnames:
  "family history" 46
  female line 99
  pronunciation 129
  Roots Surname List 98
  societies 73
  spelling variations 32, 129
  surname societies 73
  types 128
  understanding 128–9
  websites 98–9

T
tape recording 18–19
taxation records 56–7
telephone directories 15,
  106
textiles, displaying 85
tintypes 50
tombs 40
tours, organized 142
town plans 57
trade directories 106–7
trade regulatory bodies 71
travel 139–45
  diary 144–5
  equipment 142, 143
  itinerary 142
  organized tours 142
  planning 140–1

U
underclass, records of 8
uniforms *71*
United States of America:
  adoption 34
  African-Americans in
    64–5, *64*
  baptismal records 33
  cemetery records 41
  census records 52–7
  on-line 108, *109*
  death certificates 38
  land grants 69
  military service records
    68–9
  probate documents 42
  property taxes 57
United States Colored

Troops 65, 110
United States National
  Archives 65, 66, 110
unmarried couples, birth
  registration 33

V
valentine cards 13
video capture boards 93
video tapes, storage 86, 87
videotaping 19
vital records 31
  on-line 108–9

W
Wales:
  adoption 34
  baptismal records 33
  probate documents 42
wars 11
  mementoes 25
wedding photographs *135*
wills 42–3
  interpreting 44–5
  inventories 44, 45
  storage 82
Works Progress
  Administration (W.P.A.) 65
World War I 69, 111
World Wide Web 95
  census returns 54
  databases 100–3
  ethnic records 65, 110–11
  genealogy 90, 106
  general reference 106–7
  geographic records 57
  government websites
    108–9
  hyperlinks 96
  immigration records 58,
    60
  official websites 108–9
  on-line catalogs 14–15
  search engines 96–7
  surname searches 98–9
  website:
    addresses 96
    creating 112
    data for 113
WorldConnect Project 101
WorldGenWeb Project 106

Y
yearbooks, school 70, *70*
YIVO Institute 63

CREDITS

t = top; **b** = bottom; **l** = left, **c** = centre; **r** = right

Photographic Credits

1 Bettmann/Corbis; 5 Andrew Sydenham; 6/7 background: National Archives/Corbis, 6t Clive Corless/Marshall Editions, 6bl Andrew Sydenham, 6br Clive Corless/Marshall Editions; 8t Hulton-Deutsch Collection/Corbis, 9l National Archives/Corbis, 9r Brown-Forman Corporation; 10 Clive Corless/Marshall Editions, 11t Marshall Editions, 11b Ancestry.com; 12 & 13t Clive Corless/Marshall Editions, 13b Ancestry.com; 14 & 15 Ancestry.com; 18 Andrew Sydenham; 20l Corbis, 20r Clive Corless/Marshall Editions, 21b Ancestry.com; 22 Andrew Sydenham, 23 Clive Corless/Marshall Editions; 24, 25tr & 25b Clive Corless/Marshall Editions; 28/29 background: Ancestry.com, 28bl Hulton-Deutsch Collection/Corbis, 28br Clive Corless/Marshall Editions, 28/29 Ancestry.com; 30 Phil Schermeister/Corbis; 32l Oscar White/Corbis, 32r Clive Corless/Marshall Editions; 34 PEMCO-Webster & Stevens Collection; Museum of History & Industry/Corbis, 35t Philip Gould/Corbis; 37t Hulton-Deutsch Collection/Corbis; 38 Bettmann/Corbis, 39c Chris Linton/Sandra Cronan; 42 Andrew Sydenham, 43 Clive Corless/Marshall Editions; 44 Bettmann/Corbis, 45 & 46 Clive Corless/Marshall Editions; 50tl & 50r Science & Society; 52t Bettmann/Corbis, 52b Ancestry.com, 53; 54 & 55 Bettmann/Corbis; 56 Hulton-Deutsch Collection/Corbis; 58 Michael S. Yamashita/Corbis; 60 Corbis, 61t Bettmann/Corbis; 63 & 64t Corbis, 64b Flip Schulke/Corbis, 65 Science & Society; 66t Corbis, 66b Ancestry.com, 67 Corbis; 69 Ancestry.com; 71r Clive Corless/Marshall Editions; 72t Philippa Lewis; Edifice/Corbis, 72b Society of Genealogists, 73t Ancestry.com; 74/75 background: University Products Inc, 74/75 Clive Corless/Marshall Editions; 76t Ancestry.com, 76b Unversity Products Inc, 77t & 77c Clive Corless/Marshall Editions, 77b, 78t & 78b University Products Inc, 79t & 80 Ancestry.com, 81t & 81c Roy Flooks, 81b Andrew Sydenham; 82b University Products Inc, 83 Morgan River Ltd tel: 020 7274 7607; 84t Clive Corless/Marshall Editions; 86t Ancestry.com, 86b Kodak Collection/HMPFT/Science & Society, 87 National Museum of Photography, Film & TV/Science & Society; 88 Bruce Mackie, 89 Ancestry.com; 90, 91, 92 & 93 Andrew Sydenham; 94/95 background: easyEverything, 94tl John Lewis of Hungerford, Artisan Kitchens & Furniture, 94tr New York Public Library, 94b Ericsson; 96t Chicago Public Library, 96b easyEverything; 97 Bruce Mackie; 98 Horace Bristol/Corbis, 99b Bettmann/Corbis; 100b Lucien Aigner/Corbis, 101t Cyndi's List, 101b Minnesota Historical Society/Corbis; 102t Bettmann/Corbis, 102b Ancestry.com; 103 Auto Express; 104 Mike Good, 105b easyEverything; 106t Clive Corless/Marshall Editions, 106bl WorldGenWeb, 106br Ancestry.com, 107t Norman Brand/Marshall Editions, 107b Clive Corless/Marshall Editions; 109 Ancestry.com; 110 Hulton-Deutsch Collection/Corbis, 111t Jerry Cooke/Corbis; 113 Ericsson; 114/115 background: Ancestry.com, 114b Ancestry.com; 116 Phil Schermeister/Corbis, 117t Clive Corless/Marshall Editions, 117b, 118, 120 & 122 Ancestry.com; 125t University Products Inc; 126/127 background: Archivo Iconografico,S.A./Corbis, 126t Araldo de Luca/Corbis, 126l Ancestry.com, 126cr Bettmann/Corbis, 126br Clive Corless/Marshall Editions; 129t Ancestry.com; 133 Clive Corless/Marshall Editions; 137b Araldo de Luca/Corbis; 138/139 background: Ancestry.com, 138c Gail Mooney/Corbis, 138b Lee Snider/Corbis; 140 Ancestry.com, 141t John M. Dibbs/The Plane Picture Company, 141b Dave Bartruff/Corbis; 143 Andrew Sydenham; 144t University Products Inc, 145 Ancestry.com

Illustrators

97 Tim Loughhead; 103 Kuo Kang Chen; 105 Kevin Jones Associates; 130 Lynn Chadwick; 133 Roy Flooks

The publishers would like to thank the following people for kindly supplying material for this book:

Ainslie Baker
Graham Bebbington and Christine Hold
Hilary Bird
Garvin Brown
June Campbell
Fehmi Comert
Robert Dinwiddie
Ellen Dupont
Michael and Peter Fall

Dr. Ian F. Hancock
Victoria Harrison-Carr
Karen Horslen
Amanda Mackie
Janet Mehigan
Hilary Mandleberg
Malcolm Miller
Michael Nyberg
Cindy O'Brien
David Roth
Emily Salter
Juliana Smith
Lou Szucs
Janet Tabinski

John Whitehouse
Jennifer Utley
Matt Wright
Lenny Yodaiken